Understanding
Oriental
Philosophy

Books by James K. Feibleman

DEATH OF THE GOD IN MEXICO
CHRISTIANITY, COMMUNISM AND THE IDEAL SOCIETY
IN PRAISE OF COMEDY
POSITIVE DEMOCRACY
THE MARGITIST
THE THEORY OF HUMAN CULTURE
THE REVIVAL OF REALISM
AN INTRODUCTION TO PEIRCE'S PHILOSOPHY
JOURNEY TO THE COASTAL MARSH
THE LONG HABIT
AESTHETICS
ONTOLOGY
PHILOSOPHERS LEAD SHELTERED LIVES
TREMBLING PRAIRIE
THE DARK BIFOCALS
THE INSTITUTIONS OF SOCIETY
THE PIOUS SCIENTIST
INSIDE THE GREAT MIRROR
RELIGIOUS PLATONISM
FOUNDATIONS OF EMPIRICISM
BIOSOCIAL FACTORS IN MENTAL ILLNESS
MANKIND BEHAVING
THE TWO-STORY WORLD
MORAL STRATEGY
GREAT APRIL
THE REACH OF POLITICS
THE WAY OF A MAN
THE NEW MATERIALISM
SCIENTIFIC METHOD
THE QUIET REBELLION
UNDERSTANDING PHILOSOPHY
COLLECTED POEMS
THE STAGES OF HUMAN LIFE
UNDERSTANDING CIVILIZATIONS

Co-Author of

SCIENCE AND THE SPIRIT OF MAN
THE UNLIMITED COMMUNITY
WHAT SCIENCE REALLY MEANS

Understanding Oriental Philosophy

A Popular Account for the Western World

JAMES K. FEIBLEMAN

HORIZON PRESS  New York

For Richard L. Barber

Preface
Approaching the Orient

There have been many books explaining oriental religions, but oriental philosophy has been much neglected. Philosophy is the inner nature of human culture as religion is its outward expression. Nowhere is this more evident than in the Orient, and that is why I have sought to explain the culture of India and of China and Japan by discussing both their philosophies and religions. Only so is it possible to understand all other aspects of their life.

The "inscrutable oriental" and the "mysterious east" are fortunately fast disappearing as stock phrases because we have been increasingly involved in that part of the world. If mystery remains, it is only because the culture of the Orient is so different from our own. The flavor, the quality, the feeling, of oriental philosophy is unfamiliar to us and cannot fail to broaden our outlook. Exposure to it is like a trip abroad; it becomes more meaningful after you return home. Reading about it helps us to understand the differences when we meet them.

Much in these pages is strange to our way of thinking.

Western Europe's general outlook has spread to the United States and many other places, to the countries of South America, to Canada and Mexico, even out to Australia and New Zealand. Most of us have never moved outside the limits of western culture and so we have come to think of it as the only kind.

But there is of course another kind, even older than the one to which we have grown accustomed. Asia—what we call the Far East—contains at least two civilizations older than our own, as old in fact as civilization itself. India and China are the oldest of those countries which have survived in a single place; they are also the largest. India today has 600 million people, and China 800 million: to us almost inconceivable numbers. But what is perhaps more inconceivable is how different their beliefs and their ways of life are from ours. The difference is underscored by the Japanese people, who inherited the civilizations of China and India and then tried to combine these with western culture. To show the differences and what they mean to us is the reason for this book.

Religion and philosophy are names for fundamental beliefs and for the ways in which they are practiced. Understanding requires some degree of sympathy. No one could believe in all the conflicting philosophies nor practice all the religions, but to get to the essence of any of them it is necessary momentarily to accept each in turn, to be a Confucian, then a Buddhist, at least long enough to see what Confucius was getting at and what Buddha was recommending. Even the process of understanding and then rejecting them all finally will have enriched one's awareness of profound thoughts.

I have tried therefore to present in clear, readable form the philosophy I have found in the thought of the Orient, and I have not failed to consider how much of that philosophy is to be found in oriental religions.

Just what is a religion? First of all, we may say, it is a revelation and a creed, authorizing and sometimes enforcing a morality, reinforced by a ritual, a clergy and a church. The revelation and the creed contain, in addition to a theory of knowledge and a metaphysics, the morality to which they lead. The activities of men are always in conformity with what they hold to be primarily real. What we have here, then, are some of the principal elements of a philosophy. I am not claiming that philosophy is all there is to a religion, but it does lie at its center. There are supernatural elements in revelations, and the social institution of the church. We shall not be concerned here with the two last, only with the first.

What is anyone who belongs to a religion expected to believe about it, and what can be said in judgment of those beliefs from the outside where logic and fact prevail? Confining my inquiry to the oriental religions, these are the questions I intend to investigate. I shall define the religions of Asia, however much variety there may be among them, chiefly those of India, China and Japan.

Historically the connections between philosophy and religion have been closer than some religious leaders wish to admit. Religions have at times been little more than mythologized metaphysics, philosophy personified in supernatural gods; at other times they have been combined in a different way, with beliefs in the supernatural defended by means of philosophy. But there have also been religions with no reference to the supernatural, merely a moral order set forth by a leader or prophet who exemplified either by his utterance or by his behavior the way which his followers are urged to follow.

Religions begin with the words of holy men, but if they remain in existence for any length of time they accumulate philosophies which come to be regarded as sacred and inseparable from those beginnings. Yet they can be separated as philosophies and examined on their own, and in this way must stand inspection for truth or falsity.

It would be a mistake to overlook the support which churches lend to ideas. Every world religion is a living example. Sacred relics, elaborate ceremonies in connection with them, all in the housing of beautiful or imposing temples, have an emotional impact and do much to support the faith which millennia of belief continue. Anyone in search of the truth, however, must learn to clear away the accumulation of traditional possessions and procedures in order to get at the core of the ideas themselves. Oriental religions lend themselves to mystical nonsense, and while I am certainly not suggesting that all mysticism is nonsense, some of it is. I have tried to show what is factual and reasonable.

One final word. There is no substitute for the writings of the masters and their followers in the original languages, but few of us have these, and so a description, as brief as possible, is what most of us have to accept in their place.

I have omitted all the diacritical marks which indicate how the Indian, Chinese and Japanese words are pronounced in their native languages with which most of my readers will not be familiar. This is not in any case a technical work aimed at professional orientalists; it has the more humble aim of introducing the lay reader to some of the classical thoughts of Asia.

Contents

PART ONE
THE PHILOSOPHY
OF INDIA

For the Devas love mystery, yea, they love mystery.
—*The Aitareya Aranyaka*

Chapter I
Early India

The oldest civilizations, involving the culture of large populations in a single place for a long time, were in Egypt, India and China.

India is a very old country and not much is known about its history. When the Aryans, the first Indo-European peoples came to India from Iran, probably across the western passes under the Hindu Kush and through the Punjab to the east, they had been influenced by the Indus Valley civilization in the northwest and influenced further by those they found there and conquered, the dark-skinned Dravidian peoples of the south. The Indo-Aryans were tall and fair, with dark eyes, narrow, prominent noses, and long heads. They were nomads from the steppes of Central Asia, and they swept down into India about 2000 B.C. and also through Georgia into Asia Minor and Persia; they were probably also the ancestors of the ancient Greeks.

It is probable that the Dravidians were earlier invaders and that there was a more primitive native population, of short stature and broad flat noses, related to the Veddas of Ceylon and the Australian aborigines. The clues are spoken languages but the evidence from these is not altogether clear. There were also invasions of Mongoloid peoples from Tibet and China, with dark broad heads, yellow skins and slanted eyes who settled in northern India. The inhabitants of northwest India made the transition from nomadic hunting to agriculture probably as early as 4,000 B.C. It takes centuries to develop a high culture from such a primitive beginning.

The Harappa civilization of the Indus River valley, situated in what is now Pakistan, is much earlier, and has been definitely dated to 2500 B.C. As advanced as any in its time, it was almost the most extensive, for it included northern Rajasthan and even Kathiawar in western India. It was also a complex urban culture, chiefly based in the two cities of Harappa and Mohenjo-daro, though there were others. The cities were well-planned, with streets and impressive drainage systems and even with indoor flush toilets in the houses of the prosperous middle-class. The Harappa people used copper and other metals (though not iron), and raised wheat and cotton. There must have been some connection between them and the pre-Aryan Indian culture, although not much is known about it. The Indus valley civilization probably gave its name to the Hindus. The term "Hindu" may have come from the Persians who referred to India as "the land beyond the Sindhu" (the Indus), which gives some indication at least of their influence.

The civilization of the Indus valley probably contains at least an important part of the story of the pre-Aryan peoples and their religion, including a god who was later incorporated into the Hindu religion as Shiva. The invading Aryans (the term refers to a language-group and has nothing in common with its use by the Nazis to describe a mythical pure white race) reached India some time between 2000 and 1000 B.C. speaking a language derived from Sanskrit and possessed of a religion described in the *Rig-veda* (the first part of the *Vedic Hymns*). Sir Mortimer Wheeler believes that it was these people who destroyed the principal Harappa city, Mohenjo-daro, and left there the only prehistoric evidence of a massacre, which exists still today.

India is a vast subcontinent containing many climates and populations. It has become a single political unit only in modern times. Its ancient history has seen many conquests and amalgamations of peoples and cultures, and even today it includes many extremes, from the sophisticated citizen of Calcutta to the primitive Baiga of central India. Many cultures, even many religious faiths, were united by a geography which has over the centuries compelled them to live together and so to make common cause.

Two chief ethnographic divisions of mankind, the white Caucasians represented by the Aryans, and the yellow Mongolians (four if we include the Dravidians of the Deccan and the black population of the Andaman Islands, and later the Semitic Arabs who introduced Muslim speech and customs), all contributed to the making of India. Four great language groups dominated there: the Austric, the Tibeto-Chinese, the Dravidian and the Indo-European; but the *Census Report* for 1911 counts two hundred and twenty languages. If there is an Indian civilization with its characteristic religion, it is basically Hindu, for it is the Hindu civilization of the Aryan conquerors which has prevailed, though with many modifications, throughout India.

One consequence of the presence among the conquering Aryans of a conquered peoples was the caste system. Its origins are obscure, but they are probably due to the enslavement of the Dasas, whose very touch was considered defiling. The Dasas were among the aborigines who were conquered by the Aryans. The Dasas did not worship the gods of the Aryans but may instead have had a religion centered on the sacred phallus. They were flat-nosed and black, while the Aryans were white, and no doubt the color distinction contributed to the caste system. In addition we must count the effect of the division of labor among the Aryans.

In any case, below the king there were the four great castes: the priests and religious teachers *(brahmins)*, the warriors and aristocrats *(kshatriyas)*, the traders and merchants *(vaishyas)* and the farmers and slaves *(shudras)*. As early as the sixth century B.C. a caste of hunters, food-gatherers and rush-weavers lower than the *shudras* came to be recognized. They spoke their own language, were probably members of some aboriginal tribe, and constituted the out-caste of the untouchables. Despite the seriousness of attacks on the caste system from time to time, it has left its mark on Hindu society. No doubt it was a great factor in preventing the Indians from becoming a single people, as the English for instance did, and its strength continues to this day to be troublesome in Indian social relations.

There is noticeable even at this early stage a loosely organized system of related ideas regarding the nature of things. It includes a theory that the creation of the universe started from nothing, a theory which ends in complete skepticism. But as early as 1000 B.C. the beliefs which were to be carried along and developed into a Hindu philosophy were already well established.

It begins with the doctrine of *karma*, the locked sequence of causes and effects extending from the past through the present and into the future, which determines the individual's station in life. *Karma* is the background for the doctrine of reincarnation, or rebirth, according to which any individual human life is an episode in a series of lives in which the choice of caste (or even of plant or animal) depends upon the good or bad deeds done in a previous life. Both *karma* and *rebirth* are governed by *dharma*, the rule of law which determines one's duties and according to which there is no distinction between the laws of nature and those of human society. In society the caste system thus received an unusually strong endorsement.

The Aryans left no artifacts behind them except a collection of sacred writings. When they first reached India they brought religion with them. The *Vedic Hymns* were introduced into India from the outside and quickly became the first religious texts as conquerors mixed with conquered and the Indo-Dravidian population established itself and settled down to become indigenous.

The Indians have had chiefly three sacred books, the *Vedic Hymns,* the *Upanishads* and the *Bhagavad-gita.* Difficult though it may be, it is enlightening to separate out the philosophical content of each of these from the others.

Chapter II
The Vedic Hymns

Both Hindu philosophy and Hindu religion begin with the *Vedic Hymns*, the earlist recorded Indian documents and by all odds the most influential. All great religious writings have a high literary value in addition to serving as vehicles for ideas, and the *Vedic Hymns* are no exception.

The religion of the Hindus can probably be traced back to the Harappa civilization and was quite likely originated by the Aryan-speaking conquerors of India. It did not consist in any single organized church or body of doctrines but was loosely a collection of religions, all claiming the *Vedic Hymns* as their authority. Despite the obvious fact that it is a loose collection of writings, probably bearing the mark of many hands, it is supposed to have been breathed out by Brahman at his creation of the world and hence eternal. Everything may be found there, from monotheism to polytheism, from extreme asceticism to official license.

The word *"Veda"* came from the Aryan root "vid" which meant "seeing." Pre-Vedic thought was probably present among the native Dravidian peoples, who were concerned with forest deities, and contributed to the main stream of Hindu civilization. But the original Hindu thought of the Aryan invaders has its source in the *Vedic Hymns*, the products of an urban people. The dates of the *Vedic Hymns* have been variously assigned: 1200-600 B.C. by Max Muller, 1500 B.C. by Radhakrishnan, 4500 B.C. by Jacobi, and even 6000 B.C. by others. We may agree, then that they were earlier than 600 B.C. and perhaps as early as a thousand years before that—the specific dates being a matter of conjecture—which would make them as old as the Hebrew scriptures and contemporary with the first Egyptian records.

The *Vedic Hymns* are divided into four groups: *Rig, Yajur, Sama* and *Atharva.* The first books were written by wandering tribes, the second group by citizens of a settled civilization. All began as oral traditions, handed down from one generation to another until they were finally committed to writing. Such a process, although evidence of great age, is a guarantee also that they contain many errors. The first three books were manuals used by priests when officiating at sacrifices.

It is in the *Brahmanas,* which were commentaries on the formulas and actions called for in the *Yajur-Veda,* that we first find those characteristic beliefs of the Hindus which became so prominent later: a general pessimism with regard to earthly existence; a doctrine of rebirth, whereby that existence would be repeated in the future as indeed it had been many times in the past; and a search for deliverance from it. The first three *Vedas* agree in language and in much of their content, but I will discuss only the *Rig-Veda,* saving the fourth, the *Atharva,* for last.

The Rig-Veda

If we assume in a rough parallel that the *Rig-Veda* was the Bible of the early Hindus, then we can say for it that it was also polytheistic, a nature religion in which there were worship and sacrifices as well as supplication. The gods were not supernatural beings but rather naturalistic representations. There is more than a hint of monotheism if the gods be interpreted as allegorical aspects of the one supreme being. It was not a forest religion but a pastoral one, and nature in pastoral religions is apt to be represented by that part of non-human nature which is most likely to be experienced in the open country: the sun, the moon and the weather generally. The Indians of the *Vedas* were a pastoral people who ate cows, sheep and goats, and employed horses, asses and dogs as work animals. Farming and irrigation were also practiced, with bulls to pull the ploughs, and hunting continued, as indeed it long did among all peoples. Religion reflected these activities. The sacredness of the cow may have had its origin in the need to preserve the animals for milking and breeding, although no one is sure.

How close to nature the Vedic gods are! Heaven, air, and earth are represented by the astronomical bodies and the weather, including storms and rain clouds. The thirty-three gods are divided into groups as gods of the sky (Mitra and Varuna), gods of the atmosphere (Indra and the Maruts), and gods of the earth (Agni and Soma). While each of the three groups is represented by separate gods, the world they govern is one, a combination, if you will, of nature worship with a crude inquiry into nature.

In the version of the *Rig Veda* which has come down to us there are 1017 hymns, divided into ten books of unequal size, of different dates, and probably not arranged in chronological order. It is pretty well agreed that Indian philosophy begins with the tenth book, and this is the one I will be describing.

At least at first, Indian philosophy was dynamic, affirmative and on the whole this-worldly. There is a multiplicity of gods, which is, however, questioned for there is a unity among them: "He is one though wise men call him by many names." Hymn 121 is a contribution to the theory of "The Unknown God," and "Golden Child," the great God "Who."

"As soon as born alone [he] was the lord of all that is" for he established the heaven and the earth. Water is the original substance from which everything else is made. It was a time when "the great waters went everywhere, holding the germ and generating light." It is interesting that the earliest Greek philosopher on record, Thales, held much the same view.

According to the "Song of Creation," Hymn 129 reads in part:

> Then even non-existence was not, nor existence,
> There was no air then, nor the sky beyond it.
> Who covered it? Where was it? In whose keeping?
> Was there then cosmic water, in depths unfathomed?
> But, after all, who knows, and who can say,
> Whence it all came, and how creation happened?
> The gods themselves are later than creation,
> So who knows truly whence it has arisen?

There is one important aspect of the outlook of the *Vedas:* The reality of the external world is never questioned, it is assumed. There is an undertone of realism in every hymn. There is no illusion, all is real, all is out there. The later and fuller philosophy of the Hindus, with its emphasis on the self and the mind, is hardly prefigured; there is no hint here that it is coming.

Moreover, this reality holds not only for the events on earth but also for the unalterable law which is imbedded in the nature of things as their condition. The conception of an over-riding set of laws constituting a natural order of universals by means of which the gods brought order out of chaos is contained in the Vedic "Rita" which was established by the god, Varuna, but which then even he must obey. *Rita* is variously translated as "order," "law," "truth," "reality," and it pervades the whole world. It is both Plato's law above the material world and Aristotle's law within that world.

If Varuna is the god of unalterable law, Indra is the god of force, personified in Indra's constant companions, the Maruts, who have been described as similar to a tribal confederation of youthful warriors. They are in effect storm gods and are always associated with thunder and lightning, with wind and rain, playful and terrible at one and the same time. They are also the gods of battle. There are so many hymns in the *Rig-Veda* which are dedicated to the Maruts and discuss their prowess that it can hardly be understood without them. That the gods are all aspects of the one god, who appears in different guises and with different effects, is shown by a statement of Varuna's in the *Rig-Veda*, "I, Varuna, am king... I am [also] Indra. I have set in motion both worlds and maintain them." And again, "the worshipful divinity of the gods is one."

What holds for nature holds also for man, according to the Vedic philosophy. There is a *Rita*, a set of unalterable laws, for human behavior also. The *Vedic Hymns* must have been addressed to an aristocracy and were surely selected and approved by a priesthood. The social order of the caste system, which, as we have seen, probably arose from the differences between the conquering Aryans and the conquering Dasas at one time must have been a progressive step for it may have prevented further war, but it came to be a bar to progress in serving merely as a rigid class barrier which no one could cross.

For the ethics of the *Rig-Veda* are contained in the path of *Rita*, which is the good for those who follow it. The law of nature is also the law of man; the social order being only part of the natural order. Prayers are to be offered, sacrifices performed; such is the behavior demanded by the gods. The advantage of religions over philosophies is that in religions extreme differences do not have to be reconciled, they only have to be included. Vedic ritual counted on human as well as animal and especially horse sacrifices. Yet the behavior of man toward his fellow man called for kindness, charity and hospitality.

On the whole the Vedic Indians sought physical strength rather than morality and wisdom. Vice was simple disobedience of the law, but some vices were specifically condemned, gambling, for instance, witchcraft and adultery. Beyond that, the asceticism which later took such a strong hold in India was barely anticipated. The good things of this world have no harm in them, and so may be sought and enjoyed. Vegetarianism appeared much later as did also the cult of non-violence with which it was associated. The Aryans approved and practiced the custom of slaying cows in order to feed guests. Generally, there was a deep joy of life.

The quality which is to be found in the whole conception of a natural law which exists in nature and man alike is that of consistency. The world was all of a piece, and the serious distinctions which later occur, for instance between appearance and reality, did not yet exist in Indian philosophy. Again like the ancient Greeks, gods and men shared a world in which order transcended them both, and no one, neither god nor mortal, was entitled to break it. In this kind of order, the individual was bound to find a sense of belonging, a part which was under any conditions included in the whole.

The Aryans of the *Rig-Veda* were occupied with the fullness of the life they were living and had little thought for any other worlds. Apart from several brief and dubious passages, the *Rig-Veda* has nothing to say about the possibility of another life to come after death.

The *Atharva-Veda* probably represents material older than the *Rig-Veda*, perhaps containing some of the beliefs of the conquered peoples which crept into the Aryan *Vedas* and were collected at a later time. It is more religious than philosophical, a demonology or sorcery and witchcraft, with a hell of many tortures, incantations for worthy purposes and charms against evil ones, with hymns to snakes and diseases as well as to sleep, time and the stars.

There is also material here which foreshadowed the later *Upanishads*, such as a reference to the closeness of the relation between Brahman (god) and atman (the self), a female deity to supplement the predominantly male deity of the *Rig-Veda*, cow worship, and a pessimism instead of the optimism which the earlier *Veda* had proclaimed.

The rest of the *Vedic Hymns*, the intermediate group between the *Rig-Veda* and the *Atharva-Veda*, need not concern us here, for they have to do not with a religious philosophy but more with the ways in which that philosophy is preserved, administered and defended by a priestly class. Language was to hide thoughts which only the priests are privileged to reveal. The laity for whom the ceremonies were performed did not count, while the money which they supply did, for it was the priests who were the intermediaries between gods and men, and who therefore enjoyed a special holiness. The *Atharva-Veda* is full of magic and yogic practices.

The task of claiming the divine authority of the *Vedas* was finally undertaken by the *Vedas* themselves and its absolutism established as a fact. We owe to the *Yajur-Veda* and the *Sama-Veda* the birth of a tradition. Henceforth most Indian religions trace themselves back to the *Rig-Veda*. Brahman, which in the *Rig-Veda* meant simply a hymn or prayer to a god, now represented the creative force in the world. The formalization which began with the *Atharva-Veda* was continued. There were four stages in the Vedic Aryan's life: he had to be in succession a student of the *Vedas*, a householder who discharges his social duties, a hermit who spends his time doing penance, and a homeless, wandering ascetic. If we read this literally (the description occurs again and again), it means that religion as a serious practice was reserved for certain age-grades, namely the early years and the later years, first when a man was preparing for life and again in his old age when he was no longer equipped for coping with it. In his vigorous middle years he was expected to be active in the world with its economic and political as well as family affairs.

The strength of the Hindu tradition is illustrated best perhaps by the Laws of Manu, written about the first century A.D. They prescribe that, of the four great castes, the brahmins were to study and teach the *Vedas*, the *kshatriyas* were to guard the people and study the *Vedas*, and the *vaishyas* were to breed cattle, till the soil, engage in trade, and study the *Vedas*, and the *shudras* were to serve the other three castes and avoid the *Vedas* by all means.

The *Vedas* are in total an inconsistent set of writings connected with particular happenings in no way suggesting a divine origin. Yet the *Vedas* have been given an authority equal to that of the senses, and such is their authority that the authors of the six principal Hindu systems of religion and philosophy felt called upon to base their works on it.

Chapter III
The Upanishads

The Indian religions, together with their philosophies of both the orthodox and heretical varieties, have much in common despite their differences, and if they do it is because of a common inheritance. This is not sufficiently recognized by the Hindus, Jains and Buddhists. For the *Vedic Hymns* and, even more, the *Upanishads* influenced all subsequent systems of thought. The latter were probably written down between the eighth and the fourth centuries B.C. The *Vedic Hymns* celebrated the worship of nature; it is with the *Upanishads* that Indian philosophical thought properly began. There certainly are elements in the *Upanishads* and consequently in all later religions which did not originate with the Aryan-speaking peoples who were responsible for the *Vedic Hymns*. This is true of the meditations of the yogin and the belief in the transmigration of souls, evidence that the forest ascetic did not spend all his time on the mountain top. Sometimes he returned to the cities to declare the answers which he professed to have discovered in his isolation.

In general it was true, however, that after the *Vedic*

Hymns Indian thought became introverted and inner-directed, and in this state with few interruptions it remained, replacing the realism of the *Vedic Hymns* with an idealism. The realism which confronted the individual with a material world that existed independently of what he did or did not think about it was to return only twice in the history of Indian religion and philosophy, as we shall see in later chapters, where it marked only brief exceptions in an otherwise thoroughly subjective tradition.

It is the *Upanishads* rather than the *Vedic Hymns* upon which subsequent Indian thought chiefly rests. It is not a consistent body of doctrine and contains many conflicting assertions. As a result, what many Hindu religious and philosophical developments which disagree with each other have in common is that they can be traced to the influence of the *Upanishads*. They certainly represent one of the earliest attempts to give a philosophical explanation of the world. This is true of the two oldest: the Vrihadaranyaka and the Chandogya *Upanishads*.

The name, *Upanishads*, seems to have come from a phrase of three words, *upa* (near by), *ni* (devotedly), *sad* (sitting), and meant receiving secret instructions at private meetings from a great teacher. Later the *Upanishads* came to be known as the "Vedanta," it is said, either because it came at the end of the *Vedas* or because it was the purpose toward which the *Vedas* tended.

The understanding of the *Upanishads*, like so much in Indian philosophy, has to come up through texts which were corrupted before they were recorded and through a wilderness of varying interpretations. The most astute and devoted scholars have made different readings of the same terms and passages—the meanings of 'Brahman', for example, as the name for sacred utterance, for prayer, for the god or man with the power of sacred utterance, or for the creator of the world who also exists everywhere in it.

The best guess at the dates of the composition of the

Upanishads is between 800 and 600 B.C., the latter the century when Buddha lived, for he was most surely influenced by it. The essence of its teaching is the doctrine of the unity of *Brahman* and *atman,* or god and the human "self." With regard to Brahman there is a monism of the one god and a pantheism which consists in the existence of that god everywhere in nature, so that there is no break between nature, god and man. *Brahman* has now replaced the other gods, all thirty-three of them. In the *Upanishads* we read that "each god is but his manifestation, for he [*Brahman*] is all gods."

The emphasis in the *Vedic Hymns* was on the outer world, in the *Upanishads* it has shifted to the inner world of the self in relation to that outer world. Opinions differ as to whether *Brahman* is a god responsible for the material world and the individual self while at the same time transcending them, or merely an impersonal Absolute, not to be worshipped as a god but only understood as the essence of reality running through all material things and connecting them. There is some argument for both views and none conclusive enough for either.

The *Upanishads* is a book of religious beliefs rather than one of practices, and that is why it contains such a large measure of philosophy. In this it resembles the *Rig-Veda* rather than the *Brahmanas,* for the former contains doctrine, the latter ritual. The case is stronger than that, in fact, for the authors of the *Upanishads* were emphatically opposed to ritual and to all sacrifices. Their objections are based mainly on the fees paid to priests, we are told; in one passage sacrifices are compared to unsafe boats, and he who relies on ritual and sacrifices is condemning himself to old age and death, for immortality is not to be attained in such ways.

In Platonic fashion the writers of the *Upanishads* drew a distinction between two kinds of knowledge, the knowledge of the eternal and the knowledge of the temporal, the knowledge of *Brahman-atman* and the knowledge of the practical arts and sciences. The former leads to imperishable knowledge, the latter leads to—ignorance. The uninstructed are advised to seek the imperishable variety of knowledge from a competent teacher, for it has been said that the main lesson of the *Upanishads* is that knowledge is freedom, that true knowledge librates the self.

"In the beginning there was Brahman only," "Brahman, that knew its self only," "Brahman, who is knowledge and bliss." But the distinction between *Brahman* and *atman* or the self is quickly erased: "I who know the self believe him to be Brahman; I who am immortal believe him to be immortal." For it is as true to say "in the beginning this was self alone," "this self is the lord of all beings." Many authorities quote the same phrase from the *Upanishads* as the ultimate message to all human individuals. Speaking of the identification of the *Brahman* (the Absolute) with the *atman* (the self), the *Upanishads* says, "*tat tvam asi,*" which translates "you are that."

It comes to the same thing, then, "that self is indeed *Brahman*," "the self that has entered into this patched-together hiding-place, he indeed is the creator, for he is the maker of everything, his is the world, and he is the world itself." In the final analysis, "He, the self, is unattached, for he does not attach himself." Although "a person consists of desires," the man who does not desire goes to Brahman. (We shall see these two doctrines, the doctrine of non-attachment and of the absence of all desires, play a large part in later Indian philosophies.)

In the *Upanishads*, there is a definite turning toward the subject, a trend which will be increasingly emphasized and never reversed in the rest of the main stream of Indian philosophy. Gone is the god-centered interest of the *Vedic Hymns*. In its place we find a man-centered preoccupation with the implied selfishness softened only by including the relation of god to man. As F. Max Muller, the great translator of Sanskrit, has suggested, the reader of the *Upanishads* is called on to know not himself but his Eternal Self.

A term much used by students of this stage of Hindu philosophy is "non-dualism." *Brahman-atman* is the ground of all being, in a unity which permeates, includes and transcends it. There are two versions of this relation, and since they have given rise to two later schools of Vedanta, it is important to recognize the distinction on which they rest.

The "Cosmic Ideal" has god as the reality but then identifies God with the individual self, so that there is no difference: the individual *is* God, God *is* the individual. The self is as great as the world, and the world is in the self. The Absolute is the name for one end of the spectrum, the self for the other. The world and the self are equally, and even identical, emanations of the Absolute.

The "Acosmic Ideal" makes of the world a phenomenon which would cease to exist apart from God. For the reality of the world is only an appearance, it is not real. That the world of non-dualism is unsubstantial is not yet fully developed in the *Upanishads* into the theory of *maya*, which implies that all is illusion, but it is at least suggested there.

Brahman-atman is the source of the five elements: ether, air, fire, water and earth, from the five sense organs which give rise respectively to sound, touch, color, taste and odor. We experience only mixtures of these, however, not the pure elements. There are in addition to these five sense organs, five organs of action: speech, grasping, moving, excretion and generation. Consciousness gathers knowledge through all of these organs, integrates them and acts through them one at a time.

The self, we are told, is consciousness, and has no other meaning. Since the consciousness is that which knows, there is no knowledge of consciousness. For "you cannot see the see-er of seeing, you cannot hear the hearer of hearing, you cannot think the thinker of thinking." Indeed "himself no one ever sees." Moreover, after the soul departs there is no more consciousness.

In the *Upanishads* there appeared for the first time in Indian philosophy its most characteristic doctrine of *karma*, of rebirth or the transmigration of souls (the most accurate term is probably reincarnation). The soul, it was believed, migrates from one life to another. Each life with all its pain and pleasures is a result of events in a previous life and is responsible for the selection of the next life, in a locked chain of cause-and-effect. Each person's deeds accumulate and determine what will happen to him.

At the occasion of death the soul shuffles off its present body as a snake does its skin and enters into a new one. What one is depends upon the quality of one's previous life. Those who have not lived a virtuous life may have to enter the body of a lower animal, while the virtuous enter another human body. One *Upanishad* suggests that a man can be reborn as an outcaste, a dog or a swine, while another lists birds, beasts and reptiles. There are also passages which indicate that such transmigration is delayed for a while by a time spent in the higher regions of heaven or the lower reaches of hell.

The most characteristic doctrine of the Hindu philosophy is this doctrine of reincarnation. That the soul is immortal, and that it can exist outside space and time where it had no necessary connection with the material world except its passage from one life to another, is likened in the *Upanishads* to a caterpillar which reaches the end of one blade of grass only to start its journey upon another. Immortality of this sort was considered an unwanted state. Existence is not so enjoyable that a repetition of it is desirable. Life in space and time has no beginning and seems to have no end unless a release from it can be found. The ideal of the Indian, implicit in the doctrine of rebirth, was to escape from life, not to repeat it endlessly, a prospect which he found depressing.

The goal of life is *moksha*, the release of the soul from the need to be reborn, and thus freedom from the endless cycle. While it is in no sense negative, rather a state of perfect peace and of absolute bliss, there are passages in the last of the *Upanishads*, probably written much later than the others and contemporary with Buddha, which have a most pessimistic tone. Life is there described as a putrid mess of bodily tissues and of stinking sensual demands, full of pains and destructive emotions. "In such a world as this what is the use of the enjoyment of pleasures if he who has fed on them is seen to have to return to this world again and again! See fit therefore," he cries, "to take me out!"

Some passages in the *Upanishads* seem to indicate that salvation is a spiritual condition, obtainable in this life by means of asceticism and renunciation; according to other passages it can be reached only after death. In any case it represents the promise of a goal in which all diversity disappears and unity is established, attained only by substituting for the belief in the reality of diversity (which is the result of sense perception), an immediate apprehension of the unity which underlies it. It is by the cultivation of detachment that one achieves right knowledge and gets rid of the evil which results from misconceptions.

Despite the affirmative nature of *moksha*, there is some justification for the claim that it implies a negative attitude toward existence. *Moksha* is a release from bondage. Another piece of evidence in this direction is the lack of emphasis on ethics in the *Upanishads*. For such ethics as it has must be understood in altogether different terms. Another way of putting this is to say that the ignorance of unity is responsible for what is bad in human life, which is a product of the false knowledge of variety: all is one, not many.

It is ignorance of the true nature of the self which may be held responsible for immoral actions. Morality follows naturally from true knowledge of the self: if the self is not wrongly identified with the mind or the body it will not be caught up hopelessly in the wheel of birth and death. The path to the release from the wheel lies in drawing back from the shortcomings of material existence. Almost every religious book, and the *Upanishads* is no exception, eventually recommends itself. The moral life, we are told, begins with a knowledge of the Brahman acquired through the study of the *Upanishads*.

Chapter *IV*
The Bhagavadgita

We have noted that the philosophy of the *Upanishads* differs markedly from that of the *Vedic Hymns* which preceded it. In the same way the *Bhagavadgita* differs from its two predecessors. Each book is a development of the earlier work but with important additions which give it a position of its own in Indian thought. This is certainly true of the *Bhagavadgita*. Written some time between the fourth and third centuries B.C., it expresses a philosophy which is distinctly its own, and is deservedly the best-loved Indian book outside as well as inside India. Like the Bible and the Koran in other lands, the *Bhagavadgita* is used in law courts in India for the administration of oaths.

The name means "the Song of the Lord," and it is the middle part of a much longer epic, the *Mahabharata,* one of the longest and most celebrated of epics. In the opening section it claims to consist of 132,000 verses. Its durability is shown by the fact that in Hindu temples still today the text being chanted will prove to be a part of it.

Essentially it tells the tale of a battle in which many

millions are killed. Its hero, Yudhishthira, the King of Righteousness, is a personalized representation of the human conscience, and the book is about his faith in the god Krishna. Yudhishthira wishes to do his duty but Krishna is always compelling him to actions which are contrary. His conflict is between his loyalty to his principles and to his religion. It does not appear possible to honor them both.

He seeks instruction from Krishna but is told to ask the advice of Bhishma, who talks to him at length from his own death-bed. The advice is vague and contradictory. The truth is reserved for a later section, in which Krishna, who had been a silent spectator of the scene, gives the proper instruction to Yudhishthira's younger brother, Arjuna, and the substance of this advice forms the subject matter of the *Gita*.

The *Gita* consists in a long account of a dialogue which takes place between Arjuna, the great warrior, and his charioteer, Krishna, who is the embodiment of the Supreme. (Krishna, by the way, is a new god in India introduced by the *Gita*. He is not an inheritance from the Aryans and he is not mentioned in the *Vedic Hymns*.)

A great war between the Kauravas and the Pandavas is about to begin, one which Yudhishthira, King of the Pandavas, has done everything in his power to prevent, and the two armies are facing each other. Arjuna, the younger brother of Yudhishthira, who will lead the army on his side, grows faint at the thought of the many on the other side who are related to him and who will surely be slaughtered. The battle is about to be joined, but Arjuna holds back. How can I kill these men and in this way destroy their families, he asks.

Krishna the god seeks to persuade Arjuna to go into battle with a clear conscience, and offers a number of reasons. Those Arjuna will slay will not die, death is not the end. As the soul passes through childhood, youth and age, it takes on another body. Cold and heat, pleasure and pain, come and go, they do not last forever. The man who is wise makes himself fit for eternal life. He who thinks that he slays and he who thinks he is slain both fail to perceive the truth; there is neither slaying nor slain. There is no death when the body is slain. For him who is born, death is certain and certain is birth for him who died.

Therefore there is a duty to fight: there is no greater good for a warrior than to do his duty. For he acts for the sake of the action and not for its results. And he is not tempted by attachment to inaction. He must be even-minded with regard to success and failure; such evenness of mind is called yoga, which is skill in action. He is warned not to be bewildered by the *Vedic Hymns* but to strive for the insight of yoga through disciplined meditation. The seeker after the knowledge of yoga goes beyond the Vedic rule. He should get rid of all passions, all desires, remove the senses from the objects of sense, and remain intent on God by means of sense-control, free from both attachment and aversion.

There are three paths offered to the man who seeks liberation: knowledge, action, and *bhakti* or loving devotion. Men attain to their highest by doing work without attachment. A great man must set the standard for the world to follow by his example. He goes first to the senses, then to the mind, next to the intelligence, and finally to God. The third state is by far the preferable one and consists in the direct apprehension of timeless reality which is revealed in the individual once he is liberated from mortal bonds.

In a sense the *Gita* is more thoroughly Indian than the two previous holy books. For instance, while the love of God is open to all, the caste system is recognized and preserved. The duties required of a man are those that belong to his station in life, those of a lowly caste being different from those of a higher.

Shutting out all external objects, fixing the vision between the eyebrows, making the inward and outward breaths move within the nostrils, the sage who has controlled his senses, his mind and his understanding, who seeks liberation and has cast away desire, fear and anger, is forever free. Let a man lift himself by himself, then, and not degrade himself, for the self alone is the enemy of the self. He should sit in a clean place, and there make his mind one-pointed, and, controlling all thought and sense, practice yoga for the purification of the soul. Holding his body erect and looking fixedly at the tip of his nose, serene and fearless in the vow of celibacy, let him sit, harmonized, his mind on God alone.

The universe is pervaded by God but God is not limited to the world. The world is in God but God is not in the world, He is beyond it. All worlds are subject to rebirth but on reaching God there is no rebirth.

The true sage is the ascetic, living in solitude, eating but little, controlling body and mind, engaged in meditation. The aim is to master the senses and control the mind so that the self may reflect the God who is hidden in the soul. Casting aside desire and possession, egoless and tranquil in mind, he becomes worthy of becoming one with God. And finally God himself says, "Fix your mind on Me, be devoted to Me, sacrifice to Me, so shall you come to Me. I promise you truly, for you are dear to Me. He who teaches this supreme secret to My devotees he shall doubtless come to Me, nor shall there be another dearer to Me in the world."

Here, then, at the end of the *Gita* is the first example in Indian philosophy of the love of God for man. In the *Gita* there is only one god, a transcendental God for the first time in Indian thought, one who oversees both time and eternity. Arjuna finally recognized that Krishna is greater than Brahman, for he is the "infinite being, Lord of all the gods, the being and non-being and what is beyond that." He no longer strives to become identical with Brahman but to become part of Krishna.

To reach the idea of a single god from the worship of many gods seems to be a development which accompanies the progress from primitive culture to advanced civilization, itself a function of size of population. The path to him is through asceticism, in a word that renunciation of the world, substituting instead the discipline of meditation, with the promise that if successful in this enterprise the suppliant will be united with God and will not have to be reborn. Here spelled out is the physical exercise of yoga for the ascetic to practice.

Like all holy books the *Gita* contains many contradictions. I will mention one. After recommending the avoidance of inaction, we learn that after all action turns into inaction, inaction into action. Again, "having abandoned attachment, he does nothing though he is always engaged in work." Perhaps this ambivalence is what attracts such diverse followers and makes of the *Gita* an enduring influence. We shall see its influence on Buddhism and learn that it inspired Gandhi.

The last part of the *Gita* was the source of that devotional religion which needs no knowledge except unity with God. It is a mystical activity and is the one later pursued by Ramakrishna. Its acceptance outside of India, and chiefly in the west, may be due to his conviction that all religions are true and all manifestations of the absolute unity of Brahman. So Krishna and the Krishna Mission. In 1886 when Ramakrishna died he left Swami Vivekananda as his chosen successor, who had more success with disciples, spreading the word in the west and particularly in the United States.

Chapter V
Jainism

India in the sixth century B.C. was a land of religious stirrings. There were many holy men, many religious inquiries. The inherited body of religious teachings was large and fully utilized, but some men went beyond the tradition to introduce new variants of their own. Among them were the founders of Jainism, materialism and Buddhism. The first and third of these were to leave a permanent impression on Indian thought and culture and indeed to spread beyond Indian borders.

The word "Jain" comes from a Sanskrit root meaning "to conquer;" literally, one who has obtained self-mastery. It was the work of Vardhamana (more commonly, Mahavira, or "spiritual hero") born about 540 B.C. to a father who was the chief of a *kshattriya,* or warrior caste, and a mother who was the sister of a king. Of the twenty-three predecessors his tradition claimed, at least one, Parsva, is known to have existed in the eighth century B.C. Parsva is said to have lived a family life of wealth and comfort for thirty years, whereupon he left it all to become an ascetic. Mahavira followed somewhat the same pattern. He married but continued to live in his parents' house until they died, whereupon at the age of twenty-eight he entered upon the spiritual life of asceticism which he continued for twelve years until, as he said, he had obtained perfect knowledge. He spent the rest of his life teaching the members of an order of ascetics which he had organized. He died at about the age of seventy.

The most important division in the *Jaina* philosophy is that of the self *(jiva)* and the not-self *(ajiva)*, actually consciousness and the unconscious. "Jiva" means what lives or is animate; spirit and non-spirit, or self and material world, if you will.

The human individual consists of a *jiva* encased in a material body, from which it must be freed to realize its full spiritual nature. A *jiva* is a conscious substance, and there are two kinds: those which have been liberated and those still in bondage. It is only the former class that is subject to birth, growth, decay and death. The primary aim of Jainism is to show the way to self-perfection rather than to explain the world, but this cannot be done so long as there is ignorance, for knowledge includes the knowledge of an inter-dependence; knowledge is the essence of the self.

Consciousness can know everything there is to know, directly, without the aid of the senses. Human beings, unlike the higher animals, have six senses, not five; the Jains count the mind as a sixth sense. The senses are only indirect aids; what interferes with pure knowledge is the burden of *karma*, the consequences of acts performed in previous existences, which stand in the way. Enlightenment occurs when these obstacles are broken down and eliminated, for then the individual consciousness becomes all-knowing and there is absolute apprehension without the shadow of a doubt.

Ajiva, or the material world, is divided into time, space and matter, all of which exist objectively but lack life and consciousness. Time is infinite. Space is both finite and infinite—a finite space—mundane space—which contains matter, and an infinite space which does not. When at rest matter does not change; when in motion it does. It has the properties of color, flavor, odor and touch; it is eternal and consists of atoms, each of which has its own *jiva,* so that there are as many selves as there are atoms of earth, air, fire and wind, each of which has its own *jiva.* Though they are indistinguishable from one another the atoms together give rise to distinctions and difference by combination and recombination. Atoms in combination are called *skandha,* which make up the objects we ordinarily perceive.

We perceive things as they are, but how are they? The Jaina doctrine of *syadvada,* literally "may be," asserts that it is the nature of reality to be only partially known; each perspective is real but none is complete. The Jaina illustrate this with the story of the blind men examining an elephant. One thinks an elephant is the trunk which he touches, another thinks the elephant is its flank, and so on. Each has only part of the truth and thinks it is the whole. The reality is too complex for anyone to grasp. By this theory all absolutisms, all dogmas, are successfully avoided.

To understand reality, one must consider the triadic nature of all existence, a combination of appearance and disappearance with permanence: identity in diversity, unity in multiplicity. Just as there is a substance containing its attributes, there is an identity underlying all change. The Jains believe in a kind of psycho-physical parallelism: two series running concurrently, with little exchange between them, so that material events have only material causes while psychical events have only psychical causes. Thus the task of getting rid of the body in order to attain liberation *(moksha)* has to be performed by means of bodily exercises of a *yoga* character.

The main point in the Jaina ethics is that man alone is responsible for the good or bad in his life; he is, so to speak, in his own care. Unlike most religions the Jaina insist upon the ultimate solitude of the individual. "Alone he accumulates merit; alone he enjoys the happiness of heaven; alone he destroys *karma;* alone he also attains to *moksha.*" Alone, alone, alone.

The ethics of Jainism is contained in the practical discipline designed to show first how the *jiva* came to be associated with *karma* and how it might escape from *samsara,* the endless (and hopeless) repetition of lives. There are eight types of *karma;* among them are the *karma* that obscures knowledge, the *karma* that causes feelings of pleasure, the *karma* that determines one's family, and the *karma* that governs the duration of one's life.

Enlightenment leads the way to escape, and consists in right faith, right knowledge, and right conduct; none of these is considered enough without the others; together they are called "the threefold jewel." Right faith means getting rid of superstitions, right knowledge means that by knowing the true nature of things one will understand his own pure self. For the monk, right conduct contains five vows: not to injure any living things, not to lie, not to steal, to refrain from sex, and to renounce the world. For the layman the last two are relaxed; strict monogamy and contentment are substituted.

There are no castes; only two classes are recognized. One may be either a householder (layman) or a monk, according to capacity and taste. The householder must observe the five vows as closely as he can but always in moderation, but for the monk there is no moderation; all is absolute observance. In the matter of property, for instance, the monk may possess nothing and is dependent upon the householder for the food he must beg. The householder, on the other hand, may possess property but there are restrictions even for him. He must obey the principle of "limited possession," which means that he should voluntarily and in accordance with his position in society limit his property to a certain amount and offer whatever he has beyond that amount to society as a whole.

The first step, *ahimsa,* though negatively stated as non-injury, points to a community of living beings for whom it is necessary to feel and express universal love. We have encountered this principle before, but the Jains make a great point of it. *Ahimsa* must be practiced in three ways: through mind, speech and body: not to think injurious thoughts, not to utter injurious statements, not to commit injurious acts.

If the struggle to attain self-discipline is successful, then the *jiva* achieves the full glory of omniscience and finally escapes from the bondage of the body. It is now free to rise until it reaches the top of the universe where it remains in peaceful bliss forever.

Though this philosophy has been assessed as atheistic, the best term for it might be agnostic. The Jains do not assert the non-existence of God but give at least one good argument against his existence: If God created the world, then he must have felt a lack, which is inconsistent with his necessary perfection.

Chapter VI
Materialism

The period from the sixth to the fourth centuries B.C. saw the rise of the first strong kingdom of the Magadhas in what is now southern Bihar. Its conquests extended all the way to western India, and it lasted until the Mauryas took over in 321 B.C. There was considerable prosperity in the towns and fertility in the farmlands. The mercantile classes challenged the older aristocracy of the *brahmins* and *kshatriyas,* and the new religions of Jainism and Buddhism appeared, as indeed did also the less successful materialists.

It was also the period when the great epics were written, the *Mahabharata* and the *Ramayana,* which described events that had occurred much earlier when the invading Aryans did battle with the native population. Such events usually provoke reconsideration of profound beliefs, and that is why scepticism rubbed shoulders with a faith in reincarnation.

Since the prevailing philosophy in India is and always has been an idealism of one sort or another, it is not surprising that materialism seems to have existed chiefly as a whipping-boy. Yet exist it did, and there is evidence that it was taught in the period before Buddha, as early as the sixth century B.C. Indeed there are traces of materialism, though not as an established doctrine, as early as the *Vedic Hymns* and the *Upanishads,* where it is suggested that there is no supernatural power behind the visible world, that the world itself is a chaos, and that such order as it exhibits may be due to a real and objective chance.

In the *Rig-Veda* there are references to a class of men who did not believe in the gods and who refused to perform sacrifices. The sensualist philosophy known as the doctrine of Brihaspati professed to find a justification in selected passages from the *Upanishads.* It suggested that reward lasts only as long as pleasure lasts. "While life remains let a man live happily: let him feed on butter even if he runs into debt. Once the body becomes ashes, how can it ever return?"

Those who professed this viewpoint were known as Charvakas and Lokayatikas. There are no extensive writings of the Charvaka school; our only knowledge of it comes from its critics.

The Charvaka school so-called was either the name of a disciple to whom the doctrine was first passed on by its founder, or a nickname meaning "sweet-tongued," describing the persuasiveness of its position.

It seems to have made some criticisms of its own. The Charvaka materialists had some harsh things to say about traditional Indian thought, about the classics, for instance, beginning with the *Vedic Hymns* which, they insisted, were written by buffoons, and suffer from three faults: they assert what is not true, are filled with internal contradictions, and engage in useless repetition.

There is something to be said for these charges. Without the necessary caution of scepticism uncontrolled belief does not feel obliged to answer to reason and so runs riot; and the Charvaka philosophers evidently furnished the only scepticism to be found in the Indian tradition. Theirs is not a systematic philosophy—no system can be constructed on a basis of scepticism alone—but a criticism of systems.

The Sanskrit word for materialism, Lokayata, was applied to those who believed that only the world disclosed by the senses, or *loka,* exists. Sense perception, this philosophy maintained, is the only avenue of reliable knowledge. Inference is rejected and with it the claims of reason as a source of the knowledge of the external world. The properties of the material world make themselves evident to the senses and cannot be apprehended merely by thinking about them, a position most materialists would still accept, for it does not exclude thinking about the disclosures of sense experience, only substituting for them.

The material universe came about by chance, from the fortuitous combination of the four elements—earth, air, fire and water—which are eternal. Nature is the only principle underlying phenomena; there is no supernatural creator; for if there were an all-powerful and compassionate God why would he not allay doubts about his existence by revealing himself to his suppliants? If he were all-powerful he would be able to make himself manifest and if he were compassionate he would want to do so but as he does not, there seems to be no God.

The spirit of man exists, and that too comes into existence by the combination of material elements. It was nothing before this happened, and it will be nothing again after the destruction of the body. Consciousness is a property of the body. There is no such thing as atman, the soul does not exist, the body itself *is* the soul. When the body dies consciousness disappears, and therefore *karma* and rebirth are meaningless words.

The Charvaka philosophy may have been the only later one in India that did not regard this world as a place of terror, containing more pain than pleasure, and to be avoided at all costs. Most Indian philosophy is of the negative sort, and looks to release from existence rather than to the positive acceptance of existence as itself a good. Alone in this acceptance, the Charvaka has been a necessary view, if only to fill out the list of Indian alternatives. This world is not only the only world but it is a good world and the Indian is advised to accept it; he is in no need, then, of salvation. The follower of Charvaka did not seek detachment from matter, liberation from the material world of any transformation of it, for matter itself is good and spirit is not opposed to it.

Life should be lived for its own sake, the Charvaka insisted. There is no such thing as virtue. The only reality consists in enjoyment. The moral life of the individual should consist in the pursuit of pleasure and the avoidance of pain. Only the pleasure obtainable in this world is true and good. There is more pleasure than pain, otherwise no one would desire to live and would have no fear of death. Pain exists in order to heighten pleasure by contrast; in this way suffering is not an evil but serves the good.

The Charvaka philosophy was present in India earlier than those of its Greek counterparts, Aristippus, Epicurus and the Greek sceptics, in whom many of the same arguments may be found. Charvaka is one of the heterodox philosophies, inferior in influence to Buddhism and Jainism, but making a constant contrast with the orthodox six schools of Hindu philosophy, all of whom seemed to have felt called upon to defend themselves against it, surely an index to its continuing presence and influence.

A sort of epilogue exists in a more recent school of nihilists called the Shunyavadins, who advance a comprehensive view that all is emptiness. Both theism and atheism, both maya and Brahma, are equally false and promote errors. "The individual and the species, the temple and the god, all is emptiness" and "substance is no more."

Chapter VII
The Buddhism of the Buddha

We owe our knowledge of the life and teachings of Buddha, sketchy though it is, to a collection of later narratives known as the Pali Canon, set down by many hands, the earliest of which may have been the work of men who had not seen or heard the Buddha himself. The Pitakas, or Baskets of the Law, were probably not completely written down before 241 B.C.

Buddhism did not come as an entirely new departure. It was fashionable at the time to be a recluse and to seek proficiency at mind-control. Buddha was only the best among many. The Hindu religion of the brahmins was much older; by the time Buddha was born it had long been established and probably included many older elements of the Aryan invaders and even perhaps some pre-Aryan doctrines. Certainly the doctrine of rebirth was one of them: life consisted in an endless chain of repeated existences, from which a release was sought and—presumably by the enlightened—found. Such reincarnation was held to be automatic, and it makes an interesting contrast that while the western religions have eagerly pursued some form of immortality, the eastern religions have sought to escape from it.

The similarities in the life of Buddha to that of the earlier Mahavira, the founder of Jainism, has been noted, and so have the similarities of their respective doctrines. Buddha had many precedents for his idea that existence means pain. It had already been well stated in the *Bridharanyaka Upanishad:* "A person consists of his desires" but "the man who is freed from desires, he goes to Brahman." A similar idea had appeared earlier in the Samkhya-Yoga tradition, though its systematizer, Patanjali, was much later.

The loose brotherhood of wandering monks who either sought or proclaimed enlightenment was a large one indeed, and the sixth century B.C., when society was moving away from faith in the older group of religions, was a period of considerable restlessness and doubt. The region which is now South Behar, west of Bengal and south of the Ganges, which saw most of Buddha's activities, was familiar to wandering mendicants who seem to have been atheists and to have maintained the most conflicting of doctrines, believing in teachers who were possessed of superhuman insights and preaching reincarnation. Many came from the warrior caste of the *kshatriyas,* as indeed did the Buddha. This development was meaningful in a society in which religious practice as well as religious speculation occupied so large a place in the ordinary man's life.

Buddha was born into the princely family of the Gautamas about 563 B.C., near Kapilavastu on the Himalayas' lower slopes. In his early manhood he lived in great luxury. He had everything: wealth, family and high social position, yet he was unhappy; the spectacle of sickness, old age and death which he saw all around him disgusted him with earthly existence. When he was twenty-nine his wife bore him a son and he was about thirty years when he renounced his inheritance, leaving the palace for the forest in quest of ultimate truth and becoming an ascetic wanderer.

There is a lovely story about a visit paid to him by his

father who found his son in rags and asked him why he had chosen to live in poverty when he could have continued his life of luxury. Buddha is said to have replied, "It is the custom of my kind."

At first Gautama Buddha sought religious instruction under two teachers but finding one after the other unsatisfactory, tried extreme asceticism: together with five other ascetics he fasted and practiced other austerities. Buddha was in many respects a child of his times and asceticism of this sort was a favored way of life then, but at the end of six years he gave it up since it brought neither peace nor enlightenment.

Finally, one day while seated under a Bodhi tree meditating, he experienced an inner illumination which brought him the explanation he sought for the cause of human suffering. At that moment he became enlightened (hence "Buddha," which means the awakened or wise one). He left the forests for the cities and spent the remaining forty-five years of his life as a wandering religious teacher, bringing his discovery to others. In this endeavor he had many rivals, of course, but eventually prevailed over them. When he died in 483 B.C. at the age of eighty, he left behind him an order of monks and another of nuns, who shaved their heads, wore yellow robes and practiced the ascetic life in an effort to bring their message to all men.

There were yoga practices in the primitive doctrine which called on the disciple for the triple performance of morality, concentration and knowledge. One of the earliest and most reliable parts of the Pali Canon and so perhaps the nearest to the doctrine and practice that Buddha left to his disciples was a collection known as the *Patimokkha,* a set of instructions concerning the discipline which monks were expected to follow. It was to be recited at the fast day which occurred every two weeks at the new moon or the full moon. After asking three times whether the monks are pure, the rules are then repeated, seven sets of them. Typical of these rules were those which forbade sexual intercourse, obtaining what is not given, the taking of human life, making a false claim to knowledge and insight.

Buddha began by denying both a personal god and a human self, the chief characters which had played a large part in the early *Upanishads.* His approach, thoroughly pessimistic, positivistic and pragmatic, held out little hope, appealed to nothing supernatural and was entirely concerned with practice. He sought not to account for the origins of the world but only how to escape from it. His understanding of experience was very much what the English philosopher, David Hume, was to say much later that it is: states of consciousness, but no mind to organize them, no substance underlying the succession of sense impressions, and certainly no divine intervention. Our world is neither a world of being nor a world of non-being, only a world of becoming.

It was at Isipatana in the deer park near Benares that the Buddha encountered five mendicants and instructed them in his teaching. He began by cautioning against the two extremes of lust: through sensual pleasures on the one hand, and through asceticism, the self-infliction of pain, on the other. Avoid both extremes, he advised, in favor of the middle road, which leads to knowledge, tranquillity, full enlightenment and peace.

Buddha's teaching is simple enough. It consists in the Four Noble Truths.

First truth: everything in earthly existence is out of joint. Everything involved in individual existence is painful. Life itself is suffering.

Second truth: the cause of suffering is craving; this includes the desire for everything connected with separate existence, such as pleasures. It includes also the desire for superexistence (that is to say, for rebirth, immortality, and the like).

Third truth: Craving must be overcome. Give up desire so that no trace of it remains; abandon it, renounce it, become liberated from it, detach yourself from it.

Fourth truth: the road leading to the ending of desire is the Noble Eightfold Path of ascending steps, consisting in:

Right outlook: the understanding of the Four Noble Truths.

Right purpose: to reach salvation.

Right speech: not to lie and not to slander.

Right behavior: not to kill, not to steal, not to be unchaste, not to drink intoxicants.

Right self-discipline: to practice the monastic life.

Right effort: to exercise will power.

Right self-knowledge: constantly to examine one's behavior and learn to correct it.

Right self-trancendence: to meditate on the ultimate truths.

In the Four Noble Truths, the Buddha had found, he thought, the final wisdom. "I knew I had attained supreme and full enlightenment. The liberation of my mind is established, separate existence is here ended, there is not now survival [that is to say, I shall not be born again]."

In general it could be said that the Four Noble Truths were for the use of monks who were capable of austerities, while the Noble Eightfold Path was intended for the laity in whom moderation in all things would be considered sufficient.

In a second sermon to the five mendicants in the deer park at Benares, Buddha declared that "the material form of the individual is not a permanent self. Neither is sensation or consciousness. By becoming indifferent to consciousness, an instructed disciple becomes free from desire, and through non-desire he is liberated. He knows that his separate existence is ended, that the holy life has been lived, that what ought to be done has been done, that there is nothing beyond this state." This is the way to seek "the supreme peace of Nirvana which is not affected by the wretchedness of earthly existence."

In declining to describe Nirvana, Buddha avoided a characterization which at best would be misleading. It is possible to gather from other passages that he intended nothing negative, and in positive terms suggested as the result of happenings only a vague reality beyond all suffering and change, the bliss of non-existence, though he refrained from using these words also; it was in short an absolute state above and beyond all possible description.

To attempt to sum up Buddha's argument in a short paragraph: There is no consciousness of a permanent self (and, by omission, also no god). The divine life may be pursued and even reached in this world, and it excludes self-seeking. LIfe is composed chiefly of suffering. The cause of the suffering is craving: for all the material things in existence which give pleasure, such as sex, but also non-existence. Get rid of craving and you will get rid of rebirth, with its attendant ills. A life without craving brings tranquillity and peace, and in the end leads to the indescribable state of Nirvana, a kind of nothingness.

In the end Buddha looked not for salvation but for deliverance. He found life to be thoroughly miserable, but instead of trying to change it he sought to escape it, and meant that solution as a model for all.

Not the first to preach the ascetic ideal as a way of reaching to a life higher than the senses, he may have been the first to recommend it as the center of a moral order, and has been credited by his most devoted followers as preaching a doctrine of pure altruism, of being concerned not with his own welfare but only with the deliverance of others. He thought that with the proper discipline any man could reach before death a state in which he had nothing to fear from either death or rebirth.

According to the tradition, when the Buddha was asked some of the fundamental questions, in particular whether or not the world is eternal, and whether it is finite or infinite, he declined to answer, and gave as his reason that such speculations are not necessary since they do not lead to detachment, to the absence of desire, to cessation, to tranquillity, to highest knowledge, to full enlightenment, to peace. And when pressed further to answer whether he thought that by following his precepts all the world would benefit or only a half or a third part, he fell silent.

From the philosophical point of view there are a number of things that can be said about the Buddhism of the Buddha. He rejected all metaphysics as not relevant to the practical problem. Curiously, his approach was intellectual rather than emotional. The ultimate cause of suffering is ignorance, and it can be corrected only by knowledge, even though the immediate purpose of knowledge is application. For the practical problem he proposed a strict ethical solution. Thus while he did not investigate metaphysics, he did propose an ethics.

Its first principle is that life is composed chiefly of suffering. Everything hangs on that being the case; if it is in fact the case, then everything else follows logically. The second principle states that desires are the causes of suffering; it is logical that you would get rid of the suffering by getting rid of the desires.

By rejecting metaphysics he ruled out all appeal beyond his principles, which may or may not be true. I should say for instance they are *not* true. Life contains much suffering, but there is also pleasure and happiness. The affirmation of life is contained not only in pleasurable sensations but also in the *intensity of experience* where pain joins pleasure to enrich the whole. Such affirmation of life is not Buddhism, of course; for Buddhism essentially is a denial of life, and in India as well as in some other countries and perhaps in every country among some individuals, the denial of life has a deep appeal. I would suggest that it requires just as strong a character to face up to the adventure of life, considered as a whole together with everything it can bring to bear on the individual, as it does to reject life as completely and as consistently as the Buddha proposed.

Chapter VIII
The Religions of Buddhism

There are many varieties of the religion which claims the authority of Buddha. A number of accounts list no less than eighteen schools, but these resolve themselves chiefly into two main branches: the Hinayana and the Mahayana.

Before describing them, it would be helpful to tell of the events leading to the spread of Buddhism, which did not occur quickly in the years immediately following the death of Buddha. Perhaps the single factor most responsible for the spread of Buddhism was that, apart from the community of monks, lay believers were included on easy terms. There was not the rigid corporate structure common to many religions; membership was accepted without imposed conditions.

When Alexander the Great invaded India with his Macedonians he encountered a number of warring kingdoms. His death in 323 B.C. led to the consolidation of some of them and the establishment by Chandragupta Maurya of a dynasty, at which our effective knowledge of Indian history begins.

Chandragupta's rule was ruthless. Repressions by torture and death were common, and war to extend the borders of the empire were accepted as ordinary procedures. An elaborate spy structure, with a secret service extending into the lowliest villages, was organized and maintained in a complex system which has no equal in all history. We are reminded by this how oriental the Russians are, for they maintain a similar system today, not only abroad but also at home.

Chandragupta's northern empire was extended into the south as far as Mysore by his son Bindusara who succeded him in 297 B.C. and enlarged to all "the lands between the two seas" (presumably the Arabian Sea and the Bay of Bengal) by his grandson, Ashoka (274-236 B.C.).

It was probably the bloody nature of Ashoka's successful wars of conquest, in which men died by the hundreds of thousands, that led to his conversion to Buddhism. He retained in his empire the principle of freedom of religion but became a devout Buddhist himself. For having transformed a provincial sect into a "world" religion he has been compared to St. Paul. He spread it throughout India, sent out missions to Ceylon, Kashmir and Gandhara, and caused his edicts to be carved on stone pillars and rock faces throughout his empire, in this way proclaiming the conquest by *dharma* instead of by force to which he had come to subscribe calling attention to a government and a religion based on tolerance and mutual understanding. So benign did the nature of his rule become, however, that within fifty years of his death his empire fell apart.

By this time there were already many different Buddhist sects, among them the Theravada (teaching of the elders) who after several centuries claimed to have recovered the Buddha's original message. His Edicts do not mention the fundamentals of Buddhism but stress such matters as the proper reverence of pupil for teacher and the necessity of refraining from the taking of animal life. On some occasion, he recommended, each man should honor another's sect, and violence should be avoided or if this was not possible at least held to a minimum. Ashoka emerges rather as a man with an interest in the concept that life should be sane, kindly and humane than as one concerned with his soul.

The Theravada of Ceylon are supposed to have preserved the pure doctrine of the Buddha undiluted longer than any other. It is largely given in negative form: no injury, no soul, and a Nirvana which has become the cessation of the not-self.

Hinayana Buddhism

For the Hinayana Buddhists, Buddha was a man like other men, only more accomplished. After all, he made no claims to divinity. He thought he had found a moral life and he tried both to live it and to communicate it to others so that they too could benefit.

The religious orders of monks and nuns founded by Buddha before his death, which have lasted into the modern world, were predicated upon the belief that the religious life is incompatible with family life and worldly business; and it was also thought that through seclusion the members of a religious order could exercise an influence out of proportion to their numbers. Buddha enjoined on them the necessity of avoiding the extremes of asceticism and sexual excess, and of choosing the middle way: no severe discipline, no undue hardships, no seeking of converts, for instance, during the rainy season. The Buddhist monk rose early, traveled or begged his only meal until 11:30 A.M. when he retired for meditation for the remainder of the day. In the evening there were discussions and instructions.

For the Buddhist layman life was more relaxed. There was no supervision by the monks. The faithful follower was expected to avoid taking life, drinking intoxicants, lying, stealing and unchastity. He was also to use no perfumes, to sleep on a mat on the ground, and not to eat after midday. He was not expected to avoid wordly affairs but merely to be kind, temperate and prudent in all of his dealings.

Early Buddhism after the death of the Buddha concentrated on the individual without regard for the community as a whole. The ideal was the *arhat*, the enlightened one who has cast off the chains of passion and is thus liberated. The school was somewhat contemptuously named Hinayana, the "little vehicle," because it professed to carry only one passenger at a time across the treacherous seas of earthly existence. The name was bestowed on it later by the Mahayana, the "great vehicle," because the large ferry was able to carry more souls across those seas.

Hinayana Buddhism adhered as closely as possible to the teachings of the Buddha, and was the form of the religion followed most closely after his death. It remained relatively unchanged chiefly in the south of India and in southeast Asia, especially in Ceylon, Burma and Siam. The Hinayana Buddhists are fundamentalists who refuse to budge an inch beyond the literal teachings of the master. Such gods or spirits as there may be are regarded as nothing more than ornamental and uplifting.

Though it was the intention of the Hinayana Buddhists to adhere as closely as possible to the teachings of the Buddha, in this they failed somewhat. That all things are momentary and that there are no permanent entities he might have accepted, though there is no hint in his teachings that he did not believe in the reality of the external world. That all consciousness is a feeling *for* something and must therefore be wiped out he might also have accepted, though the rejection of society and of the welfare of others in favor of the solitude of a cell where a monk might pursue his self-discipline resembles only the first part of Buddha's journey toward enlightenment. It neglects the second part in which he proclaimed his mission to bring to others the truth he discovered, a mission to which he devoted the second half of his life. He would have accepted without qualification, however, the insistence that the individual determines his own destiny without the aid of any supernatural power.

Existence consists in a succession of states of consciousness, beginning in previous existences and continuing through the present existence and on to reincarnation in a number of following states. There is some small evidence that this was Buddha's view although he denied the consciousness itself, and so it was asserted that he did and did not believe in reincarnation but he could not have, since the collection of parts called the self breaks up. Yet something does not get through, though Buddha never says what.

The agnostic by definition is one who does not know about God, whether he does or does not exist. From Buddha's silence on the topic it is possible to conclude that he was an agnostic. In this regard he marks a break with the Hindu tradition which dominated Indian thought before his time, for the Hindu religion is full of gods from the *Vedic Hymns* on.

After Buddha the ranks were quickly closed again and the omission was corrected, and in a surprising way. Buddha himself was declared a god! That is to say, while Hinayana Buddhism officially denied the existence of god, in practice it allowed the worship of the Buddha as a god, and taught that there was a way to rebirth into the heavenly world of Brahman by means of grace and with the help of Buddhist saints.

Nirvana, the goal of every Buddhist, consists in two stages; the first stage in this life, the second, after death. In the first the *arhat*, or emancipated saint, has achieved sainthood despite the five constituents of the personality, the five *skandas:* body, feelings, perceptions, will and consciousness. Though no longer of this world, he lingers in the world in order to teach enlightenment to others. With death the *arhat* achieves the second stage of Nirvana, in which no *skandas* remain. It is a continuation of the first and the transition to it is held to be a trivial one, so that the *arhat* is indifferent as to whether he is in a state of life or death, for death itself is no longer important.

But the Buddha refused to describe the condition after death. Religion, like philosophy, was for him a matter of finding the proper question, not the proper answer. (Of western philosophers only Schopenhauer has provided us with the notion that the limits of the positive are not necessarily negative.)

The negative interpretation was most vigorously set forth in a work entitled the *Questions of King Milinda,* the Indian name for the Graeco-Bactrian King Menander, who ruled over the Indus valley and the valley of the Ganges from 125 to 95 B.C., and interrogated a very astute Buddhist monk named Nagasena. Considered a masterpiece of Indian prose, it is admired and used chiefly in Ceylon but often considered almost as important as the Pali Canon even though it was composed some four hundred years later.

Nagasena clung as closely as possible to the teachings of Buddha and so took a strictly negative approach to life. He held, as the great Indian historian of philosophy, N. Radhakrishnan put it, that the make-believe of religion offers no escape from the sufferings of mankind. He refused to allow the ugly truth to be disguised, and he repudiated existence in rational terms, just as the Buddha had done. He was ahead of his time in insisting on evidence for any statement and denied the existence of a soul, of a god, or of the future even for the enlightened. This was a literal reading of the master's position but it was not one the masses could live with. A more popular form of Buddhism, one that incorporated many of the Hindu beliefs which existed before Buddha's time and held out hope for the faithful was needed. Mahayana Buddhism was not long in coming.

Meanwhile, Hinayana Buddhism found a congenial home in south India and more particularly in Ceylon, where it was introduced in Asoka's time. Sacred relics were sent there. The best known as Buddha's begging bowl, but there is also evidence of a tooth which was supposed to have been Buddha's. Asoka is said to have sent it to Ceylon but it was seen in 405 A.D. at Peshawar, whence it went to Persia—it was several inches long and had most probably never been a human tooth—and eventually found its way to Portugese Goa, where the Catholic archbishop had it pounded in a mortar in the presence of the court, the fragments burned and the ashes scattered over the sea. That tooth was subsequently declared not to have been the real one, and two authentic ones sprang up in its place.

From Ceylon Hinayana Buddhism spread eastward to Burma, Siam (Thailand) and Cambodia. To the remaining islands of southeast Asia Buddhism took other routes, and had to compete not only with Hinduism, by which it was sometimes diluted, but also with Chinese influences.

Mahayana Buddhism

Just as it was the political power of Ashoka which gave such an impetus to the spread of Hinayana Buddhism, so it was the later figure of Kanishka, a Kushan king (A.D. 78-101), who performed the same service for the Mahayana during the first three centuries of the Christian era. A barbarian conqueror from the northwest he converted to Buddhism and practiced it with the zeal of a convert, perhaps like Constantine, the Roman emperor who adopted Christianity for business reasons. Kanishka called a council of monks to organize the sacred texts and these became the basis for the Mahayana tradition.

The Mahayana writings are the largest single collection of sacred texts in the world, but no one is able to say just what is included or who put it together. Even the monks were not expected to have read all of them. The language is Sanskrit (as compared with the Pali language of the Hinayana writings). The tradition insisted that there are many roads to salvation and as many guide-books. But the Mahayana writings, unlike the Hinayana, insist on their own indispensable value, their own sanctity and efficacy. There evidently was among those who were responsible for Mahayana Buddhism a tendency to compose new scriptures.

Probably what Mahayana Buddhism represents, since it

comes later than Hinayana, is the influence of Hinduism washing over and engulfing the Buddhist tradition. Roughly put, Hinayan Buddhism is objective, Mahayana subjective. According to the Hinayana the Buddha was concerned with what the mind can perceive in existing things, while according to the Mahayana the question is rather what things the mind creates. Yet paradoxically the problem of making a religion out of Buddhism meant basing a positive social order on a personal denial of life, and this the Mahayana did better than the Hinayana which it supplanted in most places and spread with great influence to China and from there to Japan.

Most of the Mahayana doctrines are not new, only newly presented, and have their origins in ancient Indian thought, particularly in the *Bhagavadgita*. Hinduism was many thousands of years old when Buddha was born and retained its strength. Actually the Mahayana was not only a religion founded on Buddhism but also a collection of the artistic and literary culture of India.

Though Buddha had always opposed all efforts by his followers to deify him, in the first century of our era his image was carved in stone and worshipped as a god. The Buddhism of the Buddha was godless, but by the time of the Mahayana Buddha himself had become a god. The Buddhism of the Buddha was a *practice*, the Buddhism of the Mahayana was a *religion*. It was held that accumulated merit could be transferred, so that rich merchants could donate caves with their elaborate statues and paintings and in this way pay for their Nirvana. These extremes could hardly be accepted by the Hinayana Buddhists, and accordingly at the Fourth Buddhist Council held in Kashmir early in the second century A.D. the division between the Hinayana and the Mahayana was recognized.

There were also tendencies in Mahayana to construct metaphysical systems and to invent deities to satisfy the emotions as well as the intellect, but the Hinayana was chiefly intellectual (though curiously non-metaphysical). Mahayana was inclined toward metaphysics, mythology and devotional piety, all foreign to the Hinayana. Probably the first great name among many who undertook a Mahayanist metaphysics was Nagarjuna who flourished between 125 and 200 A.D. He applied to the external world the same negative logic that the Buddha had applied to the soul.

The Mahayana was easier for the ordinary man to follow. It did not require him to part with his possessions and to give up the world. It was a variety of Buddhism everyone could live with and that accounts for its great success. Another element in its success is that the many gods of the older Hindu polytheism were restored though with their names changed. Now they were called buddhas and bodhisattvas, and since they were infinite in number in time and space were everywhere to be found. Many Buddhas had lived before Gautama Buddha, many more were his contemporaries throughout the universe, and there were more to come.

A classic Mahayana text, the *Lotus of The True Doctrine*, which has been said by many scholars to be typical of the school, lists 80,000 bodhisattvas, those who strive to become Buddhas in order to aid mankind, and recites many marvels and spells employed in sympathetic magic. That anyone could become a bodhisattva was a comforting idea. The Indian tendency to polytheism had its effect on Mahayana Buddhism in more ways than one: for example, the idea of worship was introduced into Buddhism for the first time. Though it had of course long been common among the Hindus, it had not been the practice of the Hinayana school. It is often true in both Hinduism and Buddhism that the many gods are represented as many manifestations of the one god, but such monotheism is hard to come by and is confined to Hinayana Buddhism and to certain forms of Vedanta.

The Mahayana, in sharp contrast with the Hinayana, teaches a belief in bodhisattvas, a code of altruistic ethics, a doctrine which holds that the Buddhas are supernatural beings widely distributed throughout space and time and innumerable, an idealistic metaphysics in which Buddhas are essences, and includes worship of images and elaboration of ritual as well as many magic formulas and charms, and, finally, salvation by faith in a Buddha through the invocation of his name.

The bodhisattvas are benevolent beings who choose to postpone the bliss of Nirvana in order to help alleviate the sufferings of others, supernatural teachers who are connected with the whole course of nature as shown by the sympathetic earthquakes which mark their progress. They play a central role because of the concept that anyone may become a Buddha. But that is not the whole story of Buddhas, for there are many other Buddhas who do not belong to our world at all but rule various remote regions, called "buddha-fields".

The Hinayana Buddhist denies the existence of the self and hence of the inner world of consciousness. The Mahayana applies this also to the outer world, and so proves that the material world does not exist. The only reality is self-conscious thought without an object, though it is necessary to deal with appearances. A subdivision of the Mahayana, called the Madhyamikas, deny the reality of both the inner *and* outer worlds, and so may be called absolute nihilists. It is only through ignorance, they say, that material things appear to be separate in the first place. Get rid of subjectivity and such things will cease to exist. What does exist is only the reality of the Buddha, variously described as an indescribable thing-in-itself and as an all-pervading essence which occasionally takes Buddha-shape. The absolute truth is a void with no properties whatsoever.

Like so many religions Madhyamika Buddhism insists on the existence of a twofold truth, a truth about everyday life and a supernatural truth. The advantage of this distinction lies in the fact that the latter cannot be judged by the standards of the former.

Religions, eastern and western, have in common a conflicting desire to avoid logic in the attempt to express the mystical and at the same time to justify its claims by means of reason. We are accustomed to this in the west: believe what is absurd, Tertullian insisted for Christianity. We can see this clearly illustrated in the most famous of the Mahayana Buddhist texts, the *Vagrakkhdika* or *Diamond Cutter,* written about A.D. 350, where it is plainly stated that a *bodhisattva* is one who denies that there are persons but is resolved to save them; his greatness is said to be his skill in combining these conflicting beliefs.

Obviously no one could do so and yet retain his rationality, but that is nearly always what the religious individual is asked to do. By defeating thought through contradictions, another bond is removed in the name of freedom of spirit. A number of these contradictions are attributed to the Buddha himself: "after I have delivered immeasurable beings, not one single being has been delivered," and again, "the fully enlightened are to be known from no-signs as signs." After the Buddha had finished preaching it was said that his words were praised by monks and nuns, by faithful men and women and by "the whole world of gods, evil spirits and fairies."

Subsequently, the two schools of Hinayana and Mahayana continued to exist side by side, with many variations in ritual and discipline accounting for the split into many sects. The influence of the older Hinduism grew in effect until in many respects it became impossible to distinguish Buddhism from Hinduism, at least on point of doctrine, and even on many points of monastic discipline.

The Buddhist influence persisted through many centuries and even survived the persecutions of foreign invaders, like the Huns in Northern India from A.D. 470 to 530, who destroyed monasteries and promoted the more irrational forms of Buddhism, such as the worship of Shiva. Buddhism and Hinduism remained relatively stronger in the safer south, where they competed with Jainism without persecution. But from the seventh century on, the decline of Buddhism throughout India, even in the south where it had been strongest, became evident. It remained strong in the western states into the twelfth century, then almost disappeared from India and gave way to the revival of Hinduism which remained the dominant Indian religion. Probably it was Buddhism which contributed to the later Hindu tradition the respect for animal life and the institution of monasteries. It continued to exist in isolated pockets here and there, but never regained its former popularity.

It was the Mahayana version of Buddhism which spread north and west, and eventually found its way to China where it exerted a strong influence—one of the most influential regions of the entire world is the area surrounding the basin of the Tarim River in what is now the Chinese province of Singkiang—as we shall see in the next part of this book where we discuss the philosophy of China. Here it will suffice to say that Tibetan Buddhism was a variety of the Mahayana. The Tibetans were the chief power in the Tarim basin from about 750 until 850 A.D. and many Tibetan manuscripts have been found there.

Tantric Buddhism

I cannot leave the topic of Buddhism without a mention of the sect which illustrates more than any other what a great variety of beliefs were included under the name of Buddha and how far many of them strayed from his doctrine.

Tantric Buddhism, which has flourished chiefly in Tibet, probably dates from A.D. 500. It probably owes much to earlier religious beliefs and practices, those of the pre-Hindu Dravidians, for instance, who as we have seen lived earlier than the writers of the *Vedic Hymns*, practiced magic and witchcraft, and maintained a cult of the mother goddess and fertility rites. Tantric literature is filled with hymns, formulas for spells, and long descriptions of mythological beings.

Insofar as Tantric Buddhism has a fixed position at all it can be stated somewhat as Professor A. Bharati has done. The universe is a unity but it works only through the mutual attraction of opposite poles: activity and passivity, for example, the male and female principles. The Tantric exercises relive this unity by means of a spiritual discipline: what is being carried out in practice is the merging of appearances, with the Absolute believed to be a short cut to salvation.

The Tantra taught that not much could be learned from treatises but that it was necessary instead to study directly under a spiritual instructor called a "Guru." He stands in the place of the Buddha and can teach the secrets and mysteries. The three activities called for from the Tantric Buddhist were the recitation of spells (called "mantras"), the carrying out of ritual gestures and dances, and the identification with gods by means of meditation in a trance-like state. A complete ritual would have to include all three because there are three sides to a human being, body, speech and mind; the body acts through the gestures, the speech through the mantras, and the mind through a trance.

There are two forms of the Tantra, right-handed and left-handed. In many ways the Left-handed Tantras are the more interesting because they represent the last extreme of the Buddhist religion. Left-handed Tantric Buddhism is distinguished by the worship of Shakris, female gods, by vast number of terrifying demons, by an elaborate ritual which must take place in a cemetery, and by an obligatory sexual intercourse. In the older Buddhism, which was exclusively masculine, it was not even possible for a woman to become a Buddha, but in the Left-handed Tantra the sexual life was employed to explain the spiritual.

The highest activity was said to be the union of man and woman, as the art produced by this school baldly portrays. There are two forms of the discipline. In one form there is the actual handling of the ingredients of the ritual: women, meat and wine. This is the left-handed form; in the right-handed the worship can be conducted through substitutes; that is to say, meditation or union in place of sex; in place of meat, cereals;

and in place of wine, some non-alcoholic drink. But it is the pious duty of everyone who subscribes to Left-handed Tantra Buddhism to have intercourse at least once each day in some out of the way place. Intercourse is a ritualistic discipline and must be with a woman who is not one's own wife; a woman of any caste is acceptable. In view of this recommended license, I should mention again that it has a serious Buddhist religious purpose, which is to bring an end to human suffering from the misery of attachment by eliminating death and rebirth.

The explanation in religious terms went somewhat as follows: if Nirvana and the world are one, then the passions, including the sexual passion, are the same as Nirvana. Indulgence in the senses, the love of self, of wine and women, and indeed of all material possessions, are justified because they serve as avenues to universal love. The passions lead to salvation. With the Left-handed Tantra, the Buddhism of the Buddha has swung round full circle.

As an important postscript to Left-handed Tantric Buddhism it should be pointed out that the most prevalent religious cultural practice in India was and remains asceticism, with the Left-handed Tantra functioning as a kind of permanent counter-culture and as evidence that the earliest tradition in Indian religious life still survived.

When Buddhism became established in India the effect at first was to improve the moral content of Hinduism as a religion that was based on the *Vedic Hymns* and the *Upanishads*. But Buddhism, by its acceptance of the popular forms of Hinduism, was so severely debased and diluted that by the year A.D. 1000 the invading Moslems found little left of it to destroy. Outside India, however, and especially in southeast Asia, Buddhism continued to flourish and to affect other aspects of culture such as the fine arts, where it furnished a magnificent stimulus.

Chapter IX

The Religions
of Hinduism I

There have been six principal schools of Hindu philosophy regarded as orthodox, most of which flourished after A.D. 200, but can be traced back to origins as early as 800 B.C. Although holding different, widely varied views—on the existence of God, on the material world as real or illusory, on the question whether individual souls can flourish without reliance on God and the world—they had much in common. All the systems objected to what they regarded as the skepticism of the Buddhist, they accepted the authority of the Vedic Hymns; all employed the same terms though assigning slightly different meanings to them; all held that there is something beyond the self, all accepted pre-existence and rebirth; all supposed that the universe obeys laws but paradoxically that intuition rather than reason is the path to understanding.

Unlike the practice in the west, religious tolerance prevented open conflict among adherents of the various views, at least in India, and all were considered legitimate paths to wisdom. In this chapter we shall look at three of the most typical and influential of the six Hindu schools, the Samkhya-Yoga, the Advaita Vedanta, and the Nyaya-Vaisesika.

The Samkhya-Yoga

The true Indian tradition moves from the *Vedic Hymns* through the *Upanishads* and on through the epic of the *Mahabharata* to the *Samkhya-Yoga,* spanning perhaps several thousand years in the process. Probable dates for the Samkhya-Yoga are about 700 B.C., where it was begun by Kakila, and somewhere between the sixth and fourth centuries, when it was chiefly the work of Patanjali; but its influences may be several thousand years earlier. Patanjali admitted that he only systematized a theory and a practice which was already much older.

The *Samkhya* is the earlier theory and the Yoga the later practice, and clearly they belong together. They have long been associated though they have two differences: *Samkhya* is atheistic whereas Yoga is theistic; *Samkhya* relies upon metaphyisical knowledge whereas Yoga relies upon techniques of meditation. Both reject the world, not for the negative reasons that the world is unworthy but because something more worthy exists: a sacred kind of being which can be uncovered. As Mircea Eliade pointed out, the Indian mystic thinks he is leading man away from the more limited to the less, toward in fact a sort of solidarity with the cosmos, a participation in a broader nature which alone could be the setting for the many rebirths to which every self is destined. The world is real enough but it is a world of becoming, and it is better to seek a kind of being apart from the world and not subject to change.

First then the *Samkhya* theory, which begins with a personal God, whose existence is proved by the fact that there is more knowledge in some individuals than in others. There must be a person whose knowledge is complete and perfect, and that person is God. He is also the reason why the *Vedic Hymns* are regarded as revealed and infallible.

Here, then, we have a supreme God with separate sources for the dualism of the physical universe and the self: *prakriti* (nature or matter) and *purusa,* (spirit or soul). Matter and individual souls existed separately from all eternity. The salvation of the soul requires it to move away from matter and toward God. The *purusas* have their being independently of *prakriti* and outside of space and time. Indeed the relations between *prakriti* and *purusa* are never explained; we are never told how spirit became involved in matter in the first place, but we do know that it has to be isolated from matter and indeed from all other spirits.

Prakriti is both matter and force, out of which the variety of the universe evolved. Cause is the principle governing all change, but is always more general than the effect which is pre-existent in it. The elements of *prakriti* always existed, there is no creation or dissolution, and they can be ascertained through reason. *Prakriti* does not depend upon God, it can evolve of itself but does not evolve *for* itself; it evolves toward *purusa*. There is only one *prakriti* but there are many *purusa*. God is only another *purusa*, and like the *purusa* unrelated to *prakriti*, which is the name for the ground of the whole material universe. The interrelations of the three qualities of nature of which *prakriti* consists, namely *sattva* (light or purity), *rajas* (energy), and *tamas* (inertia or darkness), account for the variety and infinite complexity of things.

Purusa, like *prakriti*, is eternal and always present. It is passive sensation, never active, but like *prakriti* ascertained through the reason. It involves pure consciousness, and is without any necessary references to an object. Pure consciousness can be neither externally nor internally perceived.

Material things, then, are not independent but have only dependent existence, and exist in order to satisfy a need connected with the *purusa*. There are an infinity of *purusas*, proved by the fact that the birth and death of one individual does not involve the birth and death of others. The relation of *prakriti* to *purusa* is not as clear as it might be.

As expressions of the spirit, all persons long for escape from the endless cycle of existence and that they have such longings is evidence that salvation is possible. It is the prevalence of pain that leads the spirit to long for freedom from pain; and toward that freedom the knowledge that the self is unaffected by the non-self is the first step.

The term "yoga" (or yoke—that which serves to bind together), refers to any ascetic technique which includes a kind of formal meditation. Yogic practice is first mentioned in the *Upanishads*. However, the Yoga of the *Samkhya* has to be distinguished from the general practice throughout India of similar physical and psychological exercises whose aim is well-being; they carry no religious or philosophical meanings. Yoga spread almost immediately to other schools, such as the Buddhists and the Jains, which differ from the *Samkhya* in having no personal God.

Yoga—a kind of detached action, a self-discipline aimed at the self—is the practice of *Samkhya*. It is the identity of the self with the consciousness that is responsible for those fluctuations of attention which obscure the purity and freedom of the self. To gain control over the consciousness the method is to suppress the mental activity based on the five senses. The disciplines of love, indifference to sinners, and above all *ahimsa* or non-injury; and the goal is *samadhi* or quiescence, by which the freedom of pure spirit is reached. Yogic practices were designed to teach renunciation of the world and absolute detachment from it, the highest form of which is detachment even from the distinction between the self and the not-self.

The necessary precondition for *Yoga* is the acceptance of God as the perfect model, for only by contemplating God is it possible to become like God. The practice consists in such physical aids as body postures and breath control; and the mental training that accompanies deep meditation in the effort to achieve a state of equilibrium which resembles dreamless sleep, an awareness of absolute detachment from everything including even, in the end, God and the world.

Ordinarily perception is understood as the awareness by a subject of an object. The yogic practice the direction of perception is reversed. The yogin follows the perception backward from the object to the subject until the subject itself becomes its only object.

Among the number of steps Eliade has listed in the yogic technique are: restraints, bodily postures, respiration, and concentration, to reach tranquility *(samadhi)*.

The restraints are preparatory in nature, and include not killing, not stealing, refraining from sex, and from avarice. Of these, not killing *(ahimsa)* is the most important; it means not harming any creature at any time. These restraints, moral in nature, prepare the yogin for more intense exercises.

The most important—the core of Yogic practices—is the bodily posture. The individual is seated, his right foot is on the left thigh and his left foot on the right thigh; he crosses his arms behind his back and grasps the right toe with the right hand and the left toe with the left hand; at the same time, his chin lowered to touch his chest, he gazes at the tip of his nose or at the center of his navel.

To this posture is added the discipline of respiration, by which the yogin must slow down the respiratory rhythm as much as possible, breathing in, breathing out and holding the breath, each of which should occupy equally long times, progressively retarding the rhythm until respiration is suspended as long as possible, thus producing a sensation of harmony, an awareness of the presence of his body, and a deliberate consciousness of his greatness.

Eliade thinks that the bliss attained in this fashion produces soft gestures and a kind of vegetable existence, and that sap rather than blood flows in the yogin's veins. This would represent a kind of evolutionary retrogression, which may be after all what the yogin seeks. But there is more: considerable powers are claimed by the successful practice which opens doors of reality not otherwise accessible; for instance, he can in this way have knowledge of his previous existences; he can become invisible; he can know when he is to die; he can exercise immense physical strength. But what he wants most of all is liberation through assimilation to pure being from which every attribute has been removed. The final self-revelation comes when the yogin takes possession of being in all its completeness and becomes one with it, thus realizing that identification with the cosmos which is the ambition of every mystic of whatever faith.

The Advaita Vedanta

We turn next to the *Advaita Vedanta*, the most influential of the six schools, which represents a prevailing strain in ancient Indian thought, the direct outcome of traditions that go back to the *Vedic Hymns*, the *Upanishads*, the *Bhagavad-Gita* and the *Brahma-sutra*. It is an attempt to instil new life into the Hindu religion. Its origins in the *Upanishads* led it to be called *Vedanta*, or the concluding chapters of the *Veda*. *Advaita* means non-dualism, hence a monistic interpretation of the Upanishadic tradition. Its author Shankara belongs to the eighth century of our era when, though he died at the age of thirty-two, managed to construct a very influential system of absolute idealism.

Shankara was born about 788 A.D., and was contemporary with the first of three waves of Muslim invaders, that of the Arabs, who brought not only their religion and philosophy with them but also their civilization. Their existence and dominance in the north of India was a severe challenge to Hinduism, which was able, however, to survive, even to flourish under those conditions—a tribute to its abiding strength.

There is nothing really new in Shankara's teaching. He advocated the identity of Brahman and atman, the world as an appearance, and the path of wisdom leading to *moksha* or freedom.

Brahman is supreme. Nothing much can be said about it, for Brahman cannot be found through knowledge obtained by the senses or reached through logical classifications; in a word, cannot be known. Brahman is pure inwardness, indivisible. We cannot even say that Brahman is one, except negatively: we can assert non-dualism. Brahman is being, eternal and self-existent.

Similarly, the world is not an illusion, only an appearance. For Shankara Maya does not mean illusion, it means appearance; appearances are real. The object perceived exists apart from the perception of it, the object known is independent of the act of knowing. Shankara combined an idealism of metaphysics with a realistic theory of knowledge. The world has its basis in being; that anything is real means that the world is real. The unity of Brahman and the world is not asserted, their difference is denied; they are non-dual. The world is dependent on Brahman, *is* Brahman. Maya is simply the principle which accounts for the appearance of Brahman as the world: we see the multifariousness of things where in reality there is only Brahman. The multiplicity of things in the world is compared to a stick burning at one end which when waved around gives the illusion of a circle of fire.

Ultimate reality is not unknown; it is the essence of the self. Apart from the consciousness of the self the world does not exist; it is only in the consciousness of the self that there is the certainty of existence. There can actually be a positive *experience* of the immortality of the soul. Like Descartes, Shankara denies that anyone can deny his own existence, for in the very act of doubting there is an affirmation: if he doubts, he exists. Atman is not the subject but the basis of the distinction between subject and object, the spirit discovered in the depths of the subject.

Consciousness is not amenable to time and space; death does not affect it; it is pure being. Salvation through freedom from subjection to Karma is what it always is in Indian religions—attained through detachment, the suppression of egotism, correct, disinterested social behavior, attainment of liberation or *moksha,* which can come finally only when the body has been cast off.

Shankara criticized both the Samkhya-Yoga and Buddhism, though the similarity between the *Advaita Vedanta* and certain schools of Mahayana Buddhism is clearly evident—and no wonder, when both issued from a long tradition of Hindu beliefs. The influence inside India of *Advaita Vedanta* has been considerable, though more among Indian intellectuals than with the populace. Since the Neo-Vedantins of the Ramakrishna Mission have spread the doctrine widely outside of India, it has had something of a vogue in the west.

The Nyaya-Vaisesika

The third of the classic schools of Hinduism that we shall consider is the *Nyaya-Vaisesika,* the nearest thing to a western philosophy that exists in India, and older than Buddhism. The history of the school is divided into two periods, the first about the third century B.C. beginning with Gautama and Kanada and the second about A.D. 1200 with Gangesa some 1500 years later. It resembles nothing so much as the classical western realistic philosophies of Plato and Aristotle and, among modern philosophers, C.S. Peirce and A.N. Whitehead. We will look primarily at the early period when *Nyaya-Vaisesika* was first formed, but we can offer here little more than a brief outline.

The philosophy has in it greater profundities than any I have here recorded. Curiously, the *Nyaya* and the *Vaisheshika* arose independently and were brought together only later, as we shall presently see. *Nyaya* is literally "that by means of which the mind is led to a conclusion," or, in a word, "argumentation," while *Vaisesika* comes from *visesa,* meaning "individual difference," the argument being for diversity or plurality in the universe. The *Nyaya* developed the theory of knowledge and logic; the *Vaisesika* developed the metaphysics, a system of pluralistic realism. Yet they are not far apart, for while the *Nyaya* school was concerned with formal logic, it sought by removing false knowledge to emancipate the soul and lead it to the bliss of salvation. Knowledge is not the same as reality, only the means of reaching it, but our minds are capable of achieving a trustworthy account.

The *Nyaya*, not concerned so much with how things are as with how we know what they are, seeks a reliable method of arriving at truth and then devises a defense of that method. As truth-seeking is already present in human action, all that is necessary is to understand and express it by means of general principles. Its achievements in logic formed the basis of all systematic philosophies in India, even of those which disagreed with the *Nyaya-Vaisesika* system. The *Vaisesika* by contrast sets forth a catalogue of all that there is, and tries to show the special features that each entry possesses.

The theory of knowledge is that of pluralistic realism: whatever there is, is knowable; all things are objects; all objects are independent of our knowledge of them, hence the realism; they are also independent of each other, hence the pluralism. There are two kinds of objects; material things are said to be objects, and so also are classes of things. When knowledge corresponds to the object of knowledge it is true; otherwise it is false. The test of truth or falsity is whether or not it leads to successful activity: if you wish to discover whether a substance is water, see whether it will quench thirst. This is what the Americans call pragmatism, the pragmatism of Peirce, however, rather than that of James, for the test of truth is not "what works" but what corresponds to reality.

Unconditioned perception is where all knowledge starts, and the mind (manas) is a condition of perception. The manas mediates between the self and the senses, but perception is direct and immediate, and is due not to previous experience or reasoning, but to direct contact of a material object with the corresponding sense organ; perception depends on external objects to be perceived.

There are six kinds of perception; among them the perception of the material object through its quality—when we perceive the quality as a class, and when we perceive the absence of the object. Moreover, we can perceive not only the absence of the object when our senses are directed to where it was but also the presence of the ground where it was.

Perception can be external (when brought about by the senses) or internal (when due to the contact of the mind with its proper objects). Indeterminate perception is sensible contact with an external thing without recognizing the class to which it belongs. Determinate perception is similar contact but with its class recognized.

The second avenue of knowledge, inference, resembles the classic inference of Aristotle's logic of the syllogism, the same three terms and the same relations between them, though under other names, with slight differences too technical for our present discussion. Suffice it to say that Indian logic insists that the premises be true and the conclusion true, a departure from western logic in which the relations of conclusion to premises is a matter of validity rather than truth. There are also relations to perceived and unperceived causes and effects not present in western logic, which is independent of perception and indeed also of cause and effect.

In the metaphysics of the *Nyaya-Vaisesika* being is divided into six kinds of independent realities: substance, quality, action *(karma)*, generality, particularity, and inherence.

As with Aristotle, substance is the substratum or underlying material cause of composite things. There are nine substances: earth, water, fire, air, ether, time, space, self *(atman)*, and mind. Each is composed of atoms which are eternal; the corresponding compounds are not eternal. There is a qualitative difference between atoms, of which there are as many classes as there are elements.

At the ordinary level things come into existence by combination. Nothing lasts far more than instants: it originates and endures for at least an instant, but it can cease to exist in the third instant. Thus an invisible change keeps occurring which accounts for the transcence of stable objects that we encounter.

Earth, water, fire, and air are what common experience ordinarily encounters. Time, measurable only by the movement of material objects, and space definable only by reference to such objects, are objective realities.

The self has such qualities as cognition, desire, pleasure and pain. Consciousness, the basis of all activity, belongs to the self, but only accidentally; it is not an essential attribute. With liberation, which is the aim of the self, it becomes free from consciousness and therefore from all experience. And that is the goal of the individual, the freedom of the self from all experience; *moksha* or liberation. For there is more pain than pleasure in experience, while *moksha* can be a permanent condition, reached by the self when it ceases to have experience in any form.

That there is a mind is proved by the fact that while the external senses can be in contact with many objects at the same time, the internal sense can be in contact only with a single object at a time.

There are twenty-four kinds of quality, among them color, taste and smell, and some which sound strange to western ears, such as number, remoteness, effort and tendency.

There are five kinds of action, contraction and expansion and also throwing upward and locomotion.

The metaphysics of the *Nyaya-Vaisesika* has two separate domains of being, a domain of *samanya* (universals), and a domain of *visesa* (particulars).

"Generality" *(samanya)* must receive special consideration here for it touches on one of the most familiar topics in metaphysics. *Samanya* is similar to the western "universal," or infinite class, although some authorities dispute this, and as in the west, it has been the source of much controversy. The Jains, for instance, take the view that it has a basis in the material world but cannot be elevated to its own domain: *in* things does not mean *apart* from things. The *Nyaya-Vaisesika* answer is to admit that universals are in the corresponding particulars but that could not be, if universals were not available everywhere and actualized only where the corresponding particulars occur.

"Generality" has its own being but is to be found also in substance; it is, in a word, apart from existence. It is an independent kind of being and it is eternal, residing in many. There are two kinds of generality; the highest is being itself, which includes everything and is included in nothing; the lower corresponds to the many universals which are included in being, the species of the higher genus. But at the same time it must be remembered that they are not the particulars. A fair comparison would be with Plato's all-inclusive Good, the most inclusive universal, his universals of goodness and of beauty, and good and beautiful material things which are the sensed particulars.

"Particularity" belongs to existence and is the opposite of "generality." Particulars, *visesa*, have distinctive features. As individuals, each is unique and singular, the ground upon which the whole system rests, as is shown by the fact that the system is named after them. Particulars are what exist; they impose an internal unity upon a diversity of content, and they oppose other particulars. In so far as a particular is itself always the same throughout its diversity, it exhibits universality, and this also makes it a member of a class of such particulars.

"Inherence" is a permanent relation between two parts when one is in the other. Thus the whole is in its parts, the universal is in the particular. Inherence is necessary connection, the relation between cause and effect. But accidental conjunction also exists; and so chance is equally real and objective.

In addition to the kinds of existence we have been examining (such as substance, earth, etc.), there are four kinds of negative existence: "the non-existence of a thing before it is produced," "the non-existence of an effect in the cause before it is produced," "the absence of a connection between two things," and "the mutual exclusion of two things from each other." "Negation" or "not" is a name, and what it names is the existence in reality of an absence or non-existence. The description of reality in this philosophy would not be complete without it, for it is part of the picture.

One of the distinguishing features of this Indian metaphysics which marks it as different from similar systems in the west is that physical things and living bodies exist *equally* and interact with one another in space and time. The world is governed by a moral order which applies not only to living bodies but to all physical things as well. All individuals of whatever kind are governed by the same law *dharma*, or law, so that all acts, not merely human acts, are moral. There is no break in quality or kind between natural law and the moral order. They share the same assumptions. It is *dharma* which supports or upholds the spiritual side of the self. *Dharma* and *adharma* refer to the earned merit or demerit which follows from the performances of good or bad deeds.

In the early version of the *Nyaya-Vaisesika*, that of Kanada for instance, there is no direct reference to God. The workings of the metaphysical system are explained without the need for such a reference. But the later school radically altered this starting procedure. By the time of Gangesa there is a single God in the *Nyaya-Vaisesika* system and he is pictured as a supreme self, infinite and eternal, omnipresent, all-knowing and all powerful. He created the world and continues to maintain it, like Aristotle's God, not out of nothing but out of eternal atoms in eternal space and time. Occasionally He destroys the world, only to recreate it out of the same materials. He is, in Aristotle's language, the first efficient cause of the world's existence but not its material cause, which is left unexplained in both the Aristotelian and Indian systems. God's existence is proved by the existence of composite things which must have a cause, and that cause must be an intelligent agent. The name for the intelligent agent is God.

Little happened to the Nyaya-Vaisesika philosophy between A.D. 900 and 1200, but in the period after A.D. 1200 when the two schools united there were new developments. One was the formation of a vigorous defense of the philosophy against its opponents. Perhaps the need for a common defense brought the two schools together. They also developed some fresh ideas which were incorporated in the philosophy.

One is the presence of a sign wherever that which is represented by the sign is present, and the absence of the sign wherever that which is represented is absent—an idea called invariable concomitance.

More important is the principle of "extraordinary universal perception," the notion in the theory of knowledge that not only are particulars perceived *as* particulars but also universals are perceived *as* universals. When a man looks at a cow, say, he sees that particular cow but he sees *in addition* the class "cow" of which that particular cow is a member. This is part of the theory of knowledge which strongly supports the metaphysics of realism.

Chapter X
The Religions of Hinduism II

One set of Hindu religions is centered on the worship of Vishna and Shiva and his consort, Shakti, with whom he is often even identified. The tradition goes back to the Indian classics; there are traces of it in the *Vedic Hymns,* the *Upanishads* and even in the *Mahabharata* of which the *Bhagavad-Gita* constitutes a part. There are several varieties of Shiva and Shakti worship, and I shall say only a brief word about three of them; enough, however, for the reader to get the message.

This period corresponds roughly with that of the Gupta dynasty (A.D. 320 to 467). It was a period of great prosperity, especially in the north. Under the Gupta dynasty culture generally flourished exceedingly. Poetry, painting and sculpture, most notably in the Ajanta caves, reached great heights; so did the sciences of astronomy and mathematics. There were universities, such as the one at Nalanda, with eight colleges and three libraries. And there were technological advances: iron and steel, cotton and cashmere textiles, and dyes.

But there were no new religious insights except those still furnished by the Hindus. Both Buddhism and Hinduism flourished, the former in a way which did not allow it to survive as well as the latter. Throughout the civilized customs the old religious distinctions and practices were to be found. As the Venetian traveler, Marco Polo, observed in the thirteenth century, the Indians had never learned to breed horses, they were very expensive because they were all imported, but the second Gupta king performed the horse sacrifice to celebrate his victories. An inscription dated to A.D. 658 proclaims the horse sacrifice to be the best of good deeds and the murder of a Brahman the worst of all sins.

Shiva-Siddhanta

From the sixth century B.C. the religion of Shiva existed in the Tamil-speaking country of south India. The Saivites had their own sacred books, called the *Agamas,* but they also recognized the authority of the *Vedas.* The *Shaira Siddhanta* was not systematized, however, until the thirteenth century of our era. It is in a sense a simpler system than the others. There are only three terms needed: God, soul or self *(jiva),* and matter.

There is only one God, the supreme reality. He has a number of properties: independence, purity, self-knowledge, omniscience, boundless benevolence, omnipotence, and bliss.

God is transcendent, and also immanent in the world. It is He who creates, maintains and destroys without any other means and without himself changing. He is called Shiva because he is bliss itself. He creates the world and makes it evolve so that souls may be saved by the removal of their impurities, for the whole world-process is only for the sake of the release of the soul. He has five functions, which are obscuration, creation, preservation, destruction and grace. The first four exist for the fifth. To this end He appears in bodily form. He appears exactly in the form in which He is worshipped. One of his appearances is as the teacher *(guru)* who strives to save the struggling soul from the endless round of existences *(samsara).*

Kashmiri Shaivaism

A later version of *Shaivaism* which occurred in Kashmir in the north and probably dates to the first half of the ninth century of our era, was the work of two men, Vasugupta and Somananda, and it does not recognize the authority of the *Veda*. It is mystical, it rests chiefly on free will as an ultimate principle, and its spiritual discipline is the practice of *yoga*. The material world is a manifestation of the universal mind and therefore mental; but it exists independently and is therefore real. Action is externalized will, and the actions of yogins express things independently of matter.

Vira-Shaivaism

There has been an attempt to trace this philosophy to the Indus valley civilization of 2500 B.C. If so it is the oldest Indian philosophy and the longest lasting, for it still has adherents among living Hindus, if the survival of animism and the cults of Shiva and Shakti are to be counted as evidence.

The Harappa culture of the Indus valley worshipped the *lingam,* the male sexual organ, and had a male god who may have been Shiva and a goddess who may have been Shakti. In Mohenjo Daro the population may have been the pre-Aryan Dravidians, who still survive in the south of India centered on Mysore.

The systematic presentation of *Vira-Shaivaism* seems not to have been made until A.D. 1160 when Basava accomplished the task. But its followers continued to wear models of *linga,* as the symbols of dynamic fullness or supreme reality, on their persons; the *lingam* was considered to be a symbol of all that is high and holy in the life divine.

It is the material rather than the formal or spiritual which is primarily real. There is no final end to life, except to consider it a realization contained in the consciousness of the world in its complete meaning. Philosophy presents reality in its comprehensive totality, which is also its concreteness.

God, who is intelligent, is the formal cause of the universe but not its material cause. There is a material cause which is non-intelligent and this is *maya,* the stuff of which the universe is composed. (As in the *Upanishads, maya* here does not mean illusion but rather the power by which God creates the real universe.) For the believer the liberation of the soul from bondage to the material world occurs in steps. The first is to be the servant of God, cleaning the temples for instance and rendering daily worship. The second is the performance of rites, a step which is closer to God because it offers him both love and praise. The third is the discipline of *yoga* which makes contemplation possible by withdrawing the senses from their objects and concentrating the mind on God. The supreme end is union with God which is to be gained by wisdom.

This is God's "adorable game." Making the soul fit to receive God's grace is accomplished finally by equating good with evil. The soul is now indifferent to merit and demerit, recognizing the presence of bondage in both. Through contemplation it is filled with the glory of God. Though not itself God, the soul can claim God's nature as its own, and so without becoming identical with God can enjoy God's nature.

The Shakta Philosophy

Like *Vira-Saivaism,* the *Shakta* philosophy too may go back to the Indus valley civilization. It is still a living religion in India, where Shiva or Shakti is still worshipped; and so it too has had a very long run. There are many lost works belonging to its literature, but the one that has survived dates back only to the seventh century A.D.

The worship of Shiva alternates between extreme asceticism and wild debauch. Probably due originally to a mixture of Mahayana beliefs with the superstitions inherited from early Hinduism, this doctrine was based on the assumption that spiritual results could be obtained by physical means. The Lingayats were the puritanical branch, but the best known were the tantric Shiva worshippers of the phallus, who supposed that the divine reposes in virility and generation.

Shakti is the goddess mentioned in one of the hymns of the *Rig-Veda* as the embodiment of power, the "great mother of the devotees." Shakti as the world-mother served as a protest against the ritual religion of the *Veda;* instead there was to be freedom of worship; just as "all streams flow into the ocean, so the worship of any god is received by Brahman." Shiva is consciousness and Shakti the formative energy of consciousness. Shakti is Brahman as endowed with will, knowledge and action, and so projects the material universe.

In this conception there is inherent a reality which splits itself into subject and object, as the universe follows upon the self-limitation of the divine power. The appearance of Shakti after the great cosmic darkness of unconsciousness is like the revival of memory in a sleeper awakening.

The self has to be rescued from the blinding effects of *maya* through the propitiation of the divine self by means of meditation. Salvation depends upon a reviving of the powers that lie within the self. Karma and rebirth are as usual accepted by the Shakta philosophers.

The worship of Shiva ("mild" or "auspicious" and probably intended in both meanings) is used for the supreme reconciliation of all opposites, male and female, good and evil, rest and activity, ascetic and erotic, creator and destroyer, life and death. But the nature of the God is broader than the ideal opposites, for Shiva represents the totality of all being. The other gods, Vishnu and Krishna, for example, are said to bow down in worship before the power of the phallus of Shiva. He is depicted as haunting cemeteries dressed in a tiger-skin, with a necklace of skulls, his head surrounded by serpents. His symbol is the lingam and he is represented as ithyphallic, but at the same time he is permanently chaste. Some of the Harappa seals depict a god with a permanently erect organ, and the Vedas accuse their non-Aryan enemies of worshipping the phallus. All peoples at some time have probably had the impossible dream of a permanently erect penis.

The followers of the Shakta philosophy sometimes worship Shiva's consort, Shakti, rather than Shiva. The female goddess is usually represented as the dread Kali who drinks blood from human skulls and is still worshipped today with sacrifices of goats in the great temple in Calcutta. For many millenia not only goats but also human victims were offered to Mahadevi, a consort of Shiva, and this was the practice as late as the nineteenth century.

The Shakti devotees of a later time and some still today, thinking to worship Shiva and Shakti through the imitation of those gods, engage in sexual intercourse, though without movement or ejaculation, combining strict control of the senses with the sexual act in an effort to illustrate the union of license with chastity. It is not to be understood as lovemaking, but as tantric ritual copulation in a strictly religious setting in order to show that between liberation or *moksha* and creativity of *samsara* there is no distinction when both are divinely transcended in the perfect union.

The reader may at this point be interested in a personal anecdote which perfectly illustrates the Shakta philosophy. I have a friend who is a Hindu priest who practices the Shakta philosophy. Noticing that he was making overtures to a pretty woman, I reminded him as diplomatically as I could of his vows of celibacy. He was not at all put out, and explained that while it was true that he did have sexual intercourse it was also true that there was no ejaculation and that therefore he had been faithful to his vows.

I was skeptical.

"Is there no ejaculation?" I inquired gently.

"Not officially," was his reply.

The Bhakti Movement

In the Tamil-speaking south in India there arose a religious movement which was to influence Hinduism throughout the land. It was probably in the eighth century that the *bhakti* movement got its start. The word comes from a root meaning "to share" but came to be understood as the loving devotion of God for man. The *bhakti* movement was the expression of a decided preference for devotional needs over the moral and intellectual, preferring the popular worship of a personal God to all formal religion and external worship. According to the followers of *bhakti*, God must be thought of as playful, engaged in spontaneous movement, analogous to sport and needing no explanation. Bhakti substituted prayer for meditation. The *Bhagavata* cult (Bhagavat of the Lord) was ushered in by a spiritual revival conducted by men who were called *Alvars* and who claimed an intuitive knowledge of God. They were influenced chiefly by the *Upanishads*, but there is also clear evidence of the *Bhagavadgita*. They were worshippers of Vishnu under one of his other names: Rama or Krishna, and were soon joined by a similar movement of the *Pashupata* cult whose members were worshippers of Shiva and whose sacred writings, the *Agamas*, were related to temple worship. This version of Shaivism was flourishing in the Tamil south by the end of the tenth century when it gave Hinduism a new life.

In the twelfth century a follower of *bhakti* founded the sect of the Lingayats, who were fanatical, puritanical anti-Brahmanic, and wore symbols of the lingam around their necks. But in many ways they were modern; they rejected the authority of the *Veda*, the doctrine of rebirth, and child marriages, while permitting the remarriage of widows. In both northern and central India *bhakti* cults flourished from the thirteenth to the eighteenth centuries.

From the sixteenth to the eighteenth century, no new religious or philosophical movement of a native character occurred. What did occur was another invasion from the north, this time of Turkish-Afghan peoples, resulting in the conquest of all of India except the extreme southern tip by the Mughals. These were Mongols who came from what is now Russian Turkistan, and they brought Islam with them. Babur and his later successors, Akbar and Aurangzeb, established a solid rule and an imperial splendor which had rarely been witnessed in India before. It was Akbar's grandson, Shah Jehan, who built the Taj Mahal as a memorial to his dead wife.

The uneasy combination of Hindu and Muslim cultures, with the Muslim rulers in the ascendancy brought a serious challenge to the religion of the Hindus. However, Hinduism remained undisturbed at the village level, so that it was preserved until it could rise again. The strength of Hinduism once again showed itself in its ability to conquer its conquerers. The Muslim religion never again left northern India, and eventually in the twentieth century obtained its own country of Pakistan. But India remained what it had always been: solidly Hindu.

Chapter XI
Mahatma Gandhi

From the beginning, Hinduism has been the prevailing philosophy and religion of the Indian peoples, and it continues so today. From time to time it has thrown up great epics of literature, and more recently it produced a great religious and political leader, Mahatma Gandhi.

Gandhi was born in Kathiawar, western India, in 1869, to parents who were members of the *vaisya* caste, the third of the four great castes, and they were grocers who dealt in vegetable drugs. They were Hindus but much influenced by the environing Jains. Married at thirteen to a girl slightly younger, Gandhi was sixteen when his father died, and went to England to study law against the orders of his caste leaders, who thereupon declared him outcaste, and so he remained throughout his life.

He passed his bar examinations in 1891 and the next day sailed for home. Disappointed in the practice of law in India he eagerly accepted an offer from South Africa, where he was a success among the Indian population because he devoted his efforts for twenty years of law practice to bringing the parties together and effecting compromises.

After his return to India his practice of law took a turn toward the legitimate defense of workers' grievances, as, for instance, with the indigo plantation workers in Champaran. For many years, however, Gandhi supported the British government in India—during the Boer War and again during World War I. He said that he did not like any government and that the best government was the one that governed least. "And I have found that it is possible for me to be governed the least under the British Empire" though he insisted that he did so on the basis of "equal partnership" and did not himself "belong to a subject race." He found himself always on the side of the working masses and against their oppressors, usually backed by the British in the name of an inherited order, although to many of its features he objected. He had not yet thought in any larger terms.

In the first world war, out of loyalty to the Crown he actually recruited for the British. After the war and an attack of dysentery which brought him almost to death, the repressive measures of the government, which had promised a measure of self-government but had failed to deliver, Gandhi turned rebel. The first efforts were disastrous because the masses did not understand or practice non-violence and the result was a number of clashes with the police. Gandhi now proposed a systematic policy of non-cooperation with the British. Due to his influence the Indian National Congress vowed to work for independence *(swaraj)* by peaceful means.

In and out of prison as a result of his efforts toward civil disobedience, Gandhi's authority with the masses continued to increase. The promise of Indian independence was complicated by the demand of the Moslems, under M.A. Jinnah, who took issue with Gandhi's conception of a united as well as an independent India, and now he was challenged on two fronts. Curiously, it was the second world war which got rid of many of the distinctions that Gandhi hated, such as that between rich and poor and white and "native." The political rise of labor in Great Britain and the formation of a labor government helped.

The Muslim League, however, represented dissatisfied leaders, and in 1946 riots and killings in Calcutta and other parts of Bengal amounted almost to civil war, whereupon Gandhi went to live in Bengal in order to work for reconciliation between Hindus and Moslems. June 1948 was fixed as the date for the transfer of power from the British, and against his will Gandhi had to accept an India of Hindus and Moslems who simply could not be reconciled and so were divided into two states, India and Pakistan, settled ahead of time, in August 1947.

To the end Gandhi hoped that the two countries would be united. When the transfer of power released the opposing forces, thousands in the Punjab were brutally murdered. The killings continued, Gandhi fought back with a "fast unto death," and in January 1948 he was assassinated by a young Brahmin fanatic.

The political mission of Gandhi was not his chief one; his mission as he conceived it went way beyond affairs of state; his doctrine was at base a religious one. The doctrine of *ahimsa,* or non-violence, and his attack on untouchability took him into an area which applied to all people everywhere to get rid of violence and to recognize a common humanity.

About 1930 Gandhi formed his first *ashram,* a religious community establishing a common life bound by discipline, and imposed a number of vows upon himself: to speak the truth; to practice non-injury or, as he called it, non-violence; celibacy; "control of the palate," eating only what is necessary to sustain life; non-theft, which included no possession of property not needed for immediate use; non-attachment; and poverty. There were several more rules, which amounted to vows, the first of which was *swadeshi,* to live on what is available in one's immediate surroundings and to obtain nothing beyond; fearlessness; and a vow to end untouchability.

The first five of these were identical with the vows the Jains had been taking for two thousand years. *Ahimsa* was not generally a Hindu requirement and could not be, since the duties of the second caste, the *kshatriya,* were devoted to war.

Also, the Hindus had regarded untouchability in connection with the lowest caste as an ancient and honorable tradition, dating back probably to the time of the conquered Dasa people. Finally, *swadeshi* by definition ruled out the possibility of establishing either a world state or a world religion.

Even the most rational of religious people are not dismayed by contradiction, and Gandhi was no exception. Asked once to describe the essence of Hinduism, he did so with a quotation from the *Upanishads*, which he translated as:

> "All this that we see in this great universe
> is permeated by God.
> Renounce it and enjoy it.
> Do not covet anybody's wealth or possession."

But, one might ask, would it not be sacrilege to renounce whatever is permeated by God?

The saint may be described as a philosopher in action, for he endeavors to live exactly in accordance with his beliefs. This can be unfortunate, however, when the beliefs are absolute, for absolutes in action are often apt to be socially disastrous, for the families of saints, who generally come off second-best.

The selfishness of holy men is disturbing. When Buddha left home to become a hermit he left behind a wife and infant son. Could he have had no consideration for their welfare or their feelings? When St. Augustine became a Christian priest according to his *Confessions* he abandoned his mistress of many years and her children with her, in order the better to serve the Lord and save his own soul.

Gandhi was not more considerate, but he did expect his wife to give up her sex life when he gave up his, and while it is on record that he consulted her in the matter, one cannot help wondering how much choice she had. In any case his decision was hardly flattering to her. He also made her give up the jewelry which had been given to her in South Africa by those who were grateful to Gandhi for his services to the Indian community, and by his own account she wished very much to keep them. The morality of the saint is evidently of a kind which applies only to him, and though he usually serves as a pristine example to others he often fails to respect the wishes and the welfare of his family. Certainly Gandhi's sons suffered from his refusal to allow them to get a modern education.

For him the *dharma* of the conscience was superior to the *dharma* of Hindu law; when the law endorsed the untouchability of the lowest caste, he consulted the *dharma* of his conscience against it and took untouchables to live with his family in his house to show that he meant what he said. By the use of fasting, an old weapon, he got his way with astonishing speed, over-turning old customs in the process, in which case he was no doubt right.

Yet the danger in the appeal to conscience lies in the consequence that in doing what he feels to be right his feelings may mislead him, as indeed they often do. Gandhi's conscience led him to condemn sexual intercourse as an evil in itself, but it can be argued that since man is one of God's creatures and everything about him is from God, sex too is from God and to deny it altogether as Gandhi recommended may be a sacrilege.

Not for nothing is it proclaimed by the democrats of western countries that theirs is "a government of laws, not of men." The laws can be amended, but without the establishment of laws and at least partial adherence to their authority the result is a serious conflict of conscience. It may at least be argued against Gandhi that the requirement to live without sex would be regarded by many good men as going against their consciences.

R.C. Zaehner professes to see in Gandhi a latter-day version of the king Yudishthira who in Gandhi's beloved *Gita* had to face the choice between the *dharma* of traditional Hinduism and his conscience. For Gandhi, to whom the sacred writings of the Hindus were inviolate, there was no obligation to follow the letter of the law if it seemed to him to go against "reason and moral sense"; he could dismiss as misinterpretation whatever he did not agree with, a technique practiced by religious leaders the world over when they read their own ideas back into the tradition in order to secure endorsement of them.

Gandhi was no traditionalist when he opposed his own values to those of previous generations. Though he insisted that he was an orthodox Hindu, obedient to orthodox teachings, he threw his weight against the caste distinction of the untouchables. He wished the lowest caste and its official derogation by society abolished, although the custom had the endorsement of several thousands of years of Indian history. He was against the immolation of widows on the funeral pyres of husbands; he was against child marriage; he was against temple prostitution; but he was for cow worship though it was not as old as such customs go.

Worst of all, perhaps, he rejected the industrialism of the west, which alone might have saved the hungry millions who by his action were condemned to slow death by starvation. He wished to turn progress back, and described himself as "a determined opponent of modern civilization," unlike his lifelong friend, Rabindranath Tagore, to whom truth was beauty and who, far from rejecting the best of western culture, tried to teach scientific agriculture to the peasants. The success of agricultural science in the United States and elsewhere provides strong basis for the conclusion that it could have increased the yield of grains in India to a point where want might have been abolished. In its place Gandhi backed the spinning wheel.

It is hard to defend him on these two scores. The eating of beef and the improvement in farming might have saved many lives and untold suffering; indeed they might do so today were it not for the fact that the impact of Gandhi's personality and preferences is still powerful.

A photograph of his last worldly possessions has been printed in the English edition of his autobiography and elsewhere. They consisted of little except sandals, a pair of spectacles and a rice bowl. At the time of his death he was a house guest of G.D. Birla, one of the richest men in India.

Gandhi's leadership and his enormous appeal to the Indian masses, shows the strength of the Hindu tradition in religion and of the philosophical ideas behind it. For after centuries during which alien conquerors overran the sub-continent and dominated it, after long periods of foreign rule by such as the Mughals with their Muslim religion and their Persian culture, and by the British with their Christianity and their European customs and traditions, Hinduism was able to reassert itself through Gandhi, although certainly in a much revised version tempered by reforms and with emphasis on life in this world rather than in the next. Hinduism it was at bottom and Hinduism it remained.

Possession of absolute truth leads its possessor to uncompromising actions. Truth can be revised at a later time because truth is timeless, but actions which follow from it cannot. We ought not to be too sure of the truth; it is well to soften conviction until the truth has stood the test of repetition. Because Gandhi, like so many religious leaders, was too sure, some of the consequences of his actions have been disastrous. He succeeded in gaining independence for India, but then the wars between the Moslems and the Hindus on the border between India and Pakistan have resulted in the deaths of many thousands on both sides. Nehru, his disciple and successor, was a world leader in the United Nations but refused to allow a team to come in to oversee the settlement in Kashmir. And the government of Mrs. Gandhi, when faced with the choice, preferred atomic weapons to the supply of food for a starving population. Never doubting the good intentions of the Mahatma's actions, we find it difficult to discover the good effects of his policies.

Chapter XII
Some General Observations on Indian Philosophy

Indian philosophy as expressed through its religions is so various that every attempt to give a complete description of it differs so much from others that only the familiar names exist to give them a common title. In the course of its long development it laid out many alternatives, some of them sharply in conflict with others; for example, *maya*, which began as a name for the mysterious power by which the god Varuna creates, ended by referring to the illusion that the material world is real; and it would be fair to ask what Hinayana Buddhism and Tantric Buddhism have in common except the name.

Indeed, so wide is the variety of Indian religions that, whatever preferences you may have, you will find some sect which endorses them. Consider sexual practices, for example, where the range of choice runs all the way from abstinence to official eroticism, from the Hindu ascetic to the left-handed Tantra Buddhist. Different sects of the same religion order self-mortification and sexual orgies; human sacrifices and abstinence from all killing, even of insects; belief in one transcendent god and in many gods. It is a long way from the cannibalism of the Kapalikas or Kalamukhas to the doctrine of non-violence.

This variety has an advantage. It has been observed for thousands of years by travelers visiting India that tolerance accompanies the deep interest in beliefs of all sorts. Whatever their classes, Indians have never thought that differences of belief, whether in the classic epics of the various and often divergent Hindu schools, or in Buddhism, Jainism or Muslim religions or philosophies, should be grounds for violent conflict—a sharp contrast with western practice.

It is impossible to view the religions without some degree of distortion arising from the angle of vision. What most Indian religions have in common is idealism, a belief that reality is mental, which leads them to the common error of supposing that what they think ought-to-be, is—an attitude they have in common with Germans, most of whose philosophers have been idealists; they are much like the German who protested after the loss of World War II that it did not come out right because his country was supposed to have won it. Professor A. Bharati has given as an example the belief that the caste system has been done away with because the constitution adopted by independent India abolished it, when in fact it is as strong as ever.

Religion as a special way of life has never been accepted by a vast population anywhere as much as it has in India. In different cultures religion has been added to other activities but, however deeply it may have permeated them, it has seldom replaced them as it has in India. The result of this preoccupation has been a vast collection of religious beliefs, many of them sharply in conflict with each other but none lacking vast hordes of adherents, so that religious leaders, holy men, ascetics and libertines, all claiming religious authority, are never far to seek.

A philosophy in the broad sense is the product of a whole people in their cultural setting on the land. India is no exception. If we pare down the Indian religions, each to its core

of philosophy, we find common ground: an interest in the after-
life as itself another life, and perhaps even more related to this
doctrine, a scorn for life in this world, which they see only as a
preparation for the next. When ordinary people wish to be
saved from the suffering of the material world, Indian religious
leaders assure them that the pain is not real because the material
world is only an illusion. Medieval Christianity which in belief
if not altogether in action looked at this world in much the same
way. It has been so in India for a much longer time. The
doctrine of rebirth was thousands of years old in India when
Christianity as a religion was first founded.

The idea of rebirth or transmigration runs all through the
Indian religions and philosophies and with it the further idea
that the kind of life into which the individual is reborn is
decided in advance by his *karma*, the good or bad actions he
performed in his previous lives. These two associated ideas
have been regarded for thousands of years not as dogma but as
fact—which indicates the deph of the belief in them.

More people have believed in reincarnation than in any
other doctrine, with the possible exception of astrology.
Reincarnation and astrology have in common the negative
property that there is no evidence for them whatever. But,
though many people in their mortal desperation have wished to
believe, if there is any hope for progress, that hardly seems to
be adequate basis for their validity.

Despite the influence of some modern religious teachers in
India who have enjoyed a vogue in the west, most Indian
religions are polytheistic; there are as many gods as there are
thoughts and things in material existence which need to be
represented in ritual practices of one sort or another. This is
certainly true of Hinduism and equally true of later forms of
Buddhism, such as the Mahayana. It is not contradicted by the
fact that in the Buddhism of the Buddha no god is mentioned;
that point of view is not typical of Indian religious thought, and
in any case it was corrected when Buddha himself became a
god.

Most Indian philosophy is concerned less with the world than with the self, for the self has a spiritual essence, and there is some speculative exercise able to reach it. The self is a jungle of mysticism, a profuse growth of subjective states in which are buried many supernatural ideas and forces. About metaphysical knowledge, which is knowledge of the spirit of man through his consciousness, the various schools differ as to the best way to reach it. Life is a painful predicament which philosophy can help one to avoid; otherwise every individual is condemned to a future of the endless painful existences he has suffered in the endless past. Perhaps without the doctrine of rebirth Indian philosophy might have freed itself from its utilitarian bias, but Chinese philosophy, as we shall see, though it has no such bias, is equally utilitarian.

The emphasis in Indian philosophy and religion is on the individual, despite the understanding of law as *dharma*, in which there is no break between natural law and human law. Both Hindus and Buddhists went so far as to set up religious communities, which were for monks, but there seems to have been little in the way of social or political ideas among the philosophers. The inflexibility of the *dharma* was perhaps felt longest and strongest in the caste system, which is perhaps the nearest the Indians ever came to a continuing social organization which extended beyond the rule of occasional dynasties, such as the Maurya and the Gupta. The old notion, that if every individual is good and does what is right, the collective result will be a good society, can be true of course only if social order and political organization have no reality of their own and must therefore be superfluous. There is no Indian work comparable to Plato's *Republic*, no concept that a good society might be necessary to the good life of the individual and even to make it possible.

One result has been the deplorable material conditions in which the masses in India still live. A life of inward contemplation is of course wholly individual, and leaves society to the mercy of those who would exploit it. The consequence is the general poverty and illiteracy that India has continued to experience and the great discrepancy between rich and poor.

PART TWO
THE PHILOSOPHY
OF CHINA

There is something which goes along with the
particular prestige of clouds and makes the dragon
able to ride them.   —Shen Tao, 4th century B.C.

Chapter XIII
Early China

As a homogeneous population living in the same place for almost four thousand years, the Chinese have had a remarkably long history. China's beginnings, extending back into prehistoric times, are roughly dated to the Middle Pleistocene, about 400,000 B.C. with the remains of the skull of "Peking Man" found in 1927 near Chou K'ou Tien, forty miles from Peiping. There was evidently a Neolithic culture in the great basin of the Hwang Ho, of which some remains exist. But then there is a blank in the account lasting until about 2500 B.C. when it is known that China was inhabited.

According to the tradition there was a legendary Hsia kingdom in the north around 2000 B.C. The emperor Yu who is supposed to have founded a dynasty in the 23rd century B.C. could claim descent from the sky god and subsequently all emperors were presumed to be "Sons of Heaven", endowed with spiritual powers. But the "mandate of Heaven" could be shifted, as it was when the Hsia dynasty was supposedly overthrown by a king named T'ang who also claimed miraculous origins and powers.

Broadly speaking, what is known of Chinese history falls into periods which are called dynasties because they were marked by ruling families. The earliest dynasty we can be sure of with any modest degree of certainty was the Shang, roughly between 1500 and 1000 B.C. in the lower basin of the Yellow River in northern Honan but spread as far as Shensi and Hunan, with a capital city at Anyang, when both bronze and wheat were used. There was evidently a family organization, central in importance even then, with ancestor worship and descent counted through the female line; there was slavery and there were human sacrifices. What appears to have been the Shang capital has been excavated near the modern town of Cheng-chou. It was square and had walls of rammed earth. According to later stories the last Shang ruler though an able man had allowed his court to become so corrupt that further control became impossible. Heaven at this point seems to have transferred its mandate to the militant rulers of a small western province, the Chou, who destroyed the Shang capital.

After the Shang dynasty which had ruled over a Bronze Age civilization, came the Chou dynasty, with effective dates from 1122 to 771 B.C., though it endured for some five centuries longer. The Hsia, the Shang and the Chou constitute the classical Three Dynasties.

A prominent feature of Chinese civilization was its relative isolation from the outside world for thousands of years. Invasions always came as a surprise, always regarded as exceptions. Until the lasting contact with Europeans, the Chinese had believed their culture to be superior to all others, referring to their country as the Middle Kingdom because they thought of themselves as living at the center of the world, with all other countries ranged around them and subject to their influence relative to their distance from the Chinese capital.

The Chou rulers seem to have had a talent for good government. During the youth of one a regent, the Duke of Chou, acted for him and set up an administrative organization which was a model for his successors. The lords of the Western

Chou ruled over the land in the Yellow River basin and its agricultural population, as part of a feudal system not unlike that found in the Middle Ages in Europe. Peasants, tied to the land as serfs, held it in fief to a lord, providing him with food while he furnished them protection. Together they made up an aristocratic society bound by ritual practices having both political and religious meanings. This feudal system may have fallen victim to the discovery of iron which was in wide use by 600 B.C.

After the Chou, power passed into the hands of a new merchant class. The agricultural serfs gained their independence, but not without great violence and confusion, and eventually one feudal lord replaced all of the others and became Emperor, with the sole power to gather taxes by means of an organized bureaucracy. In this way order was gradually restored.

The reign of the Chou dynasty was the longest in all the history of China, and throughout the early part of its thousand years of existence the structure of society was still feudal, with differences, a strong central government among them. Its last five centuries however, saw the weakening of this central power and the rise of three contending states, and its last centuries are known as the period of the Warring States, which ended with the victory of one of them, the Ch'in.

The Warring States period (403-221 B.C.) was marked by the gradual end of the rigid social structure of the feudal system. With the old institutions in danger of collapsing, imperial regulations were no longer held to be in force, and the laws were not obeyed; but a social order is never broken and replaced without disorder. The consequent social chaos left a vacuum, and the philosophers tried to fill it, many of them by undertaking to restore the old institutions.

The period from 722 to 481 B.C. (the Ch'un Ch'iu period), down to the beginning of the Han dynasty in 206 B.C., saw the greatest development in philosophy, a time in which most of the important philosophers who were to influence all subsequent thought, Confucius and Laotse, for example, lived. As we shall presently see, Confucius was a conservative, who looked back to the Chou for his model.

The Ch'in dynasty was shortlived, roughly from 403 to 221 B.C., but its effects were tremendous. In that short period China—the land of the Ch'in—was unified for the first time in her history; many scholars date the Chinese empire from it. The Ch'in were ushered in by a ruler, Shih Huang Ti, and his utterly ruthless adviser, Li Ssu, who was responsible for applying the political philosophy of the Legalists which, as we shall see later, was authoritarian and anti-intellectual: In a decree issued in 213 B.C. the burning of all books in the Empire was ordered, all, that is, except those in the ruler's own library. The country was organized into administrative districts and farmers were given more rights over their land but were heavily taxed. It was during this period that the Great Wall, designed to protect the peasant population against raids by the nomadic horsemen, was constructed.

For perhaps a thousand years before Confucius, who was the first philosopher worthy of the name, there was a general belief in divine beings and illustrious spirits. The belief in Heaven and with it a Supreme Emperor was accompanied by the prevalence of divination, the attempt to foretell future events by supernatural means and by magic, which sought to achieve the desired effects through the control of supernatural forces. Gradually, however, toward the end of this period more down-to-earth considerations began to emerge, the work of a small, enlightened group who seem to have proceeded cautiously. A hundred or so years before the birth of Confucius one wise man observed that "It is when a state is about to flourish that [its ruler] listens to his people; when it is about to perish, he listens to the spirits."

The Chinese of this early period thought that their rulers were intended to follow the laws laid down by Shang Ti, the Supreme Emperor who dwelled in Heaven. Sage and king were in their view one and the same, and mortal man and his state could only follow them. The belief in some kind of preferred social order, even if divinely inspired, was also the beginning of the rule of reason. No doubt the first two steps taken in Chinese civilization were those toward the individual's self-awareness and his deliberate appeal to reason. Nothing outside himself constituted a source of wisdom, though the spirits and divine creatures were still there.

Chapter XIV
The *I Ching*

Our account begins with one of the oldest of Chinese books and indeed one of the oldest anywhere, the *I Ching*, or *Book of Changes*. Some three thousand years old, perhaps older, it belongs to a period when divination was relied on to direct human affairs, probably with its beginnings in the early Chou dynasty, 1122 B.C.

Although the *I Ching* was no doubt added to and revised by many writers from the sixth to the fourth centuries B.C., much of it was attributed to a mythical emperor, Fu Hsi, and to two historical figures, King Wen and the Duke of Chou. King Wen's title was probably given to him after his death by his son Wu who overthrew the last rulers of the Shang dynasty and became the first ruler of the Chou dynasty, around 1150 B.C. King Wen is supposed to have been responsible for the work in its present form, but whether he was or not, the attribution points to the tradition of the ruler who is also a sage, which began as early as anything that can be traced in China. The models of the "Inner Sage" who has acquired virtue within himself, and of the "Outer King" who has accomplished much of good in the world, together make up the ideal of the sage-king who not only discovers wisdom but is also able to put it into practice. That is why the history of China is inseparable from the history of Chinese philosophy. Surely of no other people is this as true.

The *I Ching* was known to Confucius in the sixth century B.C. and was already by then regarded as a classic and an instrument of divination—the practice of foretelling future events or of discovering hidden knowledge by occult (that is to say, secret) means. Our interest in it here of course leans toward the philosophical side, though its survival is due perhaps more to its use in divination.

Divination in early China was done with tortoise shells heated with fire so that when they cracked the lines thus produced were read as forecasts. Because of their many irregularities the cracks were difficult to interpret and a more reliable method therefore was sought and found in the diagrams employed in the *I Ching*. It began with a practice of divination based on the use of stalks of the yarrow plant (or milfoil), long stalks for long lines ——— and short stalks for broken lines — — to mean "yes" and "no" respectively. The single lines were combined in pairs to provide greater variety.

To each of these combinations a third line was added, making in this way eight possible trigrams.

Each trigram was assigned a definite meaning, and their chance occurrence was believed to have a definite predictive value.

Very early in the history of the work the trigrams were combined in pairs, making hexagrams, of which there are sixty-four different combinations, an arrangement due supposedly to King Wen. Thus for example the hexagram for "contemplation" looks like this

```
————————
————————
——  ——
——  ——
——  ——
——  ——
```

The hexagrams were considered reflections of all that happens in heaven and on earth. What had to be accounted for were the changes which were ceaselessly taking place, hence the title, *Book of Changes*. Paradoxically, the word "changes" here means that whatever changes does so in terms of the unchanging. The changes that occur in exchanging the trigrams are said to be the same as those in transition in the physical world from one phenomenon to another.

It is not things that are represented by the trigrams but the movements of things. Such movements indicate actions to be taken. Since there is a choice to be made in each instance between right actions and wrong actions, the *I Ching* is not only an oracle but also a source of moral advice, not merely a book of divination but also a book of wisdom. Those who consult it put themselves in accord with the way and its power; by thinking through the order of the outer world, by exploring the laws of nature, they arrive at an understanding of fate. But the *I Ching* must be consulted early on, when situations are just forming, so that the individual may play a part in shaping his own destiny, which is the purpose of the book.

There are specific directions for consulting the *I Ching* by means of yarrow stalks or coins, but we are concerned here with its deeper meanings, its philosophy, contained chiefly in the commentaries which have grown up around it almost from its first appearance.

The second half of the *I Ching* is in most editions made up of commentaries, published as Appendices, generally acknowledged by scholars to have been written much later than the *I*

Ching itself, probably by Confucians, and some of them are credited, perhaps erroneously, to Confucius, though he probably did study it in his old age. In any case the Appendices were not a product of single authorship or of any one period.

When we look closely at these commentaries we can see the outlines of a philosophical system. The early Chinese had the idea of a two-story world, a world of laws (called Heaven) and a world of material events (called Earth) and they understood the influence that possessors of the knowledge of Heaven could exercise over earthly events.

The *I Ching* presents a complete image of heaven and earth in all their possible relationships, and indeed they are intended to be, as Fung Yu-lan points out, "a reflection in miniature of the entire universe." Everything comes about, we are told, through an interplay of heaven and earth. "Heaven" in this case, however, proves to be not a supernatural notion but the name for the power contained in a world of abstract forms, similar to Plato's theory of the Ideas. The laws of nature considered as natural causes belong to this set of conditions, as G. W. Leibniz, the seventeenth century German philosopher, recognized before many Chinese scholars. And they are conditions after all, for they determine the limits of actions in the material world of visible things, called "Earth" by the authors of the *I Ching.* Heaven presents itself to man as sun and moon, wind and thunder, while Earth presents itself as mountains and marshes. Water and fire are the two things most important to man. "Heaven and Earth are not benevolent. They treat all things like straw dogs," that is to say, without kindness or unkindness, and equally, and they provide for an endless cycle of material change and a basis for the understanding of all human affairs.

Events on earth consist in the interplay of two opposed forces, the *yin* and the *yang,* the female and male principles respectively, the *yin* (or "shaded") being the female, darkness, softness and inactivity, while the *yang* (or "sunlit") is male, light, hardness and activity. The interaction of these two forces together produce most of the universal phenomena. One *yin* and one *yang* together equal the Tao (the Great Ultimate). Another name for heaven is the "Creative" (the dragon symbol), the most powerful of all forces; another name for earth is the "Receptive," as the most devoted of all things in the world. When an action is in harmony with the laws of the universe, it leads to the desired goal and constitutes good fortune; if opposed to the laws of the universe, it lead to loss and spells misfortune.

The *yin* and the *yang*, represented by divided and undivided lines in the *I Ching*, are cosmic forces; from their interplay come all social as well as all physical developments, all ideas, institutions, cultures and civilizations. Thus we are told not to look for supernatural guidance but to the alternation of natural opposites whose outcome can be studied and even predicted.

There is a metaphysics here as well as a social philosophy, in effect a two-tiered universe, just as there is in Plato's philosophy, every event in the visible world being an image of an idea in the world of abstract forms, for phenomena take their forms from heaven; on earth they obey definite laws.

Chinese philosophy throughout most of early Chinese history was concerned almost exclusively with human conduct and not the universal nature of things which came much later, when it came at all, and so its presence in the Appendices is some evidence that they were written much later than the *I Ching* itself. Indeed the introduction of natural philosophy here is done with the ulterior motive of making available a guide to conduct. Given a knowledge of the laws of time, the processes on earth can be anticipated; changes can be calculated in advance; freedom of action is made possible; the future may be influenced—all by means of the *Book of Changes.* Consulting the hexagrams means preparing to deal with coming events—insofar as they affect one—by means of appropriate actions.

There is another way of looking at the *I Ching* in addition to those which have already been explored. This is to view it as a set of alternatives with respect to reality, very much like the set of alternatives presented in logic by Gottlob Frege or like the starting point of mathematics in the theory of sets. The reader may find his way through life by consulting the manner in which the various threads can be combined according to the interpretation of the 64 hexagrams of the *I Ching*, but this is somewhat obscure and it is not to our purpose here to pursue it.

Throughout Chinese history the *I Ching* continued an old tradition which included magic and spirits exercising supernatural powers. The spirits departed early, however, and with them the supernatural, after meeting the opposition of Confucius and his followers. What was left, and what continues still to be practiced, is what may be called earthbound divination—in a more western sense, gambling, which has not been sufficiently recognized as attempting to read the future. The gambler counts in one measure or another, on being able to predict what faces the thrown dice will show, which horse will run the fastest, where the ball will stop after the roulette wheel is spun. The *I Ching* no longer promises to control the future but only to predict it; therein lies its durability.

It is evidence of the value of the *I Ching* in Chinese society that K'ang-hsi, who was emperor from 1661 to 1722, began to study the book in 1680, giving three days to each hexagram, according to his own account. He used it, he said, both to tell fortunes and as a source of moral principles, and he referred to its importance repeatedly as though it were still the central work of the Chinese wisdom literature, supplemented only by the four Confucian Classics.

Chapter XV
Confucius

The classical Chinese philosopher is, as everyone knows, Confucius. His name was Ch'iu and his surname Chung-Ni but he was usually referred to by his title of honor, K'ung Fu Tzu, or "Master Kung," though we have grown accustomed to the Latin version.

What we know as the work of Confucius was edited much later and probably represented a tradition which was already old in his lifetime. How much of it is his own thought is conjectural, though a unified point of view does come through.

A considerable body of myth has grown up about him, including an ancestry which can be traced back to emperors and even to the notion of divinity, so that we no longer know how much is true; but the few ascertainable facts seem to be these:

Confucius was born in 551 B.C. near Chufu, in the province of Shantung. There may have been aristocrats among his forebears, but by his own admission his immediate family lived in humble circumstances.

When Confucius was three his father, who had been a military officer, died, and he was raised by his mother. He was largely self-taught and had to make his living at first at menial tasks, which put him in close contact with ordinary people whose suffering affected him deeply. Like Buddha, he sought ways to improve their lot, which was due, he thought, to the dislocations of the times.

At nineteen he married and earned his living first as a keeper of grain stores, then in charge of public lands. He had sons and a daughter. He was fifty when he became prime minister of the state of Lu. The story, probably false, was that he was such a success at this post that a neighboring state, fearing his influence, sent a group of female dancers to the ruler of Lu, a gift which had the desired effect for the ruler neglected his duties.

Confucius in disgust resigned his position and set off on his travels in 497, with the disciples he had succeeded in gathering around him, and his wanderings which lasted for thirteen years took him through many of the feudal states of China. He returned to his native state three years before he died in 479 B.C., and spent those remaining years in literary studies.

His work has been the basis of Chinese culture. He insisted that he was a transmitter rather than a creator, with a passion for "the Ancients," and declared that "the Chou [dynasty] had the advantage of surveying the two preceding dynasties. How great was its wealth of culture! I follow the Chou."

It was that dynasty in Western China from 1122 to 256 B.C., the longest in Chinese history, as we noted, that he chose as his ideal. Confucius had reference to its earlier years under King Wen and Wu and the Duke of Chou. It was the kind of civilization to which Confucius thought his contemporaries and their successors should conform, for he supposed that it must have had "an absolutely perfect moral power." He even dreamed, he said, about the Duke of Chou.

Was Confucius trying to "clothe his ethical insights with legendary historical authority", as Joseph Needham has suggested, or did he believe in the existence of an ideal past? We shall probably never know.

The time of political and economic troubles which followed the Chou witnessed a flurry of philosophical activity. Because prolonged conflicts between independent states had tended to erase clear outlines of custom and tradition which had sustained the Chinese even then for a long time, Confucius and others sought to preserve or restore the ancient virtues and elaborate manners which amounted virtually to ritual. Since they had been accepted primarily by the ruling class, Confucius would have to be counted a conservative, an apologist for the aristocracy, but he was also in a sense the first thinker to defend conduct by means of reason, primarily a moralist.

Someone has observed that a Golden Age looked back on is always one which never existed. Suffused with a misty glow, its hard lines softened, its errors forgotten, the past always looks much better than it was. Consider the state of affairs to which Confucius wanted his people to return: a country administered perfectly by philosopher-kings who had been set up as models of conduct and approved by the common people; a period of plenty in which no citizen wanted for anything and all were happy; an idealized state, with good laws and proper justice for all. Confucius sought to inculcate reverence for the kind of institutions he wished to restore.

He was the first thinker in Chinese history to develop an ethics, the first philosopher to be worthy of study. His interest was exclusively in man and society, not with nature, observing that if a ruler knew righteousness he did not need to know about farming. Rejected all forms of supernaturalism, retaining his skepticism to the end, Confucius may have been the first Chinese to think of education in formal terms, and want it chiefly for the government official, not to serve the ruler but to serve the people.

On the surface he was a teacher who used conservatism for a different purpose: Seeking to restore the ancient forms, he tried to infuse them with a new content. He wanted feelings to be genuine, not for outward show; for, though, men are social beings, to make the best contribution to society they must first improve themselves. He changed the meaning of the word "gentleman" so that it no longer referred to privileges but became a matter of obligation.

He did not lead men to search so much for truth as for the good, which he held consisted in correct behavior, in morality, character and manners. That he professed to find protection in social institutions of the past is something of a paradox, for he assumed that the proper social order could be obtained only through correct individual behavior.

Was Confucius an original thinker? Perhaps he was, if we consider that the perfect past he wanted to use as a model must have been to a large extent his own invention. All his thought was aimed at right conduct. There were of course social elements involved, altruism, comforting the aged, keeping faith with friends, cherishing the young; but in general it was self-improvement he was after.

The novelty he introduced was in its practical aspects, and that is why he sought help for the living rather than for the dead, preferring learning to meditation; and he was the first to advise not doing to others what you would not want them to do to you. Though he doubtless believed that the ordinary man as much as any other is a member of the great society, his advice went chiefly to courtiers: he recommended the behavior most appropriate in serving a prince or an emperor.

There is a vast difference in method between the philosopher and the religious prophet. The philosopher presents his ideas in generalities which he states as abstractly as possible in order to give them wide application. The religious prophet tells stories relating to individuals, in the hope that his hearers or readers will be able to generalize for themselves. The philosopher wishes his expression to be as clear and direct as possible, while the prophet is deliberately vague in order to lend depth to his utterances. The philosopher confines himself to what is natural; the prophet leans toward the supernatural.

In these terms Confucius is a baffling figure, for he wished to express what is natural but did so in the manner of the prophet, addressing himself chiefly to human nature though in a way which would lead people to suppose that he had transcended it. He was a humanist, who looked to the authority of a past in which there would have been no approval of humanism.

Like Buddha, Confucius was a restless, wandering teacher; both were products of their times. Almost contemporaries, they both preached an exclusively ethical doctrine with an emphasis on the practical side of human behavior; both rejected the supernatural; both rejected all metaphysical explanation. But Confucius understood, as Buddha did not, that the best individual morality in the world could fail collectively if there were not good government as well.

Following are some of the thoughts of Confucius as they were collected in the fourth century B.C., some years after his death. The numbering is from his *Analects*, the collection of maxims and aphorisms, which is all that we have of the writings attributed to him.

On learning

Wide research and steadfast purpose, eager questioning and close reflection,—all this tends to humanize a man. (XIX, 6)

Be familiar with the ancient wisdom and become acquainted with the modern; then you may become a teacher.

Love of goodness without love of learning is mere foolishness. Love of wisdom without the requisite knowledge results in an utter lack of principles. (XVIII, 8)

Learning without thought is a snare; thought without learning is a danger.   (II, 15)

We began life without any knowledge of it but should revere the past and so seek wisdom there.   (VII, 19)

To learn and then to practice what one has learned, is this not a satisfaction? To have students coming from distant places, is this not a pleasure? And those who do not understand everything that is said yet do not become unpleased, are they not men of a superior sort?   (I, 1)

On society

When you leave home, behave as though you were meeting some important guest. Deal with the common people as though you were taking part in a great religious ritual.   (XII, 2)

What you do not wish others to put on you, do not wish to put on others.   (V, 11)   What you do not desire yourself you should not encourage others to desire.   (XII, 2)

It may be necessary to sacrifice your own life in order to bring its virtue to perfection.   (XV, 8)

It does not bother me that men do not know me; only that I do not know them.   (II, 16)

I have never withheld instruction from any who sought it, even those who have come with the smallest offering.   (VII, 7)

The first men are those who come to knowledge in virtue of their birth; next those who become wise by study; then those who study without the capacity; and finally those who are so wanting in intelligence that they never learn.   (XVI, 9)

On government

Govern merely by statute, and people will be evasive. Govern by using the virtue of morality, and they will come to you voluntarily.   (II, 3)

In dealing with his ministers a prince should follow the prescribed ritual. In serving their prince the ministers should be guided by devotion.   (III, 19)

Those who do not occupy office in a state should refrain from discussing its policies.   (VIII, 14)

When asked about the essentials of government, Confucius replied, "Sufficient food, sufficient weapons, and the people's confidence." When asked if he could not have all three which would he give up, he replied, "Weapons". And next? "Food; for without the people's confidence all would indeed be lost."   (XII,7)

When asked about good government, he declared, "Where the near are content and the distant are attracted."   (XIII, 6)

On filial piety

Young people at home should show filial piety, and away from home respect for their elders. They should cultivate good will toward all, and if there is time acquire literary or artistic accomplishments.   (I, 6)

It is not when a man's father is alive but only after he dies that the son can be judged dutiful.   (I, 11)

Behave in such a way that your parents' only concern for you will be with your health.   (II, 6)

Filial piety involves more than merely seeing to it that parents are well fed. There is more to it than that.   (II, 8)

On the good

Once he returned from court to learn that the stables had burned down. "Was anyone injured?" he asked. He did not inquire about the horses.   (X, 12)

The question was raised of administering to the spirits of the departed. "While we lack the ability to minister to the living, how shall we minister to the dead?"

There is no one whose energy is not equal to pursuing goodness for a whole day.   (IV, 6)

Goodness is never very far away. You have only to wish for it and you will find that it is with you.   (VII, 29)

The peculiar burden of goodness is a heavy one, and it must be carried until the day of death.   (VIII, 7)

I have not met with any man whose love of morality was as strong as his sexual desire.   (IX, 17)

On truth

A leader must himself be correct. If he shows correctness, who will dare not to be correct?   (XII, 17)

Confucius was asked, "If the prince of Wei had ordered you to act for him, what would you do first?" He answered, "Rectify the names" (that is to say, straighten out the language). "For if language is not accurate, what is said will not be what is meant, and wrong actions will be taken. In the language of the superior man there must be nothing heedlessly irregular." (XII, 3)

What a man declares as a result of his experience is what he must be prepared to put into action.   (II, 13)

Superior men are modest in their words but profuse in their deeds.   (XIV, 29)

A man whose words cannot be trusted is of no use to anybody.   (II, 22)

On self-improvement

It is bad enough to have faults but worse not to want to correct them. (XV, 29)

When asked what makes a superior man, Confucius replied, "Self-cultivation". When asked to go further, he added, "Self-cultivation with a view to helping others". Still further, "Self-cultivation with a view to helping everybody."   (XIV, 45)

My great concern is not that men do not know me but that I lack the ability to know them   (XIV, 32)

One should not be concerned about not being in office but rather about one's capacity for holding office; one should not worry about not being known but rather about becoming worthy of being known.   (IV,14)

On tradition

Never criticize what is already past and never complain about what is now going on.   (III, 21)

Wealth and honor are what every man desires; but if these were obtained improperly they should not continue to be held. No man is superior who lacks social feeling. Never for a single moment should he desert the Way.   (IV, 5)

The moral power of the ancient Chou dynasty was the highest ever reached.   (VIII, 20)

The man who shows no respect for his elders will miss his opportunities in his prime and grow old only to be a useless dependent.   (XIV, 46)

The effect of the teachings of Confucius was to recognize in manners and ceremonies a kind of grace in acting out of one's regard for one's fellow man: it is solely in his dealings with others that the individual shows what he is; and the feelings of the inner man are made public through his behavior; if each and everyone followed these precepts, Confucius thought, the end result would be good individuals living together in a good society.

He was the first professional educator and what he taught served to popularize culture in general. Thus the teacher became identified with what he taught and his influence was widespread. The similarity of Confucius in China to Socrates in ancient Greece as a source of civilization at almost the same period in history has often been noted by scholars. But where Socrates had proposed a theory of the Ideas, Confucius talked about correct naming.

One of the chief ways men have of dealing with each other

is of course through language. To influence men correctly it is necessary to have the right words. Once the meaning of names is made clear, they will serve as standards of conduct. What Confucius called "the rectification of names" was intended primarily to have a moral effect though it operated through the medium of logical definitions. He thought that to have the correct social order, which meant keeping all social classes in line with what they ought to be, was to name them properly, for the naming of a thing defines that thing's essence.

In his view, as well as in the view of his contemporaries, he would die a failure, for he had not succeeded in establishing the state or the lives of individuals upon the moral order on which he thought both had to rest if they were to promote the welfare and happiness of humanity. Yet he belonged to that small group of quiet men whose thought and character were to influence history.

In all subsequent centuries, from the death of Confucius well into modern times, Confucianism has been the source of all moral order in China. He made it plain for all to see that manners, customs and indeed all conventions have their moral side, and he reduced religion to its moral component. In this way he made of morality something more; whether one calls it a cult or a religion, or merely a philosophy, is a matter of indifference, for its authority and acceptance must be recognized, perhaps it would be better to say: a religion centered on the moral precepts. The development of Chinese civilization would have been impossible without the Confucian tradition. It is challenged now by the Marxists.

Chapter XVI
Mo Tzu

The dates for Mo Tzu usually given are within the period from 479 to 381 B.C., shortly after the death of Confucius. There is some question about him, however, and some scholars believe that "he" may have been merely the book by that name. Suffice it to say that there were bands of Mohists in many parts of China, even in the rockbound state of Ch'in when it was the least civilized. Regular meetings were held, the master's words recited, and there is no doubt that the influence of Mo Tzu was second only to that of Confucius for many centuries.

It is possible to generate a climate of opinion in which diverse philosophies conflict but in which only those that meet certain requirements are tolerated. For two thousand years the leading schools of philosophy were the Confucians and the Mohists (the importance of the Taoists came much later). Though they were bitter rivals they had much in common. For instance, both looked back to ancient models, but where Confucius had chosen the Chou dynasty, Mo Tzu preferred the older Hsia (2183-1752 B.C.) in which the founder, Yu, is said to have made the crown hereditary.

In the *Mo Tzu Book* certain ideas stand out, perhaps not because they were original but because they were developed and defended as a body of doctrine. They concern the origins and structure of society, the strict organization of government and of the Mohist school, universal love, utilitarianism, and the existence of spirits.

When human life began in a primitive social state, Mo Tzu insisted, each man had his own ideas and no two agreed about anything. The result was confusion, struggle and violence. Nothing was shared and so surplus goods were wasted, and the disorder in the human world was the same as it was among birds and animals. Therefore one man was selected to be emperor because he was the most able and would make the most virtuous ruler. The origins of society lay in the choice of an Emperor who would determine what is right and wrong. After the establishment of the state the Emperor set absolute standards for everyone, strict obedience was required, and rewards and punishments were to be handed out accordingly. In Mo Tzu's conception there was no thought of individuality, only of "agreement with the Superior." The Emperor, as the Son of Heaven, was not only the ruler but the ultimate source of all correct teachings and ideas. In this way the Emperor put the order of his society in conformity with the ideas of Heaven (the Chinese word, we recall, for the ideal order of abstract laws). We must be clear about Heaven's purposes. How do we know them? By taking family life as the model. A man who has offended the head of his family must find another family or have no refuge, and if he offend against Heaven it is the same: he will have no refuge. And yet most people have not the knowledge to warn each other about this. To establish order in society the sage must understand disorder, whose sources he will discover in the absence of love.

Mo Tzu seems to have dictated the same strict organization and rigid rules for the Mohists as he held for society as a whole. Early in their career the Mohists were evidently an organized body of men capable of acting as a group. Mo Tzu insisted on absolute obedience. He ran his disciples like a military machine, and at one time as many as three hundred of them seem to have been under his control, every one of them expected to regard their leader as the sage they had deliberately chosen; and each hoped to be his successor. They did act as a group when it concerned them to do so. Mo Tzu was very much opposed to war as an instrument of state policy. Wars, he insisted, impoverish both sides; when the land is laid waste the victor loses as much as the vanquished. At least one of his disciples is said to have died in battle, and the only war he would countenance was defensive war, on which he wrote chapters dealing with methods.

Opposing war was a negative action, and Mo Tzu had a positive alternative to offer as well. He taught the doctrine of universal love. Most of the ills of the world arise because men do not love one another. The more skillful a man is in battle the more he should be punished. If everyone in the world loved everyone else in the world, as they should since all men are brothers, there would be no war.

He was very perceptive, however, in noting the crippling effects of limited love. He said that the love of the family, which Confucius and his followers promoted, posed a threat to universal love, as indeed did the love of any limited group, whether it be the love of a religion or even of the state. Religious zeal and nationalism, when neither is world-wide, block the path to universal love and the universal cooperation of internationalism which would inevitably go with it. The Mohist version of universal love often took strange forms. When one king who was a Mohist had a son who killed a man, the king insisted on executing his own son because, as he insisted, the law of the Mohists required it, since not to kill others is the greatest duty in the world. The preservation of life did not exclude retribution.

To someone who objected that the doctrine of universal love, though it might be good, was of utterly no use, Mo Tzu replied with a question, "How can anything that is good not be useful?" We like what is beneficial and dislike what is harmful, therefore we move toward the former and avoid the latter. Nature has placed man under the domination of two masters, pain and pleasure. (The English reformer, Jeremy Bentham, in the late eighteenth and early nineteenth centuries could have put it no plainer.)

The kind of doctrine Mo Tzu held to is known in the west as utilitarian. He insisted that before any statement could be accepted it must meet three tests. It must have a basis, it must be verified, and it must be applied. Its basis could only be in the conduct of the ancient sage-kings (no classic Chinese philosopher distinguished between sages and kings; kings were always sages); it could be verified only by the senses of the common people; and it could be applied only by being adopted by the government for the benefit of the country. Thus it would have to be traditional, simple and useful.

He held that usefulness was not the criterion, however; what was useful had to be directed toward some end worth pursing, and he named five of these: enriching the country, increasing the population, improving the social order, preventing war, and obtaining blessings from the spirits. Nothing was to be in excess; frugality and moderation in all things were counselled. Swords and boats should not be too elaborate, clothing should not be too luxurious, coffins not too thick and mourning not too long, houses only large and strong enough to keep out the weather.

China at the time was a country with a small population, only one seventh of what it is now. The superstitions of early China, the belief in ghosts, in good and evil spirits and the rest, were continued by the Mohists who were in this as in so many things opposed to their rivals, the Confucians.

Mo Tzu thought that the emotions posed a danger to the properly ordered life he was recommending. They tend to get out of hand, just as reason can when rationalism is excessive.

Emotion represented for him the "six depravities"—joy and anger, pleasure and sadness, love and hatred—which must be got rid of if man was to be guided by reason.

Mo Tzu differed from the Confucians on at least one large point. He believed in the existence of spirits, whereas Confucius, as we have already noted, did not. Mo Tzu was sure that when there are doubts as to the power of spirits to reward the worthy and punish the violently bad, sociiety would fall into chaos; and he included among spirits not only those of the dead but all sorts of ghosts and spectres as well. He insisted that spirits would have to be accepted if they made themselves known through the senses to a number of people, and this in his view they had done. He cited as evidence the case of one Chou king in the eighth century B.C. who had put to death his minister who was innocent of any wrong-doing. Three years later the minister reappeared at an assembly of feudal lords at noon in a chariot drawn by a white horse. Wearing red clothes, he pursued the king and from his red bow shot him with a red arrow which pierced his heart. All the Chou attendants saw it, and in distant places they heard of it, and it was duly recorded in the Chou Annals. Mo Tzu thought that the Annals, which also recorded in silk and bronze the beliefs of the ancient sage-kings in the existence of spirits, gave additional support for the belief in them in his time.

When people believe in something they have no difficulty in seeing it, as all those attested who saw witches riding through the air on broomsticks in Salem, Massachusetts as late as the seventeenth century of our era.

Chapter XVII
Mencius,
The Popular Confucian

The greatest of all the Confucians was Mencius, or Meng Tsu (371-289 B.C.). His career parallels that of his master to an astonishing degree. He was a pupil of Confucius' grandson. Like Confucius he travelled for forty years, urging rulers to reform, and like Confucius he ended a disappointed man, retiring to spend his last years in study.

The Confucian tradition, which has lasted until today, through periods of popularity and decline, probably owes almost as much to his influence as to that of Confucius. His writings, brought together as *The Book of Mencius*, constituted one of the four books which were for centuries considered the classics of Chinese learning and the basis of the civil service examinations.

Mencius' doctrine is on the whole derived from that of his beloved master. He said that he wanted to be like Confucius but that in this he had not entirely succeeded. He differed with Confucius on one point only, but it was so large that its development made of the philosophy of Mencius almost a separate doctrine, which was an idealistic one: briefly, that human nature is essentially good. Goodness is internal. The place to find the Way is in oneself, for when one finds it in oneself one can draw on it deeply. He said that "all the ten thousand things [that is, all things] are in me." He thought that morality begins at home, so to speak, and was more concerned with the person than with society. Benevolence, dutifulness and wisdom do not come from the outside but are in man originally; he has only to recover them from within himself. He possesss an innate knowledge of the good and an innate capacity to do good. Evil, on the other hand, is not innate but due to human failure to avoid the evil in external influences. The best that a man can hope to do is to make the most of his native endowment.

All who talk about the nature of things need only reason from the facts, Mencius declared. The great man is one who does not lose his originally good child's heart. If man does evil it is not his fault. If you let people follow their feelings they will be able to do good, for humanity, righteousness, propriety and wisdom are not drilled into us. The individual is under the obligation to recover his original nature by "seeking for the lost mind," and if he developes it to the utmost, he can in his way fulfill his destiny and serve Heaven.

The mentalism contained in this philosophy has led many to compare Mencius with Plato who lived at about the same time. Plato was not an idealist in the same sense but the late Platonists, the Neo-Platonists, certainly were. As the language was different, however, so was the outlook. Certainly in political theory there was no comparison.

The much advertised ancestor-worship of the Chinese is true of them. It is exemplified in Mencius as in so many others. A man's most important duty is toward his parents, Mencius said, but he judged a man not by how he treated his parents when alive but how he treated them when they died. The funeral of a parent is an occasion for doing one's utmost. Sacrifices for ancestors are required even after the long three-year period of mourning is over. The family is the central institution in Chinese culture, and evidence of this is given by every Chinese philosopher in some context or other. Mencius declared for instance that of all the ways of being a bad son, the worst is not to have an heir. Parents come before women and before wealth and princes, and the pleasure of parents alone can relieve anxiety. But in the end even the family gives way to one's self. The empire, he said, rests on the state, the state on the family, and the family on the self. Society begins with the individual. These are the Four Beginnings: the feeling of commiseration is the beginning of humanity, the feeling of shame and dislike is the beginning of righteousness, the feeling of deference and compliance is the beginning of propriety, and the feeling of right and wrong is the beginning of wisdom. The superior man is the one who preserves humanity and propriety. The man of humanity loves others, the man of propriety respects others. Mencius said that he liked life and also righteousness, but if he could not have them both he would choose righteousness. If each individual conducts himself correctly and practices altruism, a good society will be the result.

If a man has no secure livelihood he will not have a secure mind, and if he has no secure mind there is nothing he will not do in the way of self-abandonment, moral deflection, depravity and wild license. Humanity is the human mind, but the will is the leader of the vital force: the will is the highest, the vital force comes next.

His philosophy was largely ethical and individual, but he had almost a political philosophy and it was a startling one for his time. He was the first thinker to advocate "humane government." Opposed to despotism and utilitarianism, he wished to return the government to the people and even defended their right to rebel against tyrants.

Mencius argued that if the king governed badly then he lost his "mandate from Heaven" and could be removed from office and another would be chosen in his place. This would seem to argue that government is a matter of laws, not of men—

an early expression, certainly, of the democratic principle that political power resides in the people. The good will of the people was essential to good government, he insisted, and the voice of the people should be listened to over other voices. The Chinese scholar, Wing-Tsit Chan, states that this position made Mencius the greatest defender of democracy in the whole of Chinese history, a position which was never taken up in Chinese practice.

In many ways Mencius was ahead of his time. He entertained a cyclical theory of history long before anyone else did. "Every five hundred years a true king should arise, and in the interval there should arise one from whom the age takes its name. From Chou to the present is over seven hundred years. The five hundred mark is passed; the time seems ripe." The idea has recurred in the history of Chinese philosophy, but this account seems to have been the first.

That Mencius was more concerned with the individual than with the state is evident in his conception of greatness. A great man, he declared, would "live in the wide house of the world," follow the great Way (Tao), practice his principles only for the good of the people, but if that was not possible he would practice them alone. Wealth would not lead him to dissipation, poverty would never make him swerve from his ideals.

Chapter XVIII
Hsun Tzu,
The Forgotten Confucian

A favorite time to look to philosophers is in a period of economic and political upheaval, a "time of troubles." Confucius, Mencius and Hsun Tzu all lived during the "Period of the Warring States." It does seem to point to a deep human need for some kind of social order and stability. It is difficult to pursue individual goals when nothing is settled or seemingly permanent.

Hsun Tzu's dates are not accurately known. He is believed to have flourished some time between 298 and 238 B.C. Like Mencius he was full of praise for Confucius, but where Mencius thought most highly of Confucius' morality, Hsun Tzu preferred his love of learning, and he challenged severely Mencius' interpretation.

Like his master Confucius, Hsun Tzu looked back to the rule of the ancient sage-kings, the men of the Chou dynasty, but he gave more important justifications for doing so. As neither the social world nor human nature changes, he declared, why not revive the institutions of that ancient dynasty?

Unlike his masters, Hsun Tzu looked also to more recent

models. There was an old saying to the effect that any man in the street can become like the sage-king, and Hsun Tzu declared that this meant the practice of humanity, righteousness, and a following of laws and correct principles.

It was not enough that the philosopher should discover truth for himself. He must also and most urgently teach it to others. It was the conception of the philosopher as teacher that he emphasized. To have the right teacher is to train for good, and as we have noted, only training can instill it in the individual, who is born, as Hsun Tzu believed, programmed for evil, so to speak. The purpose of an education so understood is not merely to acquire knowledge but to influence conduct for the better. (As we shall see, the Taoist insisted that this was precisely *not* the way to do it.)

In general, Mencius was an idealist and Hsun Tzu a naturalist. The former believed that human nature is essentially good, the latter believed it to be evil. (A westerner is forcefully reminded at this point of Rousseau and Hobbes.) Yet they had more ideas in common than those which set them apart. On the question of morality Hsun Tzu believed that man can become good only through training. He is naturally envious and hates others; to follow his original instincts can result only in strife and violence. The civilizing influences of teachers and of laws, the guidance of rites and of justice, are necessary if good government is to result. This picture of human nature represents at least a half truth; that there is some evil in human nature can hardly be questioned, but Hsun Tzu went further in asserting that at birth all men are equal in every respect, even in ability. This has been disproved, the equality is now political; everyone should have the same opportunities. But the truth is Mencius and Hsun Tzu were partly right; man has conflicting impulses; the actions he performs are based on his needs; he wishes by turns to help and to hurt his fellow man for different reasons.

For Hsun Tzu, if all men try to satisfy all their desires they will run into conflict, for there is not enough of everything to satisfy everybody, and since conflict is bad, the consequences are sure to be bad also. Although he believed that human nature is inherently evil, man can become good, learning how to uphold the law and achieve uprightness. He has only to practice learning and every day add to the sum of his knowledge. It is in the nature of man to know and what he knows are the laws of the material world; only it is not always so simple, for it often happens that observation generates doubt because the things of the material world are not always apprehended clearly. Further investigation is called for.

The way of the sage is open to one and all Hsun Tzu declared. A man can become a superior man by cultivating the right habits, proper conduct and standards of justice, and thus himself become a sage in the end. Man likes what is beneficial and dislikes what is injurious. In the pursuit and avoidance that follow he knows no personal restraints. Society with its organization enables him best to satisfy his desires; its institutions provide for the division of labor, which is established by the more intelligent and accepted by the others. Self-preservation requires such a moral system. If the rules of proper conduct and of justice established in accordance with the accepted morality of society were to be abandoned nobody's desires would be satisfied. Though man is not inherently moral, society provides the necessary morality and maintains it for everyone's benefit. Thus morality for Hsun Tzu rests on an utilitarian basis. There is no kind of human life that does not have its social distinctions, no social distinctions that are not subordinate to the rules of proper conduct, no rules of proper conduct that are not subordinate to the sage-kings. Hsun Tzu leaned toward the kind of authoritarianism later advocated by the Legalists and approved of their most repressive measures. He followed Confucianism in many things, but to the extent to which he went off on his own he did more harm than good to the school. His mistake in not supposing that there is good as well as evil native to human nature in the end warped his philosophy so much that all subsequent Confucians had to reject it, so that it was for the most part forgotten, his accomplishments were neglected and his incisive analyses were not taken up, as they might have been, with advantage.

He was a thoroughgoing naturalist. He did not believe in ghosts and spirits any more than Confucius had. Beating a drum to cure rheumatism will only wear out the drum and won't cure the rheumatism, he declared. If you pray for rain and it rains, it proves nothing; it would have rained anyway. He was very clear about Heaven; it is, he said, the order of nature, and you are obeying the will of Heaven when you follow nature—intelligently.

There was a Chinese tradition of logic and the theory of knowledge, though they were not separated and were known only as the "Rectification of Names." As we have noted, both the term and the subject were the work of Confucius, who however confined their use to social classes in order to preserve clear distinctions between them. Hsun Tzu, abstracting somewhat further, carried the idea into pure logic. When we wish to speak of all things in general, he said, we call them things, and there are abstractions beyond that, until nothing more general can be found; but names were made in order that we may denote actual things and can convey ideas to one another. His emphasis Hsun Tzu was not on the names but on the things which the names are intended to describe, the correctness of names being determined only by convention. The material things are there to be reckoned with and present a stubborness which we deal with by means of language. Names, then, are secondary to recognition and it is their correctness which must be our concern.

As to the material things with which we must deal, what is the basis of their similarities and differences? Hsun Tzu asked. Why do we call an object a dog? He did not accept the Platonic type of answer that the naming was due to the ideal dog which served as the model for particular dogs. His answer sounded more modern; he said that it was due to the testimony of the senses.

He might have done even better—and so might many moderns—if he had said that we owe our knowledge of the ideals to the testimony of the senses which tell us about similarities among particular dogs which no study of dogs separately can explain, for we actually do perceive the resemblance of dogs to each other.

But this would have been too much for Hsun Tzu. He seems only to have been concerned lest the name for a thing he substituted for the thing; and in terms of some extreme claims in the philosophy of language today, his concern was justified.

Hsun Tzu's philosophy exerted a greater influence at first than did that of Mencius, until the end of the Han dynasty in A.D. 220 when he began to be considered the leading Confucian. He was a great influence in the hated Ch'in, a barbarous state which overthrew the much admired Chou but set up a dictatorship, which united China in the third century B.C. Indeed two of its ministers had been his pupils. But after that his reputation declined sharply and was not revived until the nineteenth century. Then it was Mencius and not Hsun Tzu who was thought to be the inheritor and transmitter of Confucian wisdom. Hsun Tzu's work was not one of the Four Books which were considered classics by the Chinese.

Chapter XIX
Laotse and the Tao

When a society is experiencing a time of troubles there are always thinkers who naturally seek a way of escape from the chaos that attends social conflict. We may take it that Confucius was such a thinker. There was another whose work has taken its place among the classics of Chinese philosophy, Lao-tzu, or, as he is known more commonly in the west, Laotse.

The Confucians and the Mohists were advisers to princes; they were concerned with how best to run a state and occupied themselves with law and order. The individual somehow got lost in all this, but his champions were bound to arise sooner or later. Taoism arose as a counterpart and balance to the social concerns of rival schools. Like Confucianism, it probably came out of an ancient body of traditions, beliefs, and practices, but with a different emphasis, and was more concerned with nature and the individual's place in it. It was probably much earlier than the half-legendary work of Lao Tan for instance who is said to have preached conformity with nature, the writings which bear the name of Laotse.

Since his philosophy aimed at self-effacement and namelessness, he did not write under his own name which was Li Erh. According to James Legge, Laotse was born in 604 B.C., which would make him fifty years older than Confucius. Legge thought that the two men met more than once. Later perhaps more reliable, scholarship places him within the fourth century, and dates the *Tao Te Ching* about 300 B.C., perhaps a little earlier.

Laotse, the exact date of whose birth and death are not known, was a native of the state of Ch'u, had a family and was a recluse, though not a hermit. He was one of a large number who withdrew as much as possible because they were opposed to the government. Since his work was extended by Chuang-tzu, they may be grouped together as the principal members of the Taoist school and the authors of the Taoist philosophy. No doubt their writings have suffered from editing and rearranging by the Han scholars who lived much later (206 B.C.-220 A.D.); nevertheless a somewhat consistent view emerges.

Laotse's philosophy is contained in a short book entitled the *Tao Te Ching,* in English *the Way* (Tao) *and Its Power* (Te). I have used the translation "Way," but according to Legge in the introduction to his edition of the basic texts of Taoism, "Tao" has been rendered in English by a number of other words, among them: "road," "nature," "path" and "course" or in a triple sense as at once "being," "reason" and "speech."

It is a work of some eighty-one brief chapters but it has been much more important than its size would indicate. In most things opposed to the sayings of Confucius, it has, together with the sayings, furnished the classic philosophy of ancient China, and has spread far beyond its borders. In English alone I have counted forty translations.

The *Tao Te Ching* is difficult to understand, for it was written in parables and pithy utterances many of which are contradictory and so lend themselves easily to more than one interpretation. To suggest what difficulties confront the translator, I offer seven translations of the same sentence the first line of chapter 49:

"The Sage's self is not a self for itself"—Witter Bynner

"A sound man's heart is not shut within itself"—Hermon Ould

"The Sage has no heart of his own"—(This one is Arthur Waley's, who suggests in a footnote that it could have been read to mean:

"The Sage makes no judgments of his own.")

"The Sage has no fixed (personal' ideas."—Wing-Tsit Chan

"The Sage has no decided opinions and feelings"—Lin Yutang

"The Sage has no invariable mind of his own"—James Legge

In what follows I shall suggest something of the meaning of the contents, relying upon the work of a number of the best Chinese scholars. In a word, where Confucius was interested only in human nature and conduct, Laotse was occupied chiefly with untouched nature and with its mystical overtones, but also with a direction which pointed down the road toward natural science. The paradoxes and contradictions in the *Tao Te Ching* are not there accidentally; they have a meaning which must be unravelled.

The Taoists had a theory of metaphysics, of being, or what there is, and they had an ethics and a politics which they deduced from it. In this sense their philosophy is more comprehensive than that of the Confucians, who were content to occupy themselves with human conduct. It seems more complete to have a theory of the world and then to locate the place of man and society in it than merely to have a theory of man and society as though they did not have any place in the world. Although the Taoists had a theory of society or government, the emphasis still seems to have been on the individual.

On metaphysics

There is a single unifying first principle of being and it is called Tao. The way of Tao is the way of power. Events follow the way of power, which is to reconcile opposites (*yin* and *yang*) and to exhibit unity in diversity. Tao gives rise to differences and therefore to the diversity of separate things, which is what brought the material universe into existence. Being gives rise to non-being, which is at the same time not nothing. It contains all the forms and is the source of all power, for it is the power inherent in each thing that makes it what it is. The Tao cannot be named; to name is to define and thus to delimit, and the Tao is without limit. What exists can be destroyed and the Tao is indestructible, the invariant behind all variables.

To quote selectively from the *Tao Te Ching:* "Existence and non-existence give birth, each to the other" (ch. 2). "Being comes from non-being, and all else comes from being" (ch. 40). "The softest thing in the world overcomes the hardest. Non-being penetrates that in which there is no crevice" (ch. 43). "There is always being, we have only to see the outcome. The name that can be named is not the invariable, but what is named is the source of all things" (ch. 1). "Its name is the Invisible, it reverts to nothingness" (ch. 14). "Tao is eternal and has no name" (ch. 32). "I do not know its name; I call it Tao. If forced to give it a name I call it power; being great it functions everywhere" (ch. 25).

Tao never does anything yet through it all things are done (ch. 37). "Tao is empty like a bowl, it may be used but its capacity is never exhausted. Deep and still, it appears to exist forever" (ch. 4). "Tao produces the ten thousand things. Matter gives them physical form" (ch. 51). "The all-embracing quality of the great power follows from the Tao. Deep and obscure, it is the essence of things, and the essence is very real. From the time of old until now, its name ever remains by which we may see the beginnings of all things" (ch. 21). "When all things return to their original state, then complete harmony will be reached" (ch. 65).

On the theory of knowledge

Since desires, of which the desire for knowledge is one, must be lessened, the desire for knowledge must be lessened, too. Knowledge is knowledge of the objects of desire and prevents contentment. Study only increases desire. To study what is unstudied therefore is to reach the desirable state in which there is no knowledge. To the wise non-learning constitutes learning.

To quote again from the *Tao Te Ching*, "To know and yet not to know is best" (ch. 71). "The pursuit of learning means to increase it every day, the pursuit of Tao means to decrease it every day" (ch. 48). "To know harmony means to be in accord with the unchanging. To be in accord with the unchanging means to be enlightened" (ch. 55). "When the Way was no longer observed, righteousness came into vogue and there emerged great hypocrisy" (ch. 18). "Abandon learning and there will be no trouble" (ch. 20).

Creel makes a big point of the spontaneous use of deeply held knowledge. The skills which we have practiced often enough over a long enough period become automatic and do not require conscious thought (as in the way we ride a bicycle or drive a car). The most subtle knowledge is not rational but intuitive and unconscious, a matter of feeling. As often as not taste makes judgments better than reasoning can. The Taoists advocate this kind of knowledge over the kind that is deliberate and rational. The practices of one who knows in this way are apt to be more relaxed as well as accurate.

On ethics

To live properly in the world is to find the invariants in changing phenomena. Of the rules required to maintain contact with things, one of the chief is to rely upon the action of opposites by living in a manner opposed to the end you would seek. Anything which goes to one extreme is compelled to swing to the opposite. Whoever grasps the notion of the invariant understands this. One gets rid of extremes by grasping them in order to achieve the mean. Since being is a form of doing, the goal is a state of quiescence.

To quote again from the *Tao Te Ching*, "He who knows the unchanging is all-embracing; being all-embracing, he is impartial. Being impartial, he is universal. Being universal, he is one with nature" (ch. 16). "Man takes his law from the earth, earth takes its law from heaven, heaven takes its law from the Tao, and the law of the Tao is what it is." (ch. 25). "[The ideal man] will never deviate from the eternal virtue, but return to the ultimate state of non-being, the state of simplicity akin to uncarved wood, which when broken up is turned into concrete things" (ch. 28).

"He who has found Tao will be free from danger throughout his lifetime. Seeing what is small is called enlightenment, keeping to weakness is called strength. Use the light, revert to enlightenment. This is called "holding on to the unchanging" (ch. 52). "My words are very easy to know but there is no one able to practice them. My deeds have a master in Tao" (ch. 70). "Deal with things before they appear. Secure order before disorder has begun" (ch. 64). "There is nothing softer and weaker than water, and yet there is nothing better for attacking hard and strong things. For this reason there is no substitute for it. Everyone knows that the weak overcomes the strong and the soft overcomes the hard" but no one is able to put it into practice. (ch. 78).

"When the people of the world all know beauty as beauty, they recognize what ugliness is. When they know the good they recognize evil" (ch. 2). "Cultivate plainness, embrace simplicity, avoid selfishness, reduce desires and there will be no thieves or robbers." (ch. 19).

On politics

Living in the world, we are told, requires social and political institutions to maintain man's existence. Too many institutions, however, bring about the opposite effect. The ruler must be guided by the ideal of unobtrusive facilitation. The least government is the best government because it governs without interfering. Though laws were laid down to restrain criminals, too many laws cause the criminals to rise against them in even greater numbers. Because these principles apply to laws as well as to those who would govern, the state should be small and the people should be isolated and have few possessions. A primitive culture is to be preferred to a great civilization.

Again from the *Tao Te Ching:* "The best rulers were those whose existence was barely known to the people, the next best were those who were loved and praised. The great rulers value their words lightly; nevertheless the people will say that they simply follow nature" (ch. 17). "A state may be ruled by freedom from action. The more restrictions and prohibitions, the poorer the people will be. Therefore take no trouble, and the people will prosper, have no ambition and the people will gain in simplicity". (ch. 57). "Wishing to be above men the ruler speaks as though he were below them, wishing to be before them he places himself behind them." (ch. 66). "He who assists the ruler with Tao does not dominate the world with force. The use of force will usually be met with force" (ch. 30).

"Let there be a small state with few people, no ships and carriages used, no weapons displayed. Their food should be palatable, their homes comfortable, their simple tasks pleasurable. There should be no visiting with the neighboring state" (ch. 80).

Chinese technology

The Taoists were naturalists. They retired to nature, not to learn natural law, but to find the natural way for human beings. They did not believe in experimenting with nature; the thought had probably not occurred to them as it did the classic Greeks, but they did believe in observing nature and in fitting in with it as much as possible. In a sense they wished to live as primitively as possible in an undisturbed environment rather than in the cities. The Taoists were the first to think in terms of preserving the environment.

The Tao was not the correct social order but the order of nature, the way the universe works. Man is not the measure of all things; heaven and earth are. The order of nature is not a force; things follow its path simply because that is the way they are. The age will therefore not attempt to control nature, only to observe and understand.

Joseph Needham has called attention to the unity and the spontaneity of things and events in the universe according to the Tao and its demand for a passive acceptance of nature rather than the active management of society. The supposed impartiality of nature led the Taoist to a preference for the collectivist society of the village in ancient time (a foretaste of Red China), as it might have been under the Shang dynasty, over the feudal society so dear to the heart of Confucius. As the Confucians were occupied only with man and society—with human nature—so the Taoists were concerned with non-human nature.

The interest in nature, which the Tao generated, was limited to contemplating it and so never developed the investigation of nature which produced European science. Nevertheless, it remained counter to the Confucianists who, as we have noted, confined their interest to human nature and conduct. It is well to remember that the Taoists, unlike the Confucians, believed in the existence of spirits and even of magic, and in this were only a short distance away from experimental science, which after all owed its origins to magical practices in alchemy and astrology, both wrong but in the direction of manual operations, as Needhan has suggested. Yet they veered away and sought to discover how best to fit into a natural environment while disturbing it the least.

The nearest the Chinese came to the scientific method was a philosophy of nature and a technology which was advanced for its time. The philosophy of nature was the work of Taoists, and though they do not deserve credit for the technology, only for the fact that their work was consistent with it, the Chinese in the last few centuries before our era did invent paper, irrigation, water conservation and harness for farm animals; and the three inventions noted by Francis Bacon: printing, gunpowder, and the magnetic compass as well as mechanical clocks, the casting of iron, and steel technology; and in the first 1500 years of our era the seismograph; suspension bridges; movable type. Needham has pointed out that in comparatively recent times Europe learned much of its technology from China.

Chapter XX
Two Confucian Classics

During the early years of the Han dynasty (beginning in 206 B.C.) China became unified to a degree not known until then. Despite the many inventions, China remained largely agricultural, united by the ancient patriarchal system in which the family was central and the chief occupation was farming. There was a kind of consolidation, which included the thoughts of the philosophers; Confucius and the Confucian classics became established as the basis of all higher education.

Two very short books, the *Great Learning* and the *Doctrine of the Mean,* have been influential out of all proportion to their size. They have always been considered the work of the Confucian school, and attributed to the grandsons of Confucius, but they were probably edited by government scribes during the Han dynasty. How faithful they are to the originals we have no way of knowing. It has also been believed that the *Great Learning* was written by a follower of Hsun Tzu and the *Doctrine of the Mean* by a follower of Mencius.

The Great Learning

There is a fundamental truth and a procedure very much to be preferred, inherent in the *Great Learning,* to the effect that in order to cope successfully with the practical problems of the world a period of contemplation and speculation is essential. "Only after having gained peaceful repose can one begin to deliberate. Only after deliberation can the end be attained." To think is to retire and only afterwards to carry thought into practice, a process similar to what the modern scientist does in his laboratory before the applied scientist and technologist put the results of his inquiries to work for social betterment. It is also what Toynbee meant by "withdrawal-and-return," a temporary withdrawal from the world of affairs in order to return with newly acquired power over it.

There are three clearly stated goals in the *Great Learning:* to develop a clear character, to love people and to pursue the highest good. In order to reach these goals there is a correct procedure, which begins with the extension of knowledge— this involves of course an investigation of things—from which a chain of causes and effects is set up, somewhat as follows: the will becomes sincere, the mind is rectified, the personal life is cultivated, the family regulated, the state put in order and peace is established throughout the world.

Making the will sincere meant allowing no self-deception; cultivating the personal life and rectifying the mind meant not allowing anger, fear, fondness or worry from interfering with correct reasoning; regulating the family meant not allowing the feelings to interfere with the proper consideration of close relatives; putting the state in order meant not allowing the inhumanity of families to plunge the country into disorder; establishing peace meant not allowing disorder in the state to lead to war. Thus, to attain to world peace, we must start with the individual and his search for reliable knowledge. The good society is a result of the collection of good individuals, who cannot fail to become good if they begin by extending knowledge through the investigation of things.

The individual could find his model in the perfection of the ancient rulers. King Wen was singled out for this honor. "As ruler he abided in humanity. As a minister he abided in reverence. As a son he abided in filial piety. As a father he abided in deep love. And in dealing with the people of the country he abided in faithfulness." (The translation is Wing-Tsit Chan's.)

The Doctrine of The Mean

This book has two topics: the nature of reality and the nature of humanity. Only those who are sincere (the meaning of which will become clear presently) can develop their natures, the only way by which they develop the nature of others, in turn the only way by which they can develop the nature of things and assist in transforming and nourishing the natural processes. In the end the universe and man form a unity because they are harmonious, and they are harmonious because they are balanced. Both moderation (the mean between extremes), and the Way as the natural course of things are the guide lines.

The conventional concerns for society, the efforts to perfect it in its traditional form are what concerns the author of the *Doctrine of the Mean:* the perfect ruler presiding over a society understood as a collection of large families, with five sets of obligations to cover every contingency: those between ruler and minister, between father and son, between husband and wife, between elder and younger brothers, and between friends.

The author gives nine standards by which the perfect ruler should administer his empire: to cultivate his personal life, honor the worthy, be affectionate to relatives, be respectful toward great ministers, identify himself with all his officers together, treat the common people as his children, attract artisans, show consideration to strangers and extend influence over the feudal lords.

Although ruler and sage are usually embodied in the same person in traditional Chinese thought, the *Doctrine of the Mean* lists the virtues separately: insight and wisdom, if one is to rule; generosity and tenderness, if he is to embrace all men; vigor and resolution, if he is to take a firm hold; seriousness and correctness, if he is to be reverent; refinement and penetration, if he is to exercise discrimination. If he have these virtues he will be known throughout the Middle Kingdom and even beyond.

After the model of the ruler and sage, the next in order is the superior man, whose first obligation is to cultivate the Way, called education. The proper attitude for him rests on equilibrium and harmony—equilibrium, before the feelings of pleasure, anger, sorrow and joy are aroused, and harmony after them. Equilibrium is the foundation of the world, harmony the universal path through it. The task of the superior man is to study the Way extensively, inquire into it accurately, think over it carefully, sift it clearly, practice it earnestly.

After a restatement of Confucius' silver rule, "what you do not wish others to do to you, do not do to them," the author goes on to spell out what this means socially. It will lead the superior man to do what is proper to his station in life and not make him want to go beyond it. For in traditional Confucian thought (which is almost equal to traditional Chinese thought) the idea of social mobility is not to be found even if it occurred in actual life. If the Chinese did not recognize an official caste system, one is nevertheless affirmed here. For the superior man, if he is a noble, does what is proper to the level of his wealth and social position. If he is in a more humble state, he does what is proper to that.

The *Doctrine of the Mean* undertook a metaphysical inquiry into the nature of reality: "Absolute sincerity," one passage begins, "is ceaseless." "Being ceaseless, it is lasting. Being last, it is evident. Being evident, it is infinite. Being infinite, it is extensive and deep. Being extensive and deep, it is high and brilliant. It is because it is extensive and deep that it contains all things." Etc.

Before we try to follow the meaning of this passage we must remember that what the author means by 'sincerity' is not what we mean. For him it is a term the other meanings of which are "truth" or "reality," and these meanings are relied upon interchangeably. A technical analysis of any of these meanings would be quite different from that of the others.

The point is that in all probability the Chinese language was inadequate to deal with such abstractions as truth or reality. That it may have had this deficiency has been noted by scholars and may account both for the brevity of most Chinese ventures into philosophy and for the Chinese philosopher's concern with what, from Confucius onward, they called "the rectification of names." Consider for example the attempts of scholars to translate the word *jen*. "Humanity" is the commonest English equivalent but because it is not altogether satisfactory others have been suggested: "benevolence," "goodness," "perfect virtue." Obviously, there is a clarification of thought and an enlargement of vocabulary required here, a "rectification of names."

What came to be known generally as the Confucian classics included *The Great Learning* and *The Doctrine of the Mean* as well as the *Analects* and the work of Mencius. Together these four books shaped Chinese institutions for more than two thousand years. They made the culture largely a Confucian affair for they formed the basis of the competitive civil service examinations and meant that Confucius reigned even where he did not rule. The civil service was in point of fact a unique Chinese contribution, instituted by the first Han ruler in 196 B.C., although there were evidences of its existence in a crude form much earlier. Examinations were given not only in the philosophical classics, though these lay at its center; but also in law, mathematics, poetry and calligraphy. Later the system was extended until it resembled the three degrees now offered in American universities, the B.A., M.A. and Ph.D.

The advantages of this system were that it set learning above warfare and intelligence above family connections, and undertook to form an aristocracy of brains. It later spread to Korea and Japan; indeed it would be difficult to understand any of these cultures without it. The civil service in China was a long-lasting institution; it was not discontinued until 1905.

Chapter XXI
The Legalists

The Fa-Chia (Legalist), school of philosophy has been traced to thinkers who lived as early as 645 B.C. but the name was not given to them until the first century. There were Legalists before their ideas were recorded, for the political movements which resulted in strong states certainly did have their defenders.

They were chiefly political philosophers. Such ethics as they advanced stemmed from their theory of politics, and the metaphysics they required by way of justification they borrowed from the Taoists; indeed many of them were Taoists. Bitterly opposed to the Confucians who were more concerned with individual morality, the Legalists saw things from the point of view of the state and were occupied in the main with the tasks of rulers, their power, their methods of administration, their laws. Justice, good government and even the welfare of the citizens must proceed from the top down.

The ancient conception that the ruler was also a sage the Legalists accepted completely though they were among the first philosophers who did not look back for their model to a golden age of the past. Why follow the record of the ancient rulers when they did not rule correctly? There is more than one way to rule the world, they argued, hence the sage does not practice the percepts of antiquity but discusses the affairs of his own age and deals with them accordingly.

We owe our knowledge of the Legalist philosophy to two sources, first to the writings of Shang Yang, who died in 338 B.C. and was chief adviser to the ruler of Ch'in, and of Han Fei Tzu, who died in 233 B.C., who was a member of the ruling family of the state of Han, east of Ch'in. There still exists a *Book of Lord Shang,* probably spurious, but valuable, and a work by Han Fei Tzu known by his name.

The political philosophy which the Legalists advocated would be classified today as dictatorship. As the individual was to be rigidly controlled by the state in his thoughts, feelings and actions in every moment of his waking life, Wing-Tsit Chan calls it totalitarian.

If he is to govern properly, the ruler must have authority over three functions: power, methods and laws. Any state can be governed correctly provided none of the three is neglected in favor of the others; all are to be practiced together. Gaining supremacy over the masses, administering secretly and deviously establishing laws uniformly, all are equally necessary if the ruler is to be successful. Absolute power issues from the ruler as therefore the methods of ruling and the laws. To exercise rigid control, he must have a good working knowledge of human nature. All men are motivated by selfishness and profit, they reveal calculating minds, each man acts in his own interests. Since men have likes and dislikes, they can be manipulated by rewards and punishments, the "two handles" of the ruler's administration. Commands and prohibitions insure the carrying out of the laws, which are nothing more than decrees of the ruler, who has such control of his subjects that he exercises the power of life and death over them. It is the ruler who makes the laws but after they have been promulgated he cannot change them at will. He as well as the people must abide by them in order that there may be the rule of law. Here the quiescence of the Taoists became a factor. If power is established, the method of rule operating and the laws are in effect, the ruler may practice non-activity, leading his followers into activity in virtue of his position and called upon to do little himself, but the result is that the country is properly governed.

The individual must be taught to live, work and, if need be, die for the state. He has nothing he can call his own—no possessions, no life—that is not at the service of the ruler. The citizens must be under the complete control of the government if the ruler is to grow rich and his country made ready for war. For Confucius, remember, the "Rectification of Names" meant seeing to it that every social class is what it ought to be in the hierarchy. For the Legalists it meant only that the ruler retained control over the masses. "When names have been rectified, things undergo change."

It is obvious that under this kind of rule the people could not be trusted. Do not depend upon men to do good but arrange things so that they can do no wrong. When they are selfish, vicious and inclined to wrongdoing, only by teaching can they be made virtuous and trustworthy. The severe household has no rebellious slaves, the indulgent mother has spoiled sons. From such examples, Han Fei Tzu said, we learn that only absolute power can prevent violence; virtue and kindliness will not end disorder. Under these circumstances the ruler must exercise absolute control and maintain vigilance. Even the ruler's own ministers cannot be counted on without measures to insure their loyalty. The ruler must therefore provide for a system of informers at every level. The lengths to which the Legalists were prepared to go (and sometimes did go) is illustrated by their attitude to scholarship. In a memorial to his Emperor (a written statement of facts presented to a sovereign) Li Ssu, the prime minister of Ch'in, wrote that since the independent schools of philosophy criticized the court's codes of laws and instructions and in this way threatened the order of the empire, it would be well to prohibit such activity by burning all the books except those in the imperial archives.

Accordingly, an edict to this effect was carried out in 213 B.C. Those who did not comply were to be sent to help build the Great Wall (in effect, slave labor). Scholars, Han Fei Tzu declared, ought to be punished and put to useful work. No traditional wisdom, no ancient precedents, were necessary; the teachings of the officials were sufficient. Li Ssu had his teacher and his acknowledged superior, Han Fei Tzu, arrested and jailed, whereupon the latter committed suicide.

An even more frightful illustration may be taken from the attitude of the Legalists toward war. The *Book of Shang* recommends that if the people do not like war, it is advisable to make their daily life so miserable that they will welcome war as a release. It is not necessary to study military strategy; men who read about the art of war would serve better if thrown into the line of battle. Under the guidance of this political philosophy, the state of Ch'in was able to gain control of China by a series of bloody conquests, completed by 221 B.C., and the ruler proclaimed himself Emperor of all China. He did all that he could to consolidate his rule, making the laws uniform, standardizing weights and measures and adopting an official form for written characters. The author of all this violence was the Prime Minister of Ch'in, Li Ssu, who in the end was executed by the very eunuch he had conspired with to assassinate the emperor's eldest son when the emperor died. Absolute dictatorships are evidently always turned toward war and conquest, and often end with the violent death of the leader responsible for the initiation of the system.

The similarity here to Adolf Hitler and the Nazis is painfully obvious. Hitler's conquests did not hold and neither did those of the Emperor of China. By 207 B.C., a mere thirteen years later, the Ch'in family was forgotten, and the Han dynasty, which had a long run, was initiated by an outsider. After the violence and brutality of the Ch'in dynasty, Legalism fell into disrepute and had no counterpart for the next two thousand years; but the ideals and methods of the Legalists were to have a surprising revival under another banner much later in Chinese history—actually, in our own day.

Chapter XXII
Chuang Tzu,
The Favorite Taoist

The Chinese have always loved nature and endeavored to remain close to it, but because of the passivity of their philosophers they were not led to investigate it except through contemplation. The philosopher who best exemplified this position is Chuang Tzu, who stands to Laotse as Mencius does to Confucius: the disciple whose work contains a fresh departure while maintaining adherence to the master. Though they do not seem to have been acquainted, he and Mencius were contemporaries.

The dates of Chuang Tzu's life are uncertain—probably somewhere between 399 and 295 B.C. Born in what is now Honan province, a native of Sung, his name had been Chou. He was a minor official in Meng, who is said to have declined the office of prime minister because he wished to retain his freedom.

Unlike his master Laotse, he was fascinated by the spectacle of change. What we refer to as nature is in continual movement; there is never a moment when things in the universe are not changing. This is no less true of the forms; things also change from one form to another in the process called the evolution of nature.

Some examples from the book named after him will give an idea of the man's thinking. Time, space, and the size of material objects are all relative. Objective existence has no effect and therefore need not be taken seriously.

Suppose I make a statement. How am I to know whether it belongs to one category or another? Chuang Tzu had an answer. "The knowledge of the men of old had a limit. It extended back to a period when matter did not exist." "With matter contraries arose and the Tao declined." "If there is existence, then there must have been non-existence. And if there was a time when nothing existed, then there must have been a time before that—when even nothing did not exist." Suddenly there is being and non-being, but I don't know which is which. I have just said something but I don't know whether what I have said says something or says nothing.

From his own point of view, declared Chuang Tzu, the principle of humanity and righteousness and the doctrines of right and wrong are mixed and confused. How then could he know the differences among them? Happiness for individual man consists in finding his harmony with nature. "By means of inaction the individual will be able to adapt himself to the natural conditions of existence." By following their natures both men and things reach the state of harmony. Natural is opposed to artificial. As soon as there is any artificiality the happiness which comes from according oneself with the natural is lost; there is a loss also of interest in life.

The only personal benefit the Taoists sought from the knowledge of nature was the state of tranquillity it produced; a feeling of unity with the universe always has religious overtones. They did not want to interfere with or change it in any way, only to be at ease with it, to reach a condition of equilibrium which would result in the absence of tensions. The European parallel, Needham has pointed out, was what the Greek Epicureans called "ataraxy" which translates as "serenity."

What should the individual do, according to Chuang Tzu? Nothing—at least nothing artificial. Do what comes naturally and it will be in accordance with nature. Prince Hui's cook declared that he had always devoted himself to Tao: "When I first began to cut up bullocks, I saw before me *whole* bullocks. After three years' practice, I saw no more whole animals. Now I work with my mind and not with my eye. When my senses bid me stop, my mind urges me on and I fall back on eternal principles. I follow such openings or cavities as there may be." "Bravo!" cried the Prince. "From the words of this cook I have learned how to take care of my life."

"Tao gives him his expression and Heaven gives him his form. How should he not be a man?" He should be without passions. "By a man without passions I mean one who does not permit good and evil to disturb his internal economy, but rather falls in with whatever happens as a matter of course."

"The pure men of old did not know what it was to love life or hate death. They did not rejoice in birth, nor strive to put off dissolution. Quickly come and quickly go; no more."

"Are you afraid?" Chuang Tzu was asked.

"I am not. What have I to fear? Ere long I shall be decomposed. My left shoulder will become a cock, and I shall herald the approach of morning. My right shoulder will become a cross-bow, and I shall be able to get broiled duck. My buttocks will become wheels; and with my soul for a horse I shall be able to ride in my own chariot."

"Pleasure and anger, sorrow and joy, fickleness and fear, impulsiveness and extravagance, indulgence and lewdness, come to us like music from the hollows or like mushrooms from the damp. Day and night they alternate within us, but we don't know where they come from. They are right near by but we don't know what causes them. It seems there is a True Lord who does so, but there is no indication of his existence."

Political and social institutions, being artificial, serve only to impose suffering on men. The ideal is to "let men alone," not to govern them. Government through institutions always involves the use of force. "Bring your mind into a state of indifference. Follow the spontaneity of things and hold within you no element of ego. Then the empire will be governed." The ideal is one of complete liberty, which requires also complete equality.

The path to be followed to attain complete liberty begins with the recognition that there is nothing in the world which is not good and no point of view which is not right. From the equality of all things it follows that there is no reason to prefer life to death or death to life, for they involve nothing more than a change from one form of existence to another, so there is no reason to choose between right and wrong but to let things follow their own spontaneity. The sage transcends them in an act of unity which Chuang Tzu called "following two courses at once."

What is true of the attitude which does not distinguish between life and death is also true of the attitude toward the emotions. To follow the course of nature means to be released from bondage to the emotions and not to be affected by joy or sorrow. Getting rid of distinctions and differences is what makes it possible to become one with the infinite by attaining to a view of the universe as having no beginning or end. It is eternal and so are we. The recognition of this unity is the state of pure experience. Do not listen with the ears but with the mind, not with the mind but with the spirit, which is an emptiness prepared to receive all things. In this emptiness Tao abides and that is why it is called the "Fast of the Mind." Also, it is possible to forget everything while sitting down (that is to say, to have one's mind in all things but not on oneself). To abandon the body, discard all knowledge and become one with the Tao is called "Sitting in Forgetfulness." When one is in control of these two states, "the fast of the mind" and "sitting in forgetfulness," one has reached that Mysterious Power which is identified with the great flux, the process of change with which this philosophy started.

I cannot resist a final quotation, this time in the version of Wing-tsit Chan. "An ignorant person does not know that even when the hiding of things, large or small, is perfectly well done, still something will escape you. But if the universe is hidden in the universe itself, then there can be no escape from it. This is the great truth of things in general. We possess our body by chance and we are pleased with it. If our physical bodies went through ten thousand transformations without end, how incomparable would this joy be! Therefore the sage roams freely in the realm in which nothing can escape. All endures. Those who regard dying a premature death, getting old, and the beginning and end of life as equally good are followed by others. How much more is that to which all things belong and on which the whole process of transformation depends [that is, the Tao]?"

Chapter XXIII
The School of Names

The School of Names, or, as its members were often called, the Dialecticians, are remembered chiefly because the later philosophers disputed with them. We owe our knowledge of the work of such men as Hui Shih (380-305 B.C.) and Kung-sun Lung (about 380) to the writing of others, Our main sources being the later Mohists and the *Chuang Tzu*. It may not be fair to be represented only by one's enemies, but this is the only way we know of them; their own work has long since disappeared.

The School of Names seems to have originated with the practices of debate when lawyers like Teng Hsi, who had lived somewhat earlier, argued on behalf of clients engaged in lawsuits—or so the historian Fung Yu-lan tells us. They resemble very much the Sophists of ancient Greece with whom Socrates argued, and who were accused by him of being able to make the worst cause appear the better.

They debated such questions as whether a white horse is a horse and whether hardness and whiteness can be separate. Their arguments though interesting were fallacious, and were condemned by their opponents as absurd; but were they? They were speaking of course not about particular things but about classes of such things, what western philosophers since Plato have discussed at great length and what have come to be referred to as "universals." They recognized that *chih*, which could be translated as "classes," are as real as particular members, and that while the particulars perish the classes do not; classes, unlike their members, are changeless.

But they were limited in this direction by the Chinese language which does not distinguish between singular and plural or between active and passive voices, and so what might have developed into a full-blown study of formal logic did not do so in China as it did at about the same time in Greece. Aristotle, who wrote the logic upon which we still depend so much, was a contemporary of Hui Shih and Kung-sun Lung, two of the leading Dialecticians.

It would be fair in this connection to ask whether a language which, according to some, derived its oral signals from manual gestures about the fourth millenium B.C., lends itself readily to the abstractions upon which philosophy relies. The nature of the language has retarded the formation of an alphabet; and though the end result is a language that was once inflected, Chinese grammar is not as ideal as Greek and Latin for this purpose.

Even limited as we are to looking at the work of these particular philosophers through the eyes of their opponents, it seems important because it is as close as the Chinese ever came to that side of philosophy which makes of it a professional enterprise, with important consequences in every department of human life. They failed, where the west did not, and so they never saw the eventual practical value of pursuits which do not immediately concern the practical, though they are being made to see them now, the hard way.

In debating whether a white horse is a horse, Kung-sun Lung was trying to attack one of the fundamental questions in metaphysics. In maintaining that fire is not hot (since the sensation is in us, not the fire), he was attacking one of the basic issues in the theory of knowledge. This is the kind of professional philosophy which the Greeks did so well, but the Chinese did not pursue it with the same degree of prolonged and relentless logic.

The philosophers of the School of Names debated the relation between names and the things named, as indeed did most of the classical Chinese philosophers, an interest which has come to the fore lately with the linguistic analysts who are the followers of Wittgenstein. The Chinese touched on questions of logic in so doing, but they never developed an abstract logic comparable to the one developed in European philosophy.

As it happened, the Chinese struggled to deal qualitatively with ideas that are more easily analyzed quantitatively by means of mathematics. Consider this example from Hui Shih— one of his surviving ten paradoxes. "That beyond which there is nothing greater should be called the great unit. That beyond which there is nothing smaller should be called the small unit." In western mathematics this was the basis of the infinite and the infinitesimal calculus. Nature does not yield its secrets to contemplation but only to exploration, and the explorer must be willing to interfere with natural processes, at least to the extent necessary to learn about them.

The Chinese interest in man as himself the center of human concern, though resembling nothing so much as the statement of the Greek sophist that man is the measure of all things, may not in the long run prove to be what is best for man. It is not the bedside physician but the biochemist who has made the greatest advances in medicine. The Chinese preference for balance and proportion again resembles the Greek. Aristotle for instance wished to give every human faculty its due; but there are times when it is necessary to go all out in a cause, and from this impulse much good often results. The scientific occupation often means turning away from man to look at the environment with which he must interact to survive, and this often results in gains of direct benefit to man. But the Chinese

had no room for this occupation.in their culture, and though it
has lasted for thousands of years it had that shortcoming, for
which the Chinese are now paying heavily.

The later Mohist School

The later Mohists are mentioned here because they debated
with the Dialecticians in order to refute them. Although they
differed with Kung-sun Lung on the nature of universals, for
instance, they agreed with him about the necessity for the
"rectification of names," making the point over and over that
the dialectic is not a sterile exercise but, as they said, a "conflict
over something." It has the purpose of clarification leading to
certain knowledge. "Dialectic serves to make clear the
distinction between right and wrong, to discriminate between
good and disordered government." Against the Dialecticians
they argued therefore that qualities like hardness and whiteness
are not mutually exclusive and that words do not affect the
material things to which they refer.

The debate led the later Mohists into the questions which
were centered on the theory of knowledge. Only "personal
experience" can give us certain knowledge by relating the
faculty of knowing to the things-to-be-known. Being alive, we
are told, means to have a material form and with it the
consciousness of knowing. Most knowledge comes through the
five senses, yet there is also knowledge not obtained in this
way, the knowledge for instance that things endure. The
distinction between proper names and class names is recognized, for example between one man's name and "horse." In
general, however, "knowledge is a meeting" (of mind and
object) and thinking is a kind of searching. Knowledge from
inference is internal, but names serve to make understood what
is not known, that is to say, what is external.

The later Mohists thus recognized what they called
"transference," whereby a designated name for a particular is

included as a member under a more general class—my horse, Dobbin, under the universal, "horse." "The mutual sameness of things to one material entity extends to all things in that class. Thus squares are the same, one to another," and together they share the class "square." The class serves as a model for all that falls under it. The class is an example of similarity, which is an identity of parts; but there is also difference, which separates things. The later Mohists seem to have recognized the double reference of the universal, which points both to the class and to its members, the first logical and the second material. They were well on their way to develop a full philosophical system, but they veered away and that task was left to others and elsewhere.

Chapter XXIV

Chinese Buddhism

China, before the arrival of Buddhism from India, had always been a fertile ground for philosophers. We have already noted that the tradition of sage-king was an old one. Governments followed philosophical doctrines and were frequently advised by the philosophers themselves, not always for purely philosophical reasons. It often happened that when the masses were influenced by philosophers it was because philosophy had been seen as a practical instrument of social control. Han rulers were either Confucians or professed Confucianism, so that the social triumph of that philosophy was complete, for a while at least, centuries after Confucius had lived.

Underneath the cover of Confucianism, however, was a kind of sterile scholasticism, incorporating Legalist, Taoist and even Mohist elements as well as many folk philosophies, like *yin* and *yang* and the "Five Forces," that is to say, the five elements: wood, fire, earth, metal and water; and the five directions: north, south, east and west, together with a center. The practice of divination, employing any selection of these beliefs and intended to control events, was widespread.

Confucius himself had come to be regarded as a god, accompanied by dragons.

The welter of confused beliefs that prevailed toward the end of the Han dynasty made it almost certain that some kind of relief would have to be sought. Between A.D. 220 and 589 China was united for one short period of twenty-four years. The period was one not only of philosophical confusion but also of social disruption. In a time of troubles people tend to look to some supernatural religion for refuge. They were ready for some kind of philosophical change, and that change came in the form of an import. Buddhism brought with it a more complete philosophy than had till then been available in China.

Buddha lived at about the same time as Confucius, but Buddhism did not come to China from Central Asia until the first century of our era, then spread slowly and did not become important in China until the collapse of the Han dynasty more than a hundred years later. From A.D. the fourth century until the end of the Sungs around 960, Buddhism was the only philosophy to interest the best scholars among Chinese philosophers.

So powerful was the tradition, however, that Buddhism was made over into something peculiarly Chinese. The country has had a long history of absorbing its military conquerors, as it had done with the Mongols and later the Manchus, who ruled China for long periods but only by becoming part of the native culture. The same thing happened to its leaders in the domain of ideas. Chinese Buddhism turned into something resembling the local philosophies, particularly Taoism, and containing also large elements of Confucianism.

The story of how Buddhism reached India from China is sketchy but some of it has been pieced together. The reader will recall that northern India in the first century A.D. was in the hands of the Kushans and their king Kanishka, who was claimed by the Buddhists as a royal patron. Indeed it was during his reign that a Buddhist Council was held to discuss religious doctrine. There were close connections with central

Asia, which stood athwart the land route to China, particularly through what is now the Chinese provice of Sinkiang. The area of central Asia, more particularly the lands around the Tarim River basin, is a desert surrounded by mountains, and has served excellently as a preserver of records. The libraries in caves contained books inscribed on palm leaves, birch bark, plates made of bamboo and wood, as well as leather and paper. In many languages the ancient thoughts had been kept intact until Sir Aurel Stein and others discovered them.

The Tarim basin, though sometimes under foreign rule, had no nationality of its own. Cities divided by deserts lived their own lives for the most part and enjoyed considerable prosperity under native rulers, when not submitting to Chinese, Turkish or Tibetan garrisons. Among these cities were Kashgar in the west, Kucha and Turfan to the northeast and Khotan in the southeast. By 400 A.D. Kashgar had a monastery with a thousand monks who were students of the Hinayana, and the inhabitants by 643 were all sincere Buddhists. In 383 Kucha had been conquered by the Chinese, who carried off a remarkable Buddhist monk, Kumarajiva, who became an honored adviser to his conqueror. We know that Turfan was destroyed by the Kirghiz Turks in 843 and that many Buddhist priests were massacred, for their skeletons, still wearing fragments of priestly robes, were found by Stein in vaults. But Buddhism survived there longer than in other parts of the Tarim basin, for as late as 1420 there were said to be more Buddhist temples than private houses.

Buddhism reached central Asia during Asoka's time. It came to ancient Khotan, a city in the Tarim basin, from Kashmir just before the Christian era, brought by a monk who was a Mahayanist, and subsequent years saw it flourish, though not to the exclusion of the rival school. Khotan actually received the joint influence of China and India and may have been the land route by which Buddhism, though known in central Asia earlier, passed from India to China. It certainly was the center from which Buddhism radiated to Tibet.

Hinayana Buddhism was the first to enter China but it was Mahayana Buddhism which finally prevailed there. Because it was personal and anti-social, it found special affinities with Taoism and was antagonistic to Confucianism but finally took its place alongside both as an authentic Chinese religion.

By the time of the T'ang dynasty in the seventh century A.D., certainly one of China's periods of greatest cultural development, Confucianism, Taoism and Buddhism were equally important religions and an individual could correctly subscribe to more than one. The eastern attitude always has been more than tolerant in this regard, and multiple belonging is not unusual. Mou Tzu, the Chinese philosopher who flourished in the second century A.D. insisted that while he had become a Buddhist he had not ceased to be a Confucian, and many a Chinese took part in services in different temples, often even on the same day. By the seventh century A.D. the fortunes of the three religions varied under different T'ang emperors. With the strong central government they administered, a Confucian cult was established as the state religion to bolster the large bureaucracy, but the greatest of the T'ang emperors, Li Lung-chi, was devoted to the Taoist sages and accorded fresh honors to the memory of Laotse.

But we must go back to the third century when the account of Chinese philosophy was Buddhist, though with a large admixture of Taoism, a Buddhism that probably no Indian would have recognized. By 381 nine-tenths of the inhabitants of northwestern China were Buddhists. But there were seven separate schools of Buddhism in China, each with its own beliefs and practices. All differed primarily over the metaphysical question of being and non-being.

We shall not describe all seven schools, being most concerned with the one named Ch'an (or Zen) Buddhism. Fung Yu-lan calls it "the most revolutionary and purely Chinese development in Buddhism." Ch'an is an abbreviation of the Chinese name for meditation, for a mental concentration intended to shut out the external world.

The man most responsible for Ch'an Buddhism was Shen-hui (A.D. 670-762), who had studied both the Confucian and Taoist doctrines before becoming a Buddhist priest. Zen Buddhism owed much also to Bodhidharma, who arrived in China about A.D. 520, and to Hui-neng, (638-713), whose doctrine declared that enlightenment comes from sudden illumination and the transference of thought from teacher to pupil, not from meditation, prayer or the study of books.

Zen Buddhism represented a departure from Buddhism, of course. All sorts of later developments cut across Buddhism to bring Zen into being, not the least of which was Taoism, which it so much resembled, but even so there were places in the doctrine where it touched down at the original Buddhism of the Buddha, as for instance in the aim to get free of all desire.

Our knowledge of Ch'an Buddhism is due to an extraordinary circumstance. Its classic was turned up in a Tun-huang cave in 1900, one of those already mentioned as having been explored by Sir Aurel Stein. Called *Liu-tsu t'an-ching*, "The Platform Scripture of the Sixth Patriarch" and believed to be the work of an eighth century monk who was a follower of Shen-hui, it was sent by Sir Aurel to the British Museum where it arrived sixteen months later. He has told the story of how he found it in the course of his discovery of the silk route linking the Roman Empire with Cathay (the ancient Turkish name for China) in the thirteenth chapter of his book *On Ancient Central-Asian Tracks*.

There is a legendary account of the origins of Ch'an Buddhism which traces it to a disciple of the historical Buddha, from whom it was transmitted through a succession of twenty-seven patriarchs without the use of written texts, until it finally reached China in the sixth century with the twenty-eighth patriarch. We know for a certainty only that it was popular during the T'ang dynasty from the seventh to the ninth centuries.

The Ch'an Buddhist does not deal (as does the Indian Buddhist) with the search for a supernatural ultimate reality but with the more mundane mind, though not by looking at the mind, which is itself false. Therefore direct—and sudden— enlightenment is sought. There is no regard for writing, only for intuitive understanding. Meditation, or rather "sitting in meditation," means to be free from all obstacles, not to allow thoughts to arise, to achieve complete absence of thought in order to reach non-attachment. Meditation and calmness (regarded as one and the same thing) are the methods for getting back to the original pure nature of the self. Yet the Ch'an Buddhist never *looks* toward the past, only toward the future, and he must be sure to make his future thoughts good. To be without *dharmas* (that is to say, objects of thought of any kind, material or spiritual) is to find freedom.

The physical body is an inn, not a permanent refuge. The Chinese Buddhists did not scorn the body, which Confucius had reminded everyone was an inheritance from revered parents and was to be employed in breathing properly and lowering desires. They agreed with the Taoists that diet, suitable exercises, and proper sexual techniques were the correct ways to preserve nature. "We take refuge," they said, "in the pure Law-body of the Buddha with our own physical bodies."

With enlightenment, even if it is to be had only in an instant of thought, all living beings become the same as the Buddha. Sudden enlightenment is perfect wisdom; by understanding his mind the Buddhist achieves Buddhahood in himself. To do this it is necessary for him to empty his mind. If he seeks anything he will always suffer. It is better, he is advised, not to take any action.

Most characteristic of Ch'an Buddhism is the "kung-an," the use of a statement or action intended to shock, employed by masters as a way of educating pupils. Kung-an means literally the "official document on the desk," the "platform scripture," the final determination of truth. The truth was said to be so mysterious and so irrational that only a paradoxical answer could reveal it, as when a pupil who once asked what the Buddha was, received the answer, "Three pounds of flax." Another irrelevant way to answer fundamental questions was by shouting at the inquirer or even beating him, both methods intended to broaden the understanding and to sharpen the senses so that the mind would always be prepared to comprehend the truth instantly.

And what, according to the Ch'an Buddhists, is that truth? Fung Yu-lan says that it can be stated in four negative remarks and a positive one.

"The highest truth cannot be expressed; there is no spiritual cultivation; nothing is finally gained; there is nothing much in the Buddhist doctrine." The only positive sentence is the last: "The wonderful Tao lies in carrying water and chopping wood." In this way, Ch'an Buddhism identifies the religious life with ordinary pursuits, the sublime with the commonplace, the ultimate meaning being the discovery that there is no ultimate meaning. As one monk expressed it, having passed to the other side to learn about being, you return to live on this side. What a man does is no different from what he was, it is only that he is different to begin with. The golden mean between action and contemplation consists in detached action by which the actor has nothing personal to gain. Enlightenment resides in the sudden discovery that significance is to be found everywhere and only in the ordinary, a truth that people without becoming Ch'an Buddhists cannot know.

In a word, Ch'an Buddhism calls on no disturbance of the environment; which is to be left pretty much as it was, but the attitude that requires doing this is special and a result of the discipline of the sage who, in passing beyond the three phases of *being, non-being,* and *neither being nor non-being,* reaches a special kind of understanding of his own.

Ch'an (or, as the Japanese called it, Zen) Buddhism was the chief form of Buddhism in China from the fourth to the ninth centuries, but it had a more permanent impact in Japan than it ever had in China. We shall meet with it again and in more detail when we come to discuss Japanese philosophy in general and Zen Buddhism in particular.

To the Confucian the interest was in social order, to the Taoist in natural order; they shared a desire to reach an accommodation with this world; but the Buddhist sought to escape from the world, which he held to be illusory. In the Sung (960-1279) and Ming (1368-1643) dynasties the Neo-Confucians incorporated much of Buddhism in their versions of the Confucian classics.

Chapter XXV
Later Taoism

Neo-Taoism

Philosophers sought a remedy for the first time in Chinese history when the Period of the Philosophers overlapped with the Period of the Warring States, the time which produced both social upheaval and China's first two great philosophers, Confucius and Laotse. Either they pursued the ideal of a well-ordered society (Confucius) or they sought to escape from the social world altogether into the condition of undisturbed nature (Taoism). Similarly, the later Taoists were confronted by a time which has been named the Period of Disunity (A.D. 220-590), which produced Neo-Taoism, or, as it was known at the time, the "Mysterious Learning." Later Taoism took two distinct forms, Neo-Taoism and what may be called Religious Taoism.

The Neo-Taoists started of course from the two traditional Taoists, Laotse and Chuang Tzu, but recognized the importance of Confucius, and learned more perhaps from other influences along the way, especially from Buddhism. How else explain the metaphysical ideas of Wang Pi (A.D. 226-249)?

Only twenty-four when he died, Wang Pi had already

changed Chinese philosophy, having written a commentary on the *Tao Te Ching* stating that ultimate reality consists in original non-being which is the basis of the system that unifies all phenomena. All things partake of the one; all come from being; the origin of being is non-being, to which it is necessary to return in order to have total being. It is the functioning of being that constitutes the achievement of non-being, as another philosopher of the school explained. For non-being itself is invisible, only being is visible, and all things may be reduced to oneness which derives from non-being.

Wang Pi wrote about Laotse to explain his original meaning, but he wrote about the *Book of Changes* to set forth his own ideas. In this commentary, like the later Confucians and even Buddhists, he found the doctrine of the one-is-many and the many-is-one philosophy to be fundamental. An explanation of being, he thought, was to be found in the explanation of the hexagrams, in which the mingling of the lines contain an explanation of being, and the principles for making such an analysis.

Kuo Hsiang, another neo-Taoist of the same period, criticized the Taoism of Chuang Tzu for not having achieved a level of spiritual development equal to that of Confucius. Chuang Tzu's knowledge, he objected, was not of the kind in which he succeeded in identifying himself with what he knew, and therefore did not achieve the proper state of inaction of the mind which true knowing requires. Kuo Hsiang's second criticism was based on Chuang Tsu's soliloquies, which were intended for his own satisfaction but did not meet the requirements of men in general.

The Supreme Tao is non-being, which exists eternally; but there is no time when non-being is all-inclusive, that is, when there is no being. What has being has created itself; there is no Lord of creation. The greatest force is that of change; Heaven as well as earth is continually in a state of change; non-activity means allowing everything to follow its nature, to change in its own way.

Similarly, everything is a self and for each self everything else is the other. This is true of every part of the body, which operates independently yet together the parts constitute a unity in which they cooperate by association and complete one another, though not deliberately. Correspondingly, each body needs the whole universe to be what it is. If a single principle were to be violated, no one would be able to complete his life.

(Readers familiar with western philosophy will see in these passages ideas resembling many of those of G.W.Leibniz and those of A.N.Whitehead in recent times.)

What is true of the individual is with appropriate extensions true also of social life. Morality is part of human nature; and since nature changes, morality does also; therefore to cling to old institutions is artificial. Change makes new institutions necessary. This too is natural, for everything has its appointed place in the natural order. Whether the sage uses peaceful or forceful methods to restore order from a state of disorder depends upon the needs of the times and indicates no preference for one method over another. Variety in such social matters is unavoidable. The sage will rely upon the necessity of circumstances, letting the world in this way take care of itself. "Non-acitivity simply means allowing everything to follow what is natural to it."

Together with other neo-Taoists, Kuo Hsiang regarded Confucius and not Chuang Tzu as the only real sage, and employed the general principles of classic Taoism to interpret the *Analects* of Confucius. As one of them put it, "not even to have desire for the state of non-desire is the constant quality of the sage," a remark which shows the clear influence of Buddhism.

The reputation of sage which, as we have seen, Confucius acquired firmly during the Han dynasty, was never lost again, not even in the amalgamation of Confucianism with the two schools of Taoism and Buddhism. The result of this mixture was Taoism as a new philosophy, exchanging the contempla-tive life of inactivity within nature for an active role in which ordinary human existence was counted but in ways different from those in which it had ever been counted before.

Religious Taoism

This was in a sense distinct from neo-Taoism which was chiefly philosophical, though both incorporated much of the other two schools. Centered on the early philosophical Taoism of Laotse and Chuang Tzu, it included the *yin-yang* school as well as much of Confucianism, and aimed at acquiring long life and immortality. It was already a vigorous movement by the time of the Han dynasty, but in the Period of Disunity we are looking at now it had developed into a full religious movement, with its own temples, priesthood and symbolic images. It was indeed a serious rival of Buddhism, which had been a religion ever since it entered China, for it had a complete liturgy, several kinds of "masses," officials and ceremonials. By A.D. 165, official imperial sacrifices were offered to Laotse.

Needham points to the connection between Tantrism and Religious Taoism, and ventures an opinion, based on the relative dates, that this religious practice originated with the neo-Taoists. The essence of Tantrism is sexual intercourse and its origins are usually attributed to the beginnings of Buddhism in the Hindu tradition in the sexth century A.D. The Tantra was magical and ritualistic, involving erotic elements if not open sexual practices, displayed in images and symbols of the sexual union and involving the worship of the female sexual organs. Certainly, in any case, the Religious Taoists were involved with it and there were temple rites of a sexual character almost certainly Tantric. Needham even goes so far as to suggest that the Tantric movement might have been Taoist in origin. As late as 1943 he reports visiting the galleries and shrines of the San Ch'ing Ko Taoist temple near Kunming, the capital of Yunnan province, when it was still attended by monks. At an oilfield in the northwest there was a temple to Laotse because he above all men understood nature, kept in repair during the second world war by the Kansu Petroleum Administration, and another in a similar situation at Heilungthan near Kunming where the National Academy of Peiping maintained wartime laboratories.

Where philosophical Neo-Taoism, like so much of oriental philosophy, was inward bound, Religious Taoism tended outward, seeking to control nature for human ends, encouraging magical practices, alchemy and astrology, but lacking the power to achieve what it sought, and remaining mythological rather than scientific. Yet, as Needham never tires of pointing out, science in Europe was a product of the same movement, though it never did develop in China.

Chapter XXVI
Neo-Confucianism

The period from the tenth through the sixteenth centuries was one of consolidation. Scholars agree that it was during the T'ang that Chinese civilization reached its greatest height. The empire was enlarged then to its greatest extent, almost to what it embraces now; academies were founded, such as the famous Hanlin which existed for many centuries and played a large role in the civil service examinations; printing became widespread; and the poetry and sculpture were to remain China's best. It was also the period of Buddhism's greatest influence. The Chinese were not a pure race; but they have been able to assimilate both foreign stock and foreign ideas in a way which makes them peculiarly Chinese.

One oddity of this time. Despite the many cultural novelties of the T'ang, philosophy was not among them. The greatest productive period in original philosophy had taken place much earlier, as already noted, beginning with the birth of Confucius in 551 B.C. and ending with the burning of the books in 213 B.C., and including the Period of the Warring States.

Neo-Confucianism, strong in the T'ang dynasty (618-907), did not become dominant until the Sung (960-1279) and the Ming (1368-1643). During this last period there was an effort to return to the original basis of Chinese beliefs and an attempt to bring together in a single philosophy the work of all the various schools. The *Book of Changes* was granted a new authority, becoming almost equivalent to a Chinese Bible. Four books of classics were considered the true sources of most philosophy: the *Book of Changes, Analects, Great Learning* and *Doctrine of the Mean* formed the basis of the civil service examinations from 1313 until as late as 1905, and every scholar wrote commentaries on them.

There were also many borrowings from the Taoists and Buddhists. In some cases the interpretations of the *I Ching* were made by them, and then returned with the changes to the Neo-Confucians. It is unlikely that those who studied the work of the Neo-Confucians were always aware of this. The result was a set of philosophies which leaned heavily both on the *I Ching* and on the work of Confucius, the two supreme classics of Chinese culture.

Two philosophers of this period are outstanding, Shao Yung and Chu Hsi.

Shao Yung

Shao Yung's dates, 1011-1077, place him in the Sung dynasty. His philosophy was systematic and can be characterized as a variety of formal materialism, similar in some respects to Aristotle's.

He derived his metaphysics and his cosmology from the *I Ching*, much as his contemporary, Chou Tun-yi, did. His cosmology, or world-philosophy, is too complex to describe in detail here. It is, as he said, "what antedates Heaven," and consists in three chief classifications, "Principle," "Nature," and "Destiny," or in a sense Heaven, Earth, and the direction of

Earth toward Heaven. This is very reminiscent of the American philosopher, Charles S. Peirce, with his "Possibility," "Actuality," and "Destiny."

The *I Ching* held the key to his understanding of the world. It comes into being, he said, with hexagram 24, and comes to an end with hexagram 2. Heaven is a product of movement, Earth of quiescence. *Yang* results from the first movement, and *yin* from the highest point of that movement. With quiescence softness comes, and, when softness is at its highest point, hardness. Heaven is presented by the interplay of *yin* and *yang*, Earth by the interplay of hardness and softness. *Yang* is the major movement, *yin* the lesser. The greater *yang* makes the sun, the greater *yin* the moon, the lesser *yang* the stars and the lesser *yin* the zodiacal spaces. Through the interplay of all of these bodies Heaven is completely presented.

Similarly, greater softness accounts for water, greater hardness fire, lesser softness soil and lesser hardness stone. Through the interplay of all four, Earth is completely explained. These are the fundamental building-blocks of the material universe, from which all other things are derived. Living beings are transformations of heat, both animals and plants.

Since growth and decay exist for all things, Heaven and Earth, consisting as they do of form and matter, also grow and decay. Material force is unified; it is produced by Heaven. Spirit is also a unity; it is unlimited and operates both in existence and in non-existence, in life and in death, but *always through the agency of material force.*

(This also is reminiscent of Peirce and of Whitehead, with whom Peirce shared the notion that the Platonic forms as well as material things evolve, a notion which, so far as I can discover, is not to be found in any thinker except these three.)

Shao Yung had a cyclical theory of history, probably derived from the Buddhist theory that the world is perpetually running through four periods: formation, existence, destruction and non-existence, which was given a Confucian twist by

Shao Yung who interpreted the cycle in terms of the growth and decay of the *yin* and *yang* as explained by the series of hexagrams in the *Book of Changes*.

At the present time, Shao Yung believed, the world is approaching the close of a cycle and will be replaced by the beginning of another cycle. He was very precise in his calculations, and predicted that living creatures would come to an end sometime between A.D. 46,023 and 46,383, and that the entire world would come to an end in A.D. 62,583.

On the topic of the theory of knowledge, Shao Yung was, again like Peirce and Whitehead, a realist. Consider this passage.

"The sage's ability to synthesize the qualities of all things lies in his ability to observe objectively. By such objective observation I mean an observation of things not made in terms of the self [but] in terms of those things themselves." And again, "to observe things in terms of those things: this is to follow one's nature. But to observe things in terms of the self: this is to follow one's feelings. The nature is impartial and enlightened; the feelings are partial and blind." (I have relied chiefly on Fung Yu-lan's translation.)

Chu Hsi

Of the later philosophers, the one who exercised the greatest influence was not necessarily the most original. He was Chu Hsi, whose father was a district magistrate. Born in Fukien in 1130 to a literary family, Chu Hsi died in 1200. He undertook to make a system of all previous thought, based, however, on the work of Confucius, and though he deliberately omitted all Taoist and Buddhist elements, he was influenced by them. Regarding the *Book of Changes* as a work of divination he did not recognize its philosophical content. It was he who first grouped the four Classics together, and it was due to his labors that they became the basis of the civil service examinations.

Chu Hsi's debt to the many philosophers who went before him is indeed a heavy one. I have not discussed them here for reasons of space, but their work is summarized and organized in Chu Hsi's system. Suffice it to add that while he was not an original philosopher he was a comprehensive one, and his contribution was in seeing how to bring the various elements in the tradition together.

He had both a metaphysics and a cosmology, that is to say, a theory of being and a theory of the material universe. (In what follows I have used the words in the Wing-Tsit Chan and Fung Yu-lan translations, though not in Chu Hsi's original order because I wanted to select and condense the passages.)

"There is only one Supreme Ultimate, yet each of the myriad things has been endowed with it, and each in itself possesses it in its entirety. The Supreme Ultimate is a name to express all the virtues and the highest good in Heaven and Earth, man and things." There is nothing supernatural or transcendental in Chu Hsi's philosophy as indeed there is not in the work of most Chinese philosophers. "Heaven" is impersonal, usually nothing more or less than the set of all natural laws and not a name for God.

"In the beginning of the universe there was only material force consisting of *yin* and *yang*. Principle is not visible, it becomes visible through *yin* and *yang*."

Yin and *yang*, *yin* the female principle and *yang* the male, first make their appearance early in Chinese philosophy, in the *Book of Changes*. They are not mentioned, however, in the four Confucian Classics, but they do appear in Chuang Tzu, in Mo Tzu and in other philosophical works. Chu Hsi interpreted this beginning to be "a state of undifferentiated chaos. I imagine there was only water and fire. The sediment from the water formed the earth."

He thought that what he called "Principle" was primary, by which he meant evidently something akin to the Platonic forms. "Before heaven and earth existed, there was after all Principle. As there is this Principle, therefore there are Heaven and Earth. There is Principle (*li*) before there can be material force (*chi*), but it is only when there is material force that Principle finds a place to settle. Principle has never been separated from material force." However, physical form is interposed between Principle and material force. "Principle exists before physical form, whereas material force exists after physical form."

(The nearest western analogy of principle is organization, and of material force matter and energy. This is close to modern physics, and to Whitehead's philosophy of organism.)

The Principle is the kind of form which Plato intended by the word Idea, and the matter is similar to Aristotle's substance. Principle, Chu Hsi said, is "above shapes" (the Tao), and matter is "within shapes" (the Instrument). Every material thing has its corresponding ultimate or Principle. Chu Hsi had to account for what makes Principles into material things, and he explained this by introducing an Ether. The Ether has the capacity to condense and thus create, and wherever it does there the Principle is present inside it.

Chu Hsi had a cyclical theory of the creation of the universe, no doubt a result of the belief in cycles of existence introduced into China by the Buddhists. It begins with the alternation of the twin notions of movement and quiescence, water and fire. As they open and close, come and go, the Two Forms of heaven and earth which were in a state of chaos and undifferentiated, the *yin* Ether and the *yang* Ether were mingled. Then they separated and produced heaven and earth, *yin* and *yang*. The transformations of *yang* and congealings of *yin* produced the five material elements, water, fire, wood, metal and earth. The five elements together with *yin* and *yang* "boil forth together" and so produce the material objects as we encounter them.

This account is not merely of a one-stage development. "Before the Supreme Ultimate there must have been another world, just as the night of yesterday passes into the day of today." And what was true of the remote past will be equally true of the remote future. Thus movement and quiescence have no starting point and no ending. The entire universe, once having been created, is thereafter destroyed and again in the same manner re-created. The cycle of creation and destruction evidently continues eternally.

The creation of man is accounted for in much the same way. Evolutions of the Ether made possible the union of Principle with Ether and spontaneously produced human beings, who had no forebears. The Principle though itself entirely good loses its perfection when it comes into contact with the Ether. Those who receive the Ether in its purity are sages, those who receive it in its impurity become evil. Nature includes both good and evil, for "it cannot be said that evil is not nature. There is nothing in the world which is outside of one's nature."

The human individual is part of the universe, and like it is governed by Principle and material force.

"Man's nature is nothing but Principle. There is Principle first and then material force, but Principle is basic. Man receives it and thus possesses life. The material force may be clear or turbid. The clear part belongs to *yang* and the turbid part to *yin*. The clear part becomes the individual's vital force, the turbid part his physical nature.

"What integrates to produce life and disintegrates to produce death is only material force. What we call 'spirit' and 'consciousness' are the effects of material force. Consciousness, like everything else, has its own Principle. The mind is the unifying agent between nature and the feelings. Nature refers to what is stabilized, destiny to what is operating."

"Things and the mind share the same Principle. The mind embraces all Principles and all Principles are complete in this single entity, the mind. If one is not able to preserve the mind, he will be unable to investigate Principles to the utmost. With respect to order, knowledge comes first, and with respect to importance, action. Throughout a person's handling of affairs and dealing with things, there is no point at which moral considerations are not present."

Chu Hsi's political philosophy followed traditional lines. Like most Confucians he thought that ideal government was what had been practiced fifteen hundred years earlier by the mythical dynasty of the Hsia and the more historic Shang and Chou, Confucius' favorite, by reaching complete agreement. This ideal was not attained by the more recent Han and T'ang dynasties.

In those ancient Three Dynasties the rulers succeeded in giving good government to the state and thus in establishing peace in the world. The ideal remains the same, it never varies, but human interference in a millennium and a half had prevented it from being practiced. The cyclical theory reappeared here, probably suggested by Mencius' earlier idea that every five hundred years a true king is born.

Despite Chu Hsi's rejection of Buddhism, certain Buddhist teachings crept into his philosophy, though certainly not all of them, not reincarnation, for instance, but "It is wrong to say that human desire is the same as the principle of nature. For in its original state the principle of nature is free from desire. Wherever selfish desires can be eliminated and the principle of nature operates freely, there is jen" (variously translated as "virtue," "goodness," "love").

The Neo-Confucians in general and Chu Hsi in particular understood the necessity to investigate nature without prejudice and came very close to the discovery of the scientific method. The Neo-Confucians wrote on botany, geography and mathematics, and Chu Hsi himself said that "everything should be investigated to the utmost, and none of it is unworthy of attention." As to the "recitification of names" he saw that this was a side issue. "Pay no attention to names. We must investigate into the reason things are as they are." He wrote about the nature of fossils and guessed correctly that there was evidence in the highest mountains that they were once under water.

Unfortunately, in the end he was drawn back from an impartial inquiry into nature and to an exclusive concern with human nature. "The Way exists everywhere but how are we to find it? Simply by returning to the self and discovering it within one's nature and function."

In addition to the work of the classic group of philosophers I have discussed, there were the writings of other Neo-Confucians, in particular those of Chang Tsai and the Ch'eng brothers. Listen to what Chang Tsai had to say about the brothers: "I regard them as having done great service to the scholars who have come after. The work of other philosophers can go into the discard."

The Religion of Confucius

Sacrifices to Confucius were made official by imperial edict in A.D. 59. By the time of the Han dynasty, beginning in A.D. the second century, as we have seen, Confucius had become a religion, complete with ritual and with temples appropriate to them, though without a priesthood, whose function was performed by local scholars and officials. The celebrations were in honor of an interest divided between nature deities and the worship of ancestors. The temples, which existed until recently and may still stand in some places, have been well described by Joseph Needham, when he visited some of them and even participated in the ritual observances as late as 1945. The temples consisted of a series of courtyards in the midst of buildings containing guest rooms, a library and a great hall containing stone tablets inscribed with the name of the sage and his most distinguished followers. There was a statue of the sage, the "Teacher of Ten Thousand Generations" on an altar with many lights. There was an annual sacrificial ceremony at which in a nighttime ritual an ox, pig or sheep was sacrificed, liturgies were intoned and speeches delivered. The enshrining of philosophy could go no further.

As the modern scholar, J.K.Shryock, has wryly observed, no one would have been more astonished at these proceedings than Confucius himself could he have witnessed them! It was not to be the only time that a secular philosopher who carefully avoided all supernatural references was made the center of a transcendental religion and worshipped as a god, but it was one that was to remain exclusively Chinese. Confucius was known throughout the world, but his religion remained at home.

Chapter XXVII
Later Chinese Philosophy

It is possible to trace, in the history of China through the millennia, a single strain of philosophy to which we apply the trite but accurate designation of the great tradition. It begins with the *I Ching* and continues with Confucius and Laotse and their later followers. Certain definite ideas originating with the *I Ching* may be traced throughout—simple ideas, as indeed most fundamental ideas always have been, which characterize a civilization.

Chinese thought has been tilted toward human behavior. It may be active and prefer right deeds, as with Confucius, or passive and prefer inaction, as with Laotse, but in either case it has been preoccupied with moral questions. If harmony was sought with natural law, if there were supposed to be abstract ideas which stood apart and above material events, the aim was to find for human behavior a conformity which would insure its success. Chinese thought, in a word, has been oriented around the individual. For the Confucians a good society rests upon the good ruler. Hence the concern for the appearance of the superior man as ruler; all other made up the masses, whose chief virtue was in obeying the ruler.

The Chinese philosophers inclined their people away from the supernatural, not, as we might expect, toward experimental science. Their interest in nature was entirely passive. They counselled good conduct, moderation in all things, obedience to authority—the kind of program which led to quiescence and a docile population rather than the kind of development which has produced the scientific-industrial culture of the western nations. All investigations into the nature of the physical world, which for a while in the fifth century B.C. in China looked as if they might flourish, were abandoned in favor of scholarship based on study of literary classics. Wisdom consisted in the learning which had been preserved in books; progress consisted therefore in recovering a golden age which, they supposed, lay in their remote past. What the Greeks stumbled on and developed, the Chinese (oddly enough at about the same time) considered and rejected.

The result has been a civilization in which nearly all work was manual, with no labor-saving machines and no complex institutions to accompany them. A society composed of anonymous individuals satisfied with little, in a state of contentment in low key, is what the classic philosophers produced.

In the seventeenth and eighteenth centuries China presents a picture of declining religious philosophies. Confucians were conscripted mostly from the upper class. All others had adopted a mixture of Mahayana Buddhism and Taoism, overlaid with magic and ancient superstitions in a sort of crossbreed polytheism. Confucius continued to exercise a strong central influence. It was said that spirits and dragons had presided at his birth, that he was a god and the son of a mythical emperor. As we have noted, sacrifices to him were established by royal decree as early as A.D. 59 and later there were temples where he could be worshipped, just as there were Taoist and Buddhist temples. Later neo-Confucian philosophers reaffirmed the authority of the *Book of Changes* and refused to join the Taoists and Buddhists in their quest for a comprehensive, speculative philosophy.

What finally emerged was a rough combination of elements from all three religions, Confucian, Taoist and Buddhist, with equal emphasis and a total lack of exclusion, plus older customs and superstitions involving magical elements. That these did not add up to a consistent whole seems to have bothered nobody. It was acceptable, it was traditional and therefore justified.

Matthew Ricci, the Italian Jesuit who made an extensive visit to China in the sixteenth century and left a detailed diary in which he described the civilization he found, reported that "It is evident to everyone here that no one will labor to attain proficiency in mathematics or in medicine who has any hope of becoming prominent in the field of philosophy . . . to which students are attracted by the hope of the glory and the rewards attached to it"—a statement that could have been made of no other civilization at the time or since. As further evidence of decline was the fact that the majority of followers were women. In times of strong religious belief women have not been allowed to play any large part.

Judging by the writings of the philosophers, the Chinese seem incapable of the continuity of sustained thought. The classics of Confucius and Laotse, or Mo Tzu and the Legalists, all reveal the same episodic character: a series of more or less disconnected maxims and aphorisms, with almost no lengthy essays such as are found in the west, no comprehensive treatises; all was fragmentary. As Marcel Granet, the great French sociologist, pointed out, all the language they employed was concrete rather than abstract and relied on illustration more often than on generalization.

Languages are equipped for their tasks only when the tasks come into being. English acquired its Latinisms in the fourteenth century when they were needed to express complex ideas. Why did the Chinese language not do the same thing? Perhaps because an inward-looking philosophy does not involve the sort of complexities inherent in an outward-looking one, as the mathematics employed by the physical sciences in the west suggests. We shall see when we come to examine the philosophy of China today that the situation in this regard has not changed very much.

In the last three hundred years, the extraordinary rise of great populations occurred both in the east and west, accompanying the rise of science and industrialism in the west, but not in the east. Though China grew enormously in numbers, the social and technological organization to handle them did not grow with it. That was the situation at the outset of the present century.

There are no peoples without a history of intermittent warfare, and the Chinese were no exception. The earliest records contain accounts of armed struggles between neighboring states, all exhibiting more or less the outlines of the same civilization. What held the Chinese together and marked theirs *as* a civilization, despite philosophical and political differences, was what they had in common. No matter who ruled over them, no matter what philosophy they subscribed to, their practice seems to have been uniform in certain respects. The central importance of the family, including remote ancestors, the high regard for a particular set of moral standards, elaborate ceremonials and ritual observances all connected with the family, prevailed and molded the Chinese into a single culture despite the difficulties which beset them as a result of intermittent wars.

Twice China was invaded and conquered from the north, once by the Mongols in the thirteenth century of the present era and once by the Manchus in the seventeenth century. In both cases the new overlords ruled China very much as it had been ruled, taking the place of the emperors by becoming emperors themselves and installing their own nobility in the same way, but China managed to remain China.

The Confucians were always concerned with good government, but the Taoists, later joined by the Buddhists, had always kept prepared a retreat into inwardness where the individual could find his way in a period of social disorder.

They urged him to turn away from all institutions and indeed from all striving. Both effort and society are against nature, they supposed, and what is against nature can never hope to win out. The human way was one of concession. A kind of negative anarchy accompanied it: do nothing and as a result everything will be done. In order to avoid difficulties, the individual had best locate the way of power and follow it; that is to say, find out the laws of nature, pursue them, and tranquillity will be attained by conforming to nature.

Life involves difference; in death the individual resumes that unity with the universe which had been interrupted by life. But the individual does not deny life nor try to avoid death; he accepts with equanimity the course of natural events, which bring him peace and release from bondage.

In our own times China was suddenly faced with a more difficult kind of invasion, which though not a concerted effort was engaged in separately and collectively by all her neighbors led by the European powers—a story too long to tell here and well told elsewhere. Briefly, what happened was the gradual encroachment of Great Britain, France, Portugal and Germany, and later of Russia and Japan, each claiming a piece of China's coast and inland territory, until there was little left of a viable Chinese government. Even Chinese culture was threatened. Add to this the end of two of China's oldest institutions, the monarchy and the civil service—a melancholy picture. The third most sustaining institution, Confucianism, was in decline but had not yet disappeared. China, as Kenneth Latourette says, had always been governed by philosophers, but the Confucianism which had been adopted centuries earlier had no prescription for dealing with the new multiple invasions by nations which proved stronger than the Chinese.

A Chinese resurgence under Sun Yat-sen and later under the Kuomintang led by Chiang K'ai-shek and the Soong family failed to stop the force of the new Chinese communists under Mao Tse-tung. The organized forces of a civil war embraced all of China. On one side were the inheritors of the ancient tradition of war lords, on the other there was something entirely new: a philosophy from the west which had already been adopted in Russia, the philosophy of Marx, Engels and Lenin.

In the long period of its known history, China has been invaded five times: three times by people and twice by ideas. The people were, as we have seen, the Mongols, the Manchus, the Europeans; the ideas were Buddhism and Marxism. It is not difficult to see that the ideas had more effect in the long run than the people. Paradoxically, it was Marxism, European in origin, which enabled the Chinese to rid themselves of the last wave of invaders, the Europeans.

In presenting the history of Chinese philosophy, only in two instances have I had to look away from native philosophies. I have included one variety of Chinese Buddhism though Buddhism was imported from India, because an understanding of what happened to Buddhism inside China helps to reveal the Chinese spirit. And it was Chinese Buddhism that led to the Zen Buddhism that became so powerful in Japan.

The second large import occurred in modern times. The philosophy of Marx, Engels and Lenin has played a crucial role since the communist revolution of 1919. It is my contention that in this case, as in the case of Buddhism, the Chinese have transformed it into something of their own. In China Marxism is Chinese as well as Marxist and may be regarded in a sense as an authentic Chinese philosophy even if not an entirely native growth.

The situation with respect to basic beliefs was still confused when the Marxists first appeared. The alchemy, astrology, good and evil spirits, witches and all the familiar jumble of supernatural beings, which had been the Chinese lot long before Confucius, Laotse and their followers tried to banish superstition and bring to the people a modicum of rationality, returned and were combined with a confused inheritance based on the three traditions of the Confucians, the Taoists and the Buddhists, making something quite foreign to what the founders themselves had taught—and quite unintelligible in itself. It added up to the practice of magic, with the gods consulted at every turn, with good and bad omens directing every individual's actions. A host of holy men made their living from the people. When consulted they fell into trances and communicated with the gods who could give advice, cure diseases and bring luck.

I recall a time shortly after world war II when I was quite by chance descended on by Chinese friends of friends. We were new to each other, and found ourselves thrown together, naturally bound by hospitality based on social obligations which we had in common. They were business people with the drive and aggressiveness usually attributed to Americans. They told me of their experiences in buying a lot on which they had planned to build a house in Shanghai. Having discovered one they wanted, before signing the lease they asked for a day's grace to consult what they called the "wind-and-water-professor," who, I realized as they were explaining, was a diviner who visited the site and sampled the winds in order to ascertain whether they were propitious.

It was plain to the new Marxist leaders that to clear away all this rubble of belief which had accumulated for literally thousands of years, some simple and direct faith was wanted, and moreover one that would have to justify itself in terms of Chinese history, as we can now see when we examine the shape that Marxism finally took in China.

Chapter XXVIII
Chinese Communism

It will be a long time before we are able to get along without clinging to some sort of absolute belief. It requires an educated population able to exercise a certain measure of skepticism, jealous of its freedom, and made up of individuals who guard their civil liberties. The French thinker, Jean-Francois Revel, has written that Americans are surviving *Without Marx or Jesus*, in what must be the first large secular state.

This cannot be said of the Soviet Union or of China. To accept probabilities as the greatest degree of truth attainable and to live a personal and social life on that basis, would require a degree of rationality which accepts only logic and fact, and that, their leaders have concluded, is not yet enough for the masses in Asia. They want positive answers to ultimate questions, and the success of institutions based on the work of religious prophets who have offered them just that is strong support for such a claim. Witness Christianity and Islam, to say nothing of Confucianism and Buddhism, and now the new religion of Marxism, whose founder came as an economic and political revolutionary but has been transformed into a prophet, the center of a militant, materialistic atheism by both the Russians and the Chinese.

Materialism was not common in the history of Chinese philosophy, but it was not altogether unknown. As early as the third century B.C. Hsun Tzu, as we have noted, had been something of a materialist and Chu Hsi had materialist views in the twelfth century A.D., but materialism did not receive any full expression until Wang Fu-Chih (who wrote under the name of Wang Ch'uan-shan) in the seventeenth century of our era.

Reality for him was matter in continuous motion. "Apart from phenomena," he declared, "there is no Tao." There is a material constant underlying change, which itself consists in the assembly and dispersion of parts, an account intended also to explain life and death, it was an early formulation of the conservation of matter. Materials are the essences of things and provide their methods. Before bells and chimes there were no ceremonies, before flutes and strings there was no music. All existing things function because they possess substance. All products in the world are the results of material force. Even principles are not finished products; the first time there is any principle is when it issues from some material.

But the full impact of materialism was not to be felt in China until the early decades of the twentieth century, and then it came as an import from Europe via Russia.

In China, the long eclectic epoch of the confusion of philosophies was suddenly confronted by a new and unexpected development: the necessity to face Western civilization. How it did so after many false starts and crippling encounters is the preface to the last Chinese philosophy we shall have to examine.

In a number of small wars with the European powers beginning in 1839 and lasting for the remainder of the century, it was shown conclusively that the Chinese armies were no match for their enemies, so that as a result much of China was occupied or controlled by others. There was Russia in the northwest pressing on China's borders and there was Japan in the northeast fighting a series of wars with China, both claiming territory and influence. "Spheres of interest," and "treaty ports" marked the occupation of much of her coast by various European countries. The customs service and the postal system were controlled by foreigners, and many forts were dismantled. What may have saved China from complete occupation was the rivalry between her enemies.

The cultural shock of these developments can hardly be underestimated. Having for centuries and even for millennia considered herself to be a model civilization for others to emulate, China was now compelled by events to recognize her weakness and the necessity for a change. If she was to measure up, perhaps the old forms of government were inadequate. One result was the establishment of a democracy in 1905 by Sun Yat-sen, but his Republic fell apart in a series of civil wars, and Japan conquered and controlled much of China from 1931 to 1945.

China was not a stranger to western political and social ideas. For years her leading thinkers had read and considered the writings of Darwin, Spencer, Huxley, Rousseau, Tolstoy and many others. The case for a liberal version of western democracy was revived and reinforced by the lectures which Bertrand Russell gave at Peking University in 1920 and John Dewey in the following year. For a while there was some hope of reestablishing democracy on a firmer footing. The same leaders who had at first adopted democracy as an ideal were the first to turn to Marxism because they accepted the argument that the economic mode of production determined all other social developments. Having come that far, they announced that all other political movements were attempts on the part of the ruling class to subjugate the people.

The representative government led by Sun Yat-sen was hardly more than an outward form and had led only to another period of corruption, as he himself recognized. He saw that only the Soviet Union was ready to negotiate with China on the basis of equality while the other powers could hardly conceal their contempt, and toward the end he pledged "the strength of our four hundred millions to fight against injustice for all mankind."

The interim period of a few decades witnessed a civil war between the Nationalist Chinese and the Chinese Communist Party. In the 1930s and 1940s the communists, led by Mao Tse-tung, who was joined in 1936 by Chou En-lai, waged unceasing warfare with the Kuomintang and Generalissimo Chiang Kai-shek, ending with the fleeing of the Nationalists to Taiwan (Formosa).

The political philosophy adopted by the Chinese communists and put into practice in 1949 when they had at last gained control of all of China is substantially the one the Russians had adopted some thirty years before. Before describing the differences introduced by the Chinese, it might be well to describe the philosophy itself in some detail.

The philosophy of Marx and Engels—it was a complete philosophy, with a theory of reality as well as prescriptions for social and political action—has of course come to be called "Marxism," now the official doctrine of two of the three most powerful states in the modern world, adopted also in such smaller countries as Yugoslavia, Czechoslovakia, Albania and Cuba.

The influences that went to make up the theory and practice of the philosophy which Marx and Engels wrote and which has come to be called "dialectical materialism" were many. Their virture was to see the connections and to make one grand synthesis.

They were influenced by the anarchists who recommended violent revolution but wished to substitute nothing for the governments to be overthrown. Bakunin declared that "the joy of destruction is a creative joy." They were influenced by the German philosopher, Ludwig Feuerbach, who held that only matter is real and that there is no God. They were influenced also by Hegel for whom history and indeed all events follow a zigzag course which he called the "dialectic." The difference was that where the dialectic for Hegel was ideal and therefore mental, for Marx it was to be materialistic, a movement of matter, the alternation of social classes in power. Marx said that he found Hegel standing on his head and stood him on his feet. And they were influenced by Saint-Simon, the French socialist, who advanced the theory of the class struggle, and they argued against Proudhon that poverty was a result of the class struggle and not merely a product of economic conditions.

Marx and Engels were interested in the economic and political relations of man, the stress being on man in society rather than individual man. In terms of economic interest, society has always been divided into social classes. There is always a lowest class. Anciently it was the slaves, above them the class of free men who had no property, and finally the property-holding classes, the landed aristocracy.

In Marx's Europe there were men without property whose only way of making a living was to work with their hands. In England and Germany the factory system was just coming up and with it a new laboring class, the factory workers. Marx's name for them was the "proletariat," an old Roman word for free men without property. He declared that their interests were opposed to those of the burghers, or "bourgeoisie," as the French called them, the inhabitants of the new towns that grew up around the factories. The men who owned and operated the factories collected the profits. Marx said that they collected not only their own profits but also the part of the profits which rightfully belonged to the workers whose work had produced the profits in the first place. He learned from the English economist, David Ricardo, to think that the "labor theory of value" is correct: that the exchange value of a product is determined by the labor expended in its production. (The English philosopher Locke had said something similar years earlier.) Marx gave no credit to manufacturing design, to *no credit*

capital investment, in short to all those items which, together with the labor of the workers, go to make up the profits of the factories' output.

run by most numerous

If you were a materialist, as Marx and Engels were, you would have to place first in your theory of reality those who worked closest to matter, those, in other words, who worked with their hands. Marx's idea was that since the members of the working class were first in theory, they should be first in practice, since they were the most numerous, the state should be run by and for them.

History, Marx and Engels thought, is an account of the class struggle for the control of the means of economic production. They were sure that there is no such thing as independent truth, as the philosophers had always declared. In its place there was only the "historically correct," that is to say, whatever happens is what ought to have happened. The winner is always justified by the fact that he won.

In their famous Manifesto Marx and Engels called for a revolution of the working class: "Workers of the world unite," and added, "you have nothing to lose but your chains." Their appeal to violence to make right what they considered wrongs overturned decades of humanism which had sought to eliminate violence and replace it with reason, though they had before them the spectacle of the French Revolution, which had widely proclaimed the rights of man but had succeeded only in putting another class in power; a revolution which had got rid of the monarchy and landed aristocracy by violent means without achieving the ends it had sought.

There was to be a period of socialism, of the "dictatorship of the proletariat, "to counter the previous dictatorship of the capitalists, but that would be succeeded by a classless society called communism. It was a fair society that they wanted to establish, one in which each individual would contribute to it what he could, and would take from it only what he needed. But there was much that was missing from the blueprints for a better society. Marx was so concerned with the means that he did not fill out the details of the ends. The mistake he made was in thinking that the revolution he was recommending would occur first in the industrial countries, like England. The men of theory, like himself and Engels, were succeeded by men of practice who sought to put his ideas to work and the revolution occurred instead in the most economically backward of countries, Russia. The men who made the revolution there were led by Nicolai Lenin, a unique combination of thinker and man of action, who wrote books to show how Marx's theory should be applied, and then applied it himself in the Russian Revolution of 1917.

Communism as a working government owes much to Lenin. The movement has been recognized since his day as one that follows the philosophy of Marx, Engels and Lenin. A convinced Marxist, he contributed much to its practice and he was responsible for the Party, understood as a working class elite distinct from the workers. He insisted on absolute obedience to it. And in fact it was the Party that was responsible for consolidating the political and economic gains effected by the Revolution.

Marx and Engels held that the only acceptable social organization is the economic class, but in the hands of Lenin and Stalin Marxism became a support for nationalism. In other countries nationalism was condemned for serving as an instrument of capitalistic exploitation; in the Soviet Union and afterwards in Red China it was used as a support for nationalism. This is one of the many changes that these two nations made in the political philosophy they professed to accept.

When the Chinese Communist Party seized power, there was a model to follow in the neighboring Soviet Union, but the Russians had a small industrial class; the Chinese had none. Mao Tse-tung saw that the Chinese revolution would have to have a peasant base rather than a base in the industrial working class, a rural proletariat in place of the urban proletariat that Marx and Engels had proposed. The Chinese Communist Party was organized in 1921 and was able to take power some twenty-eight years later, with Mao as head of the ruling group of the People's Republic of China whose mission it became to lead China through a period of socialist dictatorship to communism in which everyone will flourish and there will be no need for a government. Like the Russian Revolution of 1919, it was led not by a spontaneous uprising of the masses but rather by a small group of highly trained intellectuals convinced of the truth of the socialist philosophy. Many of the Chinese who took part in the communist revolution in their own country had been to school in Moscow. Of the thirteen members of the Chinese Politburo in 1951, eight had studied in the Soviet Union. True to Marxist doctrine, it was not the urban class but the peasants who supported the Chinese communists and made the success of the revolution possible. Not one of the original members of the Politburo had a peasant background; they were obviously driven not by the hope of personal gain but by idealism.

Without the Russian Revolution of 1919 and the subsequent successes of Marxism in Russia, it is doubtful that this philosophy would ever have been adopted in China, where the intellectuals were quick to see its meaning and to recognize that this was a development in the west that they could use, particularly with modifications of the Russian version to make it suitable to the needs of China. Sun Yat-sen's Kuomintang had failed chiefly because there had been no effort to enlist the consent of the masses of peasants whose support was essential in the long run to any broadly-based political movement.

The nature of Chinese Marxism marks it off as the second remove from the application of the writings of Marx and Engels, if we recognize in the Soviet Union the first remove. Those who push hardest for improvements in the common lot want to be the masters. The Chinese government is a naked dictatorship, no less so because it is dressed up with ideological justification. "Only when there is destruction can there be construction," Chou En-lai declared in 1964. If the Chinese communists wished to justify themselves by tradition, it would not be difficult to do so. Marxism can be reconciled in many respects with the philosophy of history of the Ch'in and Han periods. The rigid dictatorship imposed under the Ch'in dynasty from 221-206 B.C. with its brutality and violence by those emperors who were Legalists; the materialism of Hsun Tzu and of the unknown author of the *Lieh-tzu*, and even of the Buddhist "School of Matter as Such"; to say nothing of the tradition of the sage-king (of which more in the next chapter)— all offer the opportunity to find roots in the past. A precedent even for the dialectic of the class struggle can be traced to the alternation of *yin* and *yang* in the *I Ching*.

At present the education of the masses is confined to Marxist dogma. The shorthand version of the writings of Marx, Engels and Lenin, together with polemics against Chinese capitalists and reactionaries, including the Confucians, has taken the place of a more technical education in the sciences and humanities. The life of the peasants has been altered severely in two ways. They have been moved from private enterprise to a system of communes, and have been taught Marxism as truth. The development of a scientific-industrial culture to resemble those of western Europe and the United States has become a second consideration. Indoctrination of the masses comes first, everything else follows.

There is a determined and probably successful attempt to achieve complete egalitarianism for the masses. All institutions, whether farm, school or factory, are run in the same way: by a "Revolutionary Committee" whose members are made up in equal numbers from the workers, the managers and the Communist Party. The advice of manual laborers is held to be as important as the opinions of experts. There is to be no intellectual elite, no professionals; all are equally worthy in the most technical undertakings, and all can contribute equally by means of trial and error, by means of improvement through criticism, and through the use of refresher courses. Marxism, certainly did serve to bring a materially backward people very fast into the climate of the scientific-industrial cultures. But will communist China ever produce another original philosopher or permit one to publish even if he were to turn up?

As usual, complex social and cultural situations, there are too many variables for anyone to be able to calculate the effects. When the present leadership dies, younger and more practical men will of course take their place, presumably with greater stress on the recognition that knowledge of the dogma will not take Chinese civilization far. Communism, newer in China than in the Soviet Union, resembles the belief of the Christian fundamentalists who hold to the literal truth of every word in the Bible and consider that sufficient for all purposes. Liu Shao-ch'i in *How To Be a Good Communist*, after saying that there are those who consider Marx, Engels and Lenin and Stalin to have been "mysterious beings from birth," asks "Is this correct?" and answers "I think not." The inference he wished to leave with his readers is clear.

To interpret Chinese Marxism is to understand it as a secular religion, having the advantages and limitations of the older western variety. The first requirement is faith and the purpose of philosophy is to defend the faith. In this it differs little basically from Christianity in the European Middle Ages. Faith, as Bertrand Russell pointed out, means belief without reason. There could conceivably be reasons to accept a faith but that is not the method employed in China. Faith of this sort requires emotional acceptance first and after that a marshalling of rationalizations.

The Communist Party members constitute a new ruling class, as much in a position to exploit the masses as the old ruling class did. The state owns everything and the Party controls the state without limits or brake on the uses of power. The result is sure to include abuses, of which one of the chief is dictatorship over the arts and sciences. No great achievement in the arts, nothing original, was ever the work of a committee. It is axiomatic that there is more to human life than politics, but what is not political has been suppressed. There have been moments in the short history of Red China when its leaders considered the rights of intellectuals to a speculative life outside politics. One was briefly considered—and ended—in 1950 with Chou En-lai's lecture on "Reforming the Intellectuals." Another was introduced and quickly terminated when in 1956 Mao Tse-tung announced to the Supreme State Conference that he was willing to "let the hundred flowers bloom and the hundred schools of thought contend," a promise which was cancelled a year later when it was taken as a more or less informal license for rightists to protest governmental actions.

There is a spirit in every human being and I mean by "spirit" nothing supernatural, nothing more than "the dominant inner quality of every material person or thing"—and that spirit is stilled, often destroyed by the monolithic structure of a dictatorship, even a proletarian dictatorship intended to serve the common good. The spirit if it is live must be allowed to proliferate in many directions. Diversity is its life-blood, and freedom is a prerequisite of diversity.

There is no doubt that the masses are living better in both countries than they did under the Czars in Russia and under the emperors and war-lords in China; they have more food, better housing, medical services and other amenities. It is certain that neither population would choose to return to previous conditions voluntarily. Russia was a more advanced industrial country than China when the communist revolution began. However, the transition from a largely agrarian society to a modern scientific-industrial one has cost the Russian people much, and consumer goods are still to some extent sacrificed to military hardware. It remains to be seen whether a communist regime can also be a peaceful one. Russia has shown no signs of moving in that direction, if we consider the fate of the Baltic states. Even the Russian satellites are oppressed: in 1975 Russian army divisions were still occupying Czechoslovakia. The Chinese invasion of Tibet is no indication of a pacific disposition.

History is continually being rewritten by every large group

in power which happens to be anxious to justify its position. The facts about Greek and Roman civilizations, indeed many of their greatest achievements, have had to be recovered from the debris of distortion imposed upon them by centuries of Christian dogma in the Middle Ages. We are witnesses to the same phenomenon in our time.

The split between the Chinese and Russian communists dates from 1958, when the Russian leadership suggested taking over the military control of Red China. Nationalism was not as dead as all that. The deep division which opened up between Communist China and the Soviet Union has done a great deal of harm to the absoluteness of Marxist doctrine. International communism, it was promised, would end all wars, for war was declared to be a capitalist contradiction. Neither Chinese nor Russians would ever admit that this hope has been smashed by their rivalry, or that nationalism continued to be a strong influence or that they are in many ways following toward each other policies laid down earlier by czars and war-lords.

Events modify rigid political forms. Would it be fair to describe the English government as a monarchy even though it still has a king; to accept Marx's picture of capitalism as a description of democracy as it is now practiced in the United States; to think that the absolute rule of Party leaders acceptable to Lenin in the Soviet Union and in China would be what Marx and Engels had in mind?

When the stage of socialism no longer requires the dictatorship of the proletariat and the state as a consequence "withers away" in the presence of a classless society then, it is said, communism will have been achieved. The citizen who has become accustomed to economic mobility and freedom of thought and expression would find Marxism intolerable. That is why it has to be rejected as a program for European countries or for the United States.

When Russia and China have achieved the same degree of industrialization achieved by the nations of western Europe and America, it is possible that their practices will soften and that differences of opinion will be permitted again. It is possible that the arts will be revived with something of their former glory in China and perhaps even philosophy will become again a native growth. Who can predict with certainty anything in a social situation of such vast proportions? One can only hope.

Chapter XXIX
Mao Tse-tung

The account of the history of Chinese philosophy as well as of the present-day adoption of the philosophy of communism would not be complete without a closer look at its chief advocate. Mao Tse-tung, born on December 26, 1893 in the village of Shaoshan in Hunan province, was the son of a man who began life as a poor peasant but worked himself up to the position of rich peasant and grain merchant. He did not get along with his father, who wished him to stay on the farm and not to be ambitious for an education. He had been working part time in the fields from the age of six, but at the age of thirteen he was compelled by his father to leave his studies and to work full time in the fields. At sixteen he was back in school away from home. In 1911 he joined the army and remained in it for six months, without doing any fighting. Back in school for half a year, he withdrew again, this time to read in the library for another half-year. In the spring of 1913 he entered the Fourth Provincial Normal School in Changsha, graduating five years later and the following year in Peking became a professional revolutionary. He had always written poetry and continued to do so throughout his life, but it was at this point that he added political writing to his activities.

Like many other Chinese intellectuals of his day, he began by working toward a western-style liberal democracy, for which he then substituted a mixture of anarchy and Marxism. When some of his friends, including Chou En-lai, went to France to study under a scholarship, he chose to remain behind, saying that he was not good at languages and anyhow did not know enough about his own country. Though not yet interested in the peasants, Mao had become a populist in the broad sense of the term, considering the Chinese people as a whole to be the progressive force. He became a magazine editor and political student organizer and supported himself as a laundryman.

In 1920 he became director of a Normal School and married. By that time, he said, he was a Marxist, and added to his educational career that of part-time labor organizer. He returned to Changsha as First Secretary of the Chinese Communist Party for Hunan province when there were only seventy members in all of China! A collaboration was arranged between the Party and Sun Yat-sen's Kuomintang, which was to end later in the defeat of that moderate body.

After conversations with Borodin, a Russian adviser, Mao turned in 1924 to the organization of peasant associations. By 1929 the Chinese Communist had less than two thousand members, mostly industrial workers. If the Party was to have a mass base it would have to be drawn from the peasants. The story of the ups and downs of the subsequent years of struggle are too long to relate here. At times in favor with the Party and at times out, it was because Mao saw that he must act on his own for its good that he survived.

The first "Party Congress" was held by a handful of Communists in July 1921, and was so small that when chased out of a girl's school in the French Concession in Shanghai they fled to Shaohsing and finished by meeting in a boat on a lake. Of course all was not smooth sailing. There was a false start when it looked as though the communists might gain control of the Kuomintang, but under the leadership of General Chiang Kai-shek the more moderate wing won out. When the General married the sister of Sun Yat-sen's widow, Miss Soong, whose brother became Minister of Finance and whose sister was married to the Minister of Industry, there was talk of a Soong dynasty.

Though troubled by dissent, the Kuomintang managed to give some semblance of unity to the country. The increased territorial claims of foreign powers weakened the regime, such as it was, and the demands of the Japanese were the worst of all. The world war of 1914-1918, which China joined on the side of the Allies against Germany, gave her a breathing spell because both her enemies and her foreign friends had been weakened. There were border disputes with the Soviet Union. The undeclared war fought by the Japanese from 1931 to 1937 suddenly blanketed all other considerations.

Meanwhile the communists, expelled from the Kuomintang in 1934 and hard pressed by the forces of Chiang Kai-shek, undertook their famous "Long March," some 6,000 difficult miles, much of it over mountains, to Yenan in the northwest where they found refuge with other communists. With them of course went Mao and his friend Chou En-lai, and many others of the Party leadership. The Japanese war continued, by 1937 the Japanese controlled most of the coast of China and its navigable rivers, and were in a position to choke off all resistance; yet the resistance moved west and continued.

By the autumn of 1935 Mao Tse-tung was in control of his own party. Mao's superior prestige was due to the ability to mobilize the Chinese masses which showed itself so strongly when they were confronted with the Japanese invasion. He proposed to end the struggle with Chiang Kai-shek by a new policy of collaboration, which, however, broke down, and there followed a struggle on two fronts: with the Japanese and with the Kuomintang. To gain control and keep it, Mao had to fight in one way or another on two fronts. He had to fight the opposition from the Kuomintang and the efforts of the Russians to direct Chinese communism from Moscow. In both directions he was successful.

The Chinese were saved by the second world war and the defeat of Japan. The rest of the story has often been told and continues today. Our concern with Mao Tse-tung here is chiefly as a philosopher, how he has lived and what he has come to stand for. How he managed to combine the ancient inheritance of sage-king with his development as Marxist revolutionary is what we need now to unravel.

In proper Marxist fashion Chairman Mao recognized the dictatorship and advocated violence in defense of "the revolution." "A revolution is not a dinner party, or like doing embroidery; it cannot be so refined, so gentle, so temperate and kind... Political power grows out of the barrel of a gun. The seizure of power by armed force, the settlement of the issue by war, is the central task and the highest form of revolution." The words of Mao were plain enough; victory of course was always assumed. According to his figures there were in 1958 ten million Party members in a population of six hundred million. He insisted that his aim was to achieve peace and hoped to accomplish it by opposing war with war and in this way to get rid of war—the classic claim of those who resort to war in the hope of imposing the conqueror's peace.

Almost everyone who ever resorted to war insisted that its goal was peace, a peace imposed by the conquerors. But can a movement which advocates violence ever turn to peace? Can a Party which has once exercised absolute control ever relinquish it? That remains to be seen, but the outlook is not an optimistic one. People are prone to alternations of periods of violence and peace, and there is nothing in Marxist doctrine to urge a permanent peace upon them.

According to Marxist doctrine, wars are all started by imperialists over booty, and this would apply to the imperialistic ambitions of China and the Soviet Union. A war on the border between the two countries could escalate into a war over the leadership of the communist movement, which is the basis of the conflict. Here ancient antagonisms reassert themselves, and the enemies of their forefathers remain their enemies still. A Russian Czar is no less a Czar because he has changed his title, and an emperor is no less an emperor because he is called a Chairman.

The cult of Chairman Mao was as we have seen, widely encouraged. Someone has observed that China is now a country with a single author and a single book. The "little red book" of *Quotations from Chairman Mao*, a publication of the armed forces, the political department of the People's Liberation Army contains expressions of facets of orthodox Marxism, taken from essays and speeches of Mao, all short pithy and fragmentary, with nothing particularly original in it. First issued in 1964, it was reprinted the following year, and in the three years, 1966 to 1968, 740 million copies were published. As the Chinese claimed in 1971 to have a population of some 830 million, that is a little less than one copy for each citizen.

What emerges from a study of the "little red book" is Marxism in its most extreme Leninist form: The revolution is violent, a standing arrangement, a kind of permanent war. The identification of the Party with the masses is absolute. The transition in China has gone from feudalism to a socialist dictatorship.

Stuart Schram reported that in July 1945 Mao anonymously contributed an article to the Yenan press in which he affirmed that the people of China wanted to follow "Mao Tse-tung's way." In 1964, there was opposition to Mao within the Party itself. It seems to have been the conviction of many, among them Liu Shao-ch'i, that while Mao's leadership had been well-suited to the tactical period when it was necessary to lead guerrilla fighters, it was hardly adequate to the construction of a rational industrial economy.

Mao responded to this challenge in a number of ways. He initiated a revolt within his own Party and encouraged the public to participate in a period of self-criticism. He conscripted high school students into a new organization of

Red Guards distinct from the Army and the Party, and owing allegiance only to himself. Its task was to effect a new "proletarian cultural revolution" while a handful of his most loyal followers built a cult of the Chairman. He was declared to be infallible and his thought synonymous with Marxist-Leninist truth. The Red Guards undertook to "turn the world upside down and smash it" and in this way to create a chaos, as part of the cultural revolution, a movement from which Mao hoped to emerge with safeguards against undertakings by the bureaucracy opposed to him. The movement spread so wildly that it threatened to get out of hand, and at this stage Mao called in the Army, which consolidated his hold and in general gave new impetus to the revolutionary spirit that was so badly needed. Though the Red Guards were disbanded the cult remained, reinforced.

While Mao rejected the civilization of ancient China, he was the embodiment of one side of it, the concept of a vast nation understood as an enlarged family, with an autocratic head who is both military ruler and religious leader, a supreme political authority. Elevated to the status of sage-king, he was the inheritor of a tradition which can be traced back to King Wen and his son the Duke of Chou who lived, as we saw, as early as 1122 B.C. and were much admired by Confucius.

There can be little doubt that in rejecting Confucius and his influence Mao meant to turn his back on China's past while himself being directly in the line of its inheritance, a sage-king who renounced the tradition of sage-kings. The suppression of the ancient culture of China with the prevention of all attempts to add to it, in favor of worthless specimens of the arts sponsored by Mao's wife, resembled the rigid dictatorship of the brief-lived Ch'in dynasty, when at the outset the burning of the books was ordered by the ruler, Ch'in Shih-huang, and his Prime Minister, Li Ssu, the regime as a matter of fact most admired by the Maoists.

When in 1965 the protein, insulin, was synthesized at almost the same time in Peking, at Brookhaven on Long Island

and in West Germany, the Peking chemists said that their work was accomplished while "holding aloft the great red banner of Chairman Mao." The basis of psychiatric practice has been the *Quotations from Chairman Mao*. Patients who seemed nervous while undergoing surgery employing acupuncture anesthesis were given the "little red book" to hold for comfort. A child with emotional problems was treated by being asked to repeat the sayings of Chairman Mao. Literary courses are still devoted to its study; in one reading room in a library a visitor counted 17 translations. In universities the chief responsibility of the administrators was to insure the proper study of Mao's thought.

The Christian translators of the King James Bible, aiming their observation at the Pope, wrote, "it is a terrible thing to fall into the hands of a living god." And, it could be added, there is nothing more dangerous than a God who calls for an absolute belief in a system of philosophy. Such a call lies behind the great religions of the world and now it lies behind the Marxist political movement. For an absolute belief no one would hesitate to kill those who resist conversion. It was true of the Spanish Inquisition and now it is true of the Russian and Chinese Marxists. It is the favorite way in which philosophy can come to stop all inquiry into philosophy, for no one who has the final truth feels under the necessity to seek it.

Toward the end of the *Quotations* Mao recognizes that "works of art which lack artistic quality have no force, however progressive they are politically," and deplores "the poster and slogan style which is correct in political viewpoint but lacking in artistic power," but his intentions were reversed by his wife, the former actress Lan-p'ing, now Comrade Chiang Ch'ing, who emerged from retirement to become a member of the Central Committee as well as head of the group responsible for the cultural revolution. The reform of the opera and ballet under her guidance robbed them of aesthetic quality and left them vehicles for communist propaganda of the crudest sort, the poster and slogan style, as anyone who saw them knows.

Chairman Mao embodied in his own person an extraordinary paradox for the Chinese people. On the one hand he advocated orthodox Marxism as stated by Russian ideologists, and on the other was in his own person a version of the ancient tradition the Chinese have revered for several thousand years, almost a reincarnation in terms of modern political doctrine.

Stuart Schram has pointed out that following Mao's lead the keynote of Chinese Marxism has been the elevation of the will of man over a rational examination of the facts. Observers who returned from visits to China in 1975 reported that progress in abstract thought was at a standstill. The universities were at the level of vocational and technical schools.

Chapter XXX
Some General Observations on Chinese Philosophy

Philosophy was imbedded in Chinese society in a unique way. The pervasive influence of manners and the design of the bureaucracy were due to the philosophies which developed by the professionals. Philosophy was closer to the lives of the people than is usually the case. This may have come about because it was largely a native product. For several thousand years, although China was invaded many times, foreign ideas were not imported—until the first century of our era when Buddhism was introduced from India.

This tradition produced characteristics not found in the west.

The first of these is that the preoccupation with morality caused the emphasis to fall on attitudes rather than on behavior. Correct behavior would follow naturally from the correct attitudes (without the necessity of introducing the will) displayed toward others and toward non-human nature.

The governing principle was, in a word, balance or proportion. The Chinese seem to have felt most comfortable with aesthetic morality; the test of appropriateness was preferred. The suitability to oneself of attitudes and actions, as well as others, has been the prime criterion, with priorities arranged accordingly.

The second is its discovery of a two-tiered universe long before Plato had such a conception. The Chinese version gives the names of 'Earth' and 'Heaven' to the two tiers, understanding, as has been shown throughout these pages, that 'Heaven' was not supernatural but a set of causal laws which do not change while everything on 'Earth' does.

The third is its matter-of-fact materialism. The Chinese have never been much interested in supernatural gods and they not been occupied with living in this world as preparation for the next. Human values must be pursued here and now. The exception has been the occasional belief in spirits both good and evil, but such creatures hover over the living and do not concern any other existence, even they were dismissed by most Chinese philosophers who either ignored them or attacked them headlong.

In this they differed of from the Indians, who had a taste for the mystical and transcendental. While India philosophies tended to be treated like religions, in China religions tended to be treated like philosophies.

The fourth is that it sought a model in some golden age in the past. Some early dynasty was selected from emulation and to it all the virtues of man and society were attributed. It is the mythical part of their long history—the part which antedates definite knowledge—which has supplied the ideal. It can never be disproved, and if it can never be proved it may still serve as inspiration in the present.

The fifth is its preoccupation with the family. The stability of the culture throught the millennia rests on a firm belief in the continuing presence of ancestors to be honored and emulated. The Chinese family, like few others, extends in both directions from the present; to ancestors and toward descendants. A man has dishonored his father if he does not produce any sons.

The sixth is the affirmation of the absolute rule of an

emperor. Aside from the family and the emperor little is worthy of real veneration. The vast bureaucracy in China in the past still there and more important than ever, never occupied a position of importance in the considerations of individual human behavior. Good conduct always includes the correct attitudes toward parent and emperor, good government always conceived of in terms of a just and devoted ruler with absolute power. The idea that rule need not be absolute nor in the hands of a single ruler seems not to have gained much consideration. Social behavior is often a matter of acting out the game of truth and consequences. The possession of the absolute truth justifies the absolutely ruthless actions which follow from it.

The seventh is the intense polarization of philosophy, which was interested either in man and society, as with the Confucians, or in untouched nature, as with the Taoists. The idea of man as an integral part of nature, shaped by it both by birth and by life—responses is not typically Chinese.

In understanding Chinese philosophy today it is helpful to measure the present rulers of China against this picture which historical features have been retained and which abandoned.

Briefly, the third, sixth and seventh have been retained; the first, second, fourth and fifth attacked or abandoned.

Mao and the other rulers of Red China have abandoned the importance of attitudes, do not believe in a two-tiered universe, look to the future rather than the past, and have made impossible the preoccupation with the family. On the other hand, they have retained in Chinese culture its down-to-earthness, its adherence to absolute rule, and its separation of man from nature in order to concentrate on man in society.

The golden age has been moved from the past to the future, in according to the belief in Marxism, which is utopian in accepting the idea that a perfect future for all people can be attained in this world. Though they profess to be moving toward it, it is difficult to see the Chinese permitting the state to wither away. It has permeated their lives so thoroughly that the individual is asked to give up his family as a central concern and has been compelled to do so.

One comes from an examination of Chinese philosophy with an impression of human dignity and timeless value. Perhaps that is after all the great Chinese contribution to philosophy.

PART THREE
THE PHILOSOPHY
OF JAPAN

"If you want to obtain a certain thing, you must first be a
certain man. Once you have become a certain man
obtaining that certain thing will not be a concern of yours
any more."
                                        —Zen master

Chapter XXXI
Early Japan

Little is known about the early history of Japan. The Ainu, now inhabitants of the northern island of Hokkaido, were once spread over all the islands. They must have been of Caucasoid stock, may have come from eastern Siberia—no-one is certain—and were driven north, after many wars and some reversals, by a mixed population on the mainland. In neolithic times the Korean coastline had been peopled by Mongol tribes. It is probable that the Stone Age was coming to an end in western Japan during the first century B.C., but the military nature of the Japanese occupation of the islands began early and lasted for some time, and it was not until the beginning of the ninth century that the northern frontiers were secured.

The use of bronze was a hundred years reaching Japan from China by way of Korea, but properly speaking it was iron which replaced the use of stone, so Japan never went through a true Bronze Age. The reason for the fairly uniform civilization there at the time may have been the combining of the Chinese, the Mongols and others in Korea into a single people before crossing to the islands.

The key to early Japan (and to the Japan of a much later period) was the culture of the Chinese. It came to the islands via Korea where it was doubtless first influential and then considerably altered, and altered again when it reached Japan, but it remained in its chief elements fundamentally Chinese.

The Chinese of course knew about the Japanese. As early as 108 B.C. a Han dynasty report tells of Japanese exchanges with the Chinese colonies in Korea nearest Japan and in A.D. 297 there were reports of the "people of Wa [Japan] who live on mountainous islands in the middle of the ocean". Japan became the inheritor of a long line of Chinese influences from the Han dynasty onward, including the T'ang, Sung and Ming. Always there can be noted the strong changes in these cultural influences effected by the Japanese, who were astute borrowers but never slavish imitators, always altering what they borrowed. It will be our task in this Part to determine what consistency the Japanese were able to bring to bear on what they acquired from others as a result of tendencies toward certain feelings, thoughts and actions.

The earliest reliable dates are those in the *Records of Ancient Matters* (the *Kojiki*), written in 712, and the *Chronicles of Japan* (the *Nihongi*), written in 720, when the Chinese language and literature had already been known for some three centuries. The two books contain legends and fables, the former reciting an age of the gods, the latter the reigns of the emperors, and besides to the genealogical accounts there was much erotic material. A great deal of what they record is myth and legend rather than history, for instance that the empire was founded by Jimmu Tenno, a great-grandson of the Sun Goddess, Amaterasu. All subsequent emperors have been dated from him, so that all are divine, and the Japanese were so taught until the emperor Hirohito renounced his divinity in 1946.

Jimmu Tenno—Tenno means "Son of Heaven," a title which has been applied posthumously to all emperors ever since—is believed to have been an historical chieftain who brought many local clans under his rule, and to have flourished about A.D. 300. He worshipped his ancestor the Sun Goddess in his own palace, and the practice of combining religion with rule in this way was continued by his successors. The earliest Japanese word for government (*matsurigoto*) meant religious observance.

The earliest trace of philosophy in Japan is contained in the preface to the *Kojiki*, where we learn that after heaven and earth first parted and the Three Deities began the act of creation, the yin and the yang developed, two spirits who became the ancestors of all things. The *Nihongi* recites much the same process. The yin-yang teaching, combined with much astrology; the five elements: wood, fire, earth, metal and water, were matched against the planets, against the directions, against the seasons, against the signs of the Zodiac. Chinese religious influences were not confined to this tradition but extended also to the Confucian and Taoist classics. It is also worth noting that astrology, though not as organized in Asia as it was in early western tradition, was equally widespread. The least substantiated of all beliefs has also been the most popular and longest lived, for of course it still exists today not only in Asia but throughout the world. Evidently the human species would rather invent its beliefs than limit them to the evidence.

The native religion of the Japanese people is called Shinto, "the Way of the Gods," and while its origins are uncertain they are known to date before the coming of any Chinese influences. Shinto was not at first the name of an organized religion but of an aggregate of many diverse cults, and this remained true well into historical times. It embraced varieties of animism and shamanism as well as the worship of ancestors and heroes. Gradually however the various cults merged, and the Sun Goddess became the principal deity for both nature worshippers and ancestor worshippers.

Shinto with its "eight hundred gods" was a polytheistic animism, a nature worship, however, of imperial ancestors and tribal deities as well as nature gods. The Shinto priests, always a small group, retained their ordinary pursuits which they interrupted only for their religious duties, the emphasis of which was on ritual purity. Death in particular was defiling, also disease and wounds, and so were sexual intercourse, menstruation and childbirth. After a funeral all the family went into the water to bathe, and friends came to dance and sing. No morality was advocated, only custom and ceremony. There were two important acts of worship, the first consisting in sweeping out the shrine to chase out evil spirits, the second in the washing of the body. There was also recitation of formulas and prayers.

In addition to ritual purity there was a positive idea of fertility. Ceremonies were performed that were meant to be favorable to the success of farmers and fisherman. Besides attendance at the shrines, there were offerings of the first fruit of the season or the first catch of fish or the spoils of war. All efforts were directed toward the production of food; the chief festivals had to do with food. In these early religious efforts of the Japanese there was general phallic worship, probably because the phallus represented fertility; phallic symbols have been uncovered from early stone age grave sites and phallic meaning found in trees and stones with suggestive forms. The oldest center of Shinto was the Izumo Shrine on the eastern seacoast close to Korea, but the Shrine at Ise devoted to the Sun Goddess came to be the most important. The buildings were simple wooden structures, usually single large rooms raised from the ground and entered by steps. They housed sacred objects called *kami* which might be visible or invisible and which symbolized extraordinary and even magical powers.

It is difficult to exaggerate the extent of Chinese influence on the formation of Japanese civilization. For instance in A.D. 450 Chinese writing carried by Korean scholars reached the Japanese islands, and for a while all records were kept in Chinese. In the sixth century there was an administrative revolution in which the government was remodelled along lines laid down by the Chinese bureaucracy.

It was during the reign of the Empress Suiko (592-628) that her remarkable nephew Prince Shotoku, who ruled as regent, gave the country a constitution. It was not an organized document but its ethical intent makes clear that it was aimed at ending a general anarchy. Shotoku was a devout Buddhist, there is evidence of Buddhist thinking in the articles of the constitution, but he used chiefly the Confucian teachings. The Confucian morality, in which the family was central and all private life was guided by filial piety, lay at its foundation. Women at the time were in a definitely subordinate position. The Confucian philosophy was further supported by the foundation of a university in which the principal studies were of Chinese history and philosophy. Shotoku did much to establish Buddhism in court circles, but he accomplished much more; he founded monasteries and temples, encouraged the introduction of Chinese arts and technological practices, was responsible for the adoption of the Chinese calendar, and for sending an embassy to the Chinese court of the Sui dynasty in 607. An entry dated 689 in the *Nihongi* mentions a state "department of Shinto." The first hint of nationalism is contained in Shotoku's statement that Japan was the root and trunk of civilization, while China was its branches and leaves and India its flowers and fruit.

We can see in this period the emerging shape of Japanese society. Buddhist beliefs were combined with Shinto observances in a society governed by Confucian teachings. This mixture, in which the Japanese saw no contradictions or conflicts, remained the established order throughout the centuries, and to a lesser extent prevails today. All such influences of course continued to be transmitted through Korea where Japan at the time had a foothold as early as the third century A.D. But the Japanese were driven out for once and all by the mid-sixth century.

The most significant single occurrence in Japanese history was the introduction of Buddhism which is officially dated at A.D. 552. Buddhism reached Japan via China and Korea. The

king of Paichke in southwest Korea was hard pressed and
sought help from the Japanese court. To aid his cause he had a
Buddha made of gold and copper sixteen feet high (the
traditional size) and sent it as a gift to the emperor.

The Soga clan was the first to gain control of the court by
intermarrying with the royal family until the two groups were
all but indistinguishable. No matter how strong a clan was,
however, it needed the emperor because of the tradition that
his authority was divine by way of his descent in an unbroken
line from the Sun Goddess.

The great minister, Soga no Iname, was the one who had
introduced the convention of being the real power behind the
throne and of ruling in the name of an apparent but less able
emperor, a convention which was to have a history that has
lasted as long as that of Japan itself.

It was Soga's family which took the lead in favoring the
new religion. He had political reasons, seeing it as an
instrument to help him in breaking the power of opposing clans
and establishing the emperor and his appointed ministers. As
early as 594 Buddhism was proclaimed the state religion and in
587, several generations later, the Emperor Yomei openly
adopted it. Subsequent rulers saw to it that Buddhism was
established in court circles, and though it took longer to reach
the people, things moved quickly enough. In 616 the oracle of
Miwa announced that Buddhist priests were the appropriate
persons to perform funeral rites. The *Nihongi* claims that by
623 there were in Japan 46 Buddhist temples, 816 priests and
569 nuns.

In 710 it was decided that Japan should have, like China, a
capital city, and accordingly one was established at Nara,
somewhat east of the present city of Osaka, laid out on lines
adopted from the Chinese T'ang capital at Ch'ang-an. In the
earlier centuries there were no cities, only villages of thatched
huts, the Emperor's capital being only a larger village. But now
there would be a center not only for the rapidly increasing
bureaucracy but also for the accumulation of Chinese culture.

In the seventy-five years during which Nara remained the capital, Chinese influences were consolidated in every walk of life; the architecture of temples and palaces, the reading of the Indian sutras, the costumes at court, and even court rank, all were Chinese in origin. There is some indication of the relative force of Indian and Chinese culture in relation to that of Japan when we recall that Buddhism and Confucianism were already much more than a thousand years old when they reached the shores of the Japanese islands. They had been long established in the home countries when they were first imported and had a fresh impact on a culture that was almost wholly lacking in such ideas.

Two of the principal Buddhist sects were introduced at this time, the Kegon and the Ritsu. The former was an interpretation of the Kegon sutra, which held to the doctrine of the supreme Buddha, universal and omnipresent, dwelling upon a lotus flower of a thousand petals, each of which represents a universe in turn containing a thousand worlds. This is the Locana Buddha (in Japanese, Roshana). The Roshana Buddha was compared to the position of the emperor in his state, an effort to identify religion with politics. The Emperor Shomu in 749 decreed that henceforth the Kegon scripture was to be the official one and caused the great Kegon Temple, the Todaiji, to be erected accordingly.

The Ritsu sect was more concerned with outward observances, and gave its chief attention to monastic discipline and ritual succession. Although the Todaiji remained for some time the center of the state religion of Buddhism in Japan, provincial governors were ordered to install Buddhist shrines throughout the country.

Hinayana Buddhism, closer to the strict teaching of the Buddha, never exercised much influence in Japan beyond its use as forms of academic discipline for the preparation of the priesthood. It was of course the Mahayana which took hold. In Part I of this book where Mahayana Buddhism is discussed, the point is made that the Mahayana can be viewed either as a development and extension of Hinayana Buddhism, the Buddhism of the Buddha, or as a different philosophy using the same name. I prefer the last interpretation. Buddha never considered himself a god but according to the Mahayana he was; indeed he was many gods. Also the Mahayana taught that external reality is so changeable that it can lead only to deception; material things must be negated until all becoming is denied. In place of this there is the harmony which comes from the penetration of all related things by the Buddha.

The *Sutra of the Golden Light* brought together the most original of the ideas contained in the affirmative doctrine of the Mahayana. We read that the omnipresence of the Buddha makes itself felt in everything that exists, that the gates of the Paradise of the Lotus where Buddha lives are open to all humanity, and anyone can become a Buddha. The doctrine is a curious mixture, for in the midst of all the symbolism there appears an appeal to the life of reason. It is reason which is called on to distinguish good from evil and right from wrong, and self-sacrifice is understood as the highest expression of the life of reason.

Nara Buddhism brought more than religion to Japan; it brought the best of Chinese civilization. Under the influence of the Buddhists the Japanese built bridges and highways, employed irrigation, constructed public baths, practiced cremation, and introduced many medicines, all in imitation of the Chinese technology which the Japanese Buddhist priests learned in China and brought back with them.

Chapter XXXII
The First Buddhist Sects

Buddhism was ushered into Japan by Chinese monks, many of whom introduced special versions of it. The earliest sect was the Sanron, which was brought to Japan in 625 by a Korean monk who had studied in China. Little is known of the Kusha, which may or may not have resulted in the establishment of a sect.

Of those sects which survived and still have adherents today, the first was the Hosso introduced into Japan in 650 by a Japanese student-monk, Dosho. This doctrine of the Hosso was that the *only* reality is consciousness. In accordance with the teaching of Nagarjuna, the members of the Hosso sect did not believe in the existence of the external world at all, even the motion of the stars was held to be only a creation of human minds and therefore could not be looked to for guidance, it could only deceive. The method consisted in the successive denial of all the things that change and of all becoming, until all that remains is the permanence of perfect knowledge.

The trouble with the Hosso sect was that it became an aristocratic religion in which only properly situated persons were eligible for Buddhist perfection. There was no mass appeal in such a doctrine. Its most influential monk was Gyogi (670-749) who not only saw the possibility of reconciling Shinto with Buddhism but also spread Chinese technology, and was responsible for the building of bridges and dykes, introducing many other Chinese inventions.

The Ritsu sect was brought to Japan by a Chinese monk named Ganjin. At the urging of Japanese monks he planned many trips to Japan but did not succeed until the sixth try in 753 when he was sixty-six years old. The Ritsu, chiefly concerned with promoting discipline and more occupied with observances than with doctrine, was an immediate success and numbered among its converts the dowager-empress. The Tosho-Daiji temple where Ganjin spent his last years and died in 763 is to this day the head-temple of the Ritsu.

The Kusha sect stood for a realistic philosophy of the Hinayana type according to which the material world is as real as consciousness, while the Hosso sect accepted the Mahayana doctrine which confined reality to consciousness. The austerities of Hinayana Buddhism proved too difficult for most people to accept. Accordingly, the less orthodox but more adaptable Mahayana came to take its place altogether. This was accompanied by a move from one capital to another, chiefly to escape from the threat of militant monks who now wished to usurp governmental power.

As the Buddhist temples and monasteries in Nara increased in wealth and influence, its inmates grew more worldly, and the armies of monks became for the first time a menace to the government. This was a practice new to Buddhism and a development peculiar to Japan. The Emperor Kammu (781-806), who had been trained by Confucians, moved the capital in 794 to a new city which he ordered to be laid out at Uda in an effort to get rid of the growing power of the Buddhist monks at Nara. It was only twenty-five miles from Nara but that was considered sufficient to put it outside the immediate reach of the militant monks. Renamed Heian-kyo, the "City of Peace," it stood on the site of the present city of Kyoto, and lasted until 1191. It too was built in imitation of Ch'ang-an and followed *yin-yang* principles, being divided into eight streets and nine avenues, with a palace surrounded by nine walls. There was a bureaucracy with nine departments of state, each with eight ranks of officials.

The chief developments of the Heian period were: an increase in the practice of dual rule, of abdicated emperors exercising more authority than the established emperors; a flourishing of the arts; the leadership of the powerful Fujiwara clan; and the emergence of a permanent warrior class.

Heian culture in the late eighth and early ninth centuries was extremely sophisticated but it was largely a court affair, an aesthetic center of delicate sensibilities set down in the midst of a rude peasant country which was at best only half civilized. The Fujiwara ruled through skillful intrigue rather swordplay and the show of force. They were enormously wealthy and worked hard and successfully at politics. The emperor remained as usual a figurehead, but the Fujiwara saw to it that his empress was always one of their daughters.

Though its buildings were made entirely of wood, Heian-kyo quickly became one of the largest cities in the world. Much of the eighth century was devoted by the government to the construction of palaces and the completion of the conquest of the Ainu in the north, who had proved more stubborn than had been anticipated. More than one military force had to be sent against them.

The practice of having a powerful ruler who was not the nominal head of the state, a practice which as we have seen had been begun by the Soga clan, was almost the standard practice under the Fujiwara and for the same reason: the Fujiwara, during the three hundred years that they ruled Japan, also needed the reinforcement of an emperor who could claim divine authority because of his descent from the Sun-Goddess.

There was one severe limitation to the Fujiwara rule, however. Despite the almost slavish imitation of all of the elements of Chinese culture, the system of government by men of merit selected by civil service examinations never became the custom in Japan. Instead hereditary privilege was the general practice, and it did not produce men of outstanding ability. The best posts went instead to the Fujiwara, and after them to the other powerful clans.

The members of the minor nobility, excluded from the highest offices of the state, became warriors, scholars and artists. It was they who formed the basis of the new middle class which was to have an influential future. Below them were the farmers, artisans and slaves. The Japanese, like the Chinese of the time, were slave-holders.

Since the burden of taxes increased, the free peasants drifted downward and tended to merge with the slaves, while the Fujiwara absorbed everything above. In this way there occurred a dangerous polarization of society. Both sides were weakened, the aristocrats through luxurious living, the workers through grinding poverty, and the middle class came to the fore and, beginning in the tenth century, constituted the new power in the state.

Another significant development of Heian culture was the rise of a Japanese written language. Official documents were written in Chinese. The Japanese vernacular was not deemed worthy and was left to the ladies, who composed the first distinguished fiction. We still have the "Pillow Book" of Sei Shonagon and above all the classic tale of Genji, the *Genji Monogatori* of Murasaki Shikibu, a court lady-in-waiting, written some time between 1008 and 1020. It is a great novel and an astonishing picture of court life with its sophisticated intrigues and romances.

The most influential of the new developments that seem to have been precipitated by the movement to Heian-kyo was the introduction of the Tendai and Shingon sects of Buddhism, both of which were Chinese imports to become more closely associated in Japan than they had originally been in China. Tendai (its Chinese name, *T'ien-T'ai*) was founded in Japan in

754 by Saicho, a Japanese priest who had studied in China applied for a license to found a new sect in 802, and was responsible for the building five years later of a monastery on Mount Hiei, despite the vigorous opposition of the Nara clergy, with whom he had to contend. In 827, he was posthumously granted the holy title of *Daishi* ("Great Teacher") and henceforth known as Dengyo-Daishi.

In the monastery on Mount Hiei Saicho kept his monks in training for twelve years. He divided them into three classes according to their various abilities, the first consisting of those who were most gifted in actions and words, who were to remain on Mount Hiei and serve their country through the maintenance of religious practices. The members of the second class were to return to secular life to become teachers, while those of the third class were to undertake agricultural and engineering projects.

The Tendai teaching was based on the *Lotus-Sutra*. It is a complete philosophy, with a theory of knowledge and a metaphysics as well as an ethics. The theory of knowledge consists in the contention that our perceptions and thoughts are identical with the absolute reality. This does not mean that the material world is unreal, it means rather that appearances and the absolute truth are one and the same.

(In early Japanese Buddhism we can already find the three standard alternatives in the theory of knowledge with respect to the reality of consciousness and the external world. For the Kusha, as we have seen, the material world is as real as consciousness; indeed the two are equally real. For the Hosso it was true that only consciousness is real and there is no real external world. The Tendai effected a compromise: while consciousness is real for them, the appearances of the external world are real also, which leaves entirely open the question of whether there is a reality behind the appearances.)

According to the Tendai metaphysics, there are three forms of existence: the void, the temporary and the middle. All elements of existence depend upon their relations; none is independent. The relations of the void and of the temporary are fragile but the relations of the middle are dependable and permanent.

On the individual side the Tendai sect taught that all men are able to become Buddhas and indeed all should strive in this direction. No matter how wicked a man is he is at least potentially a Buddha and can attain perfection by following Buddha's example in a life of pure morality and contemplation; of charity to all beings, an attitude of sublime forbearance, and a sense of the emptiness of things. The Mahayana doctrine that the Buddha nature is present in every individual, who has only to look inward to develop it and to become a Bodhisattva, was accepted. But many stages had to be passed through before any individual could reach Enlightenment. There were ceremonies that resembled baptism with water, including initiation and vows; there were formulas to be recited; ritual to be performed. The revelation was a stage affair and went through eight steps, the first, or sudden, step involving teaching without preparation but only to the highest intelligences, such as the Bodhisattvas, who understand immediately, the last step, involving gradual teaching, was more suitable to the ordinary individual.

The monk Kuya in 951 and Genshin (942-1017) after him preached the horrors of hell and the glories of paradise, and they could pass emotionally from one to the other quite easily. They spread the doctrine of the "Pure Land" and the worship of the Amida Buddha. To die for the faithful means to be reborn into the Land of Purity where, like a blind man who suddenly is able to see, he finds himself surrounded by dazzling lights and valuable jewels in an atmosphere in which the Buddha is seen seated on a golden lotus, surrounded by his saints.

This doctrine of the after-life, which came to prominence toward the end of the Heian period was especially influential at the Heian Court. Screens depicting the torments of hell were especially popular, as were Genshin's own graphic drawings of the horrors to be encountered there. In the eleventh and twelfth centuries, however, the attention shifted from hell to heaven, and the monks taught that entry into heaven depended not on good works but on simple faith.

The spirit of religious conflict is already present in the Lotus-Sutra, where it is baldly stated that while the Mahayana saves all creatures, the Hinayana could never save a single one. The Buddha himself is in the Mahayana. The conflict hardly seems large enough, but the pugnacious spirit it engendered is perhaps responsible, at least at the start, for the opposition of the other Buddhist sects in Japan. This situation steadily worsened and, as we have seen, militant monks began to be attached to the monasteries. During the reign of the emperor Shirakawa (1072-1086) and for a century later the "warrior-monks" of the Tendai sect fought frequent battles with those of the Hosso sect, which certainly was as contrary to the spirit of Buddhism as anything could be.

The companion sect of Tendai was Shingon, introduced into Japan at about the same time by Kukai (774-835), who named it after its Chinese original *Chen-yen*, Shingon or "True Word," and founded a monastery on Mount Koya which was still in 1952 one of the most flourishing in Japan. At first Saicho tried to make friends with Kukai and even sought to learn from him but was finally repulsed and died a bitter man. Shingon, which had come into existence in China, no doubt under Tantric influence, was a mystical doctrine not reducible to words, but given to the use of magic in the form of incantations, spells and ritual gestures all containing secret meanings. The mysteries of the mind were handed on from master to disciple but not written down. Hence they were considered esoteric (for the initiated) rather than exoteric (for the public). Kukai has told how his Chinese master, Hui-kuo, waited almost until his death until he found in the young Kukai a proper disciple. Unfortunately, not all of Kukai's borrowings were good. He also imported into Japan spells guaranteed to prolong life, which was certainly contrary to the teachings of Buddha. A later branch of the Shingon called the Tachikawa school, influenced by the Chinese yin and yang and the Tibetan Shaktists, taught that sexual intercourse was the secret way of becoming a Buddha, but in 1335 the Tachikawa leader was exiled and Tachikawa books ordered to be burned. Evidence of it is said to linger still in some Buddhist sects.

Kukai despite the secrecy managed to write a book, the *Ten Stages of the Religious Consciousness*, describing the progression toward Enlightenment. (It must be noted here that Kukai counted on six elements rather than the usual five: earth, water, fire, air, space, for he added consciousness.) For the first stage he described a purely animal life of uncontrolled passions, Confucianism was the second stage and Taoism the third; then after two Hinayana stages, there were two others including a Mahayana, Tendai for an eighth, Kegon a ninth, and of course Shingon for the tenth and final.

The Shingon taught that life is an affair of constant change, either upward toward Buddhahood or downward toward hell. The compassion of the Buddha led the enlightened ones away from their ordinary existence as "butting goats" and toward salvation, but the magical formulas took precedence over doctrine and adherents saw in it an easy way to salvation, particularly since it provided a reconciliation with the native Shinto gods, and so was encouraged by Shinto priests. Early Shinto had resisted the importation of Buddhism from Korea and China, but the Shingon doctrine found the Shinto and Buddhist gods to be identical, and so the two religions became harmonized. Its tendency to regard every natural phenomenon as a divine manifestation which could be represented by the image of a particular deity made it especially acceptable to Shinto. Shingon was regarded as that branch of Buddhism closest to Shinto, and so beginning in 937 there came into existence a kind of Shinto called *Ryobu* (or dual) Shinto, combining the two religions. This remained the most powerful religious movement until the Meiji Restoration of 1868.

Kukai's aesthetic approach won more favor at court than

the more moral Tendai school. A many-sided and gifted man, he was, in addition to his central religious interest, a scholar, a sculptor, a painter, a poet and an inventor. In fact he thought of Shingon in terms of the arts, saying that his Chinese master, Hui-kuo, had informed him that only through art could the esoteric teachings be properly conveyed: the obscurities and secrets of the doctrine can be depicted and hence understood only in terms of paintings and sculptures. Music and literature were to be included along with gestures and other symbolic acts. Kukai saw Shingon as a religion that composed a whole civilization, not merely a part of it.

Chapter XXXIII
The Sects of
the Middle Ages

By the middle of the twelfth century there was a marked change in Japanese politics. The long rule of the Fujiwara clan came to an end, a period of feudal militarism was begun, with a struggle of some years between the Taira and Minamoto clans. The conflict was intensified by the militant Buddhist monks from two monasteries of the Tendai sect who not only fought with each other but also descended from their mountain retreats around Kyoto to terrorize the capital. After many battles with the Taira and much bloodshed, Yoritomo Minamoto was victorious and procured for himself the title of *Sei-i tai Shogun* (usually shortened to Shogun) meaning "barbarian-subduing Generalissimo." A military man, he meant to rule Japan by military government from his old base at Kamakura, and therefore established the practice of "Bakufu" or tent government, a simple soldier's rule, in contrast with the luxurious ways of the court.

Yoritomo died at the end of the twelfth century and was succeeded by two incompetent sons, but thanks to the skill of his widow the rule passed into the hands of her capable father-in-law, Hojo Tokimasa, as regent. The government was now twice removed from the emperor, first by a military dictator and then by a regent who represented him. The Hojo regents were capable administrators and managed to dominate the government for the next hundred years. Historians like Sansom are full of praise for the working of justice under them. They operated under a code of law designed for the military and adopted in 1232 (there already was one for the civilian officials and the monasteries), but it was not a systematic body of law, only a collection of maxims and rules, which favored the feudal lords and was kept a secret. The guiding principle was corporate expediency rather than general justice, but it did protect some of the rights of the peasants, who otherwise would have had none.

One of the least desirable features of the Hojo regency was the continued brawls and raids conducted by the militant monks. Ecclesiatical troops, sometimes even of the same sect though attached to different monasteries, would conduct skirmishes. Armed monks descended on the capital more than twenty times during the thirteenth century and were only kept in check by the army of the Bakufu. The result of the fierce quarrels would often be the intimidation of the lay populace and often even of the court.

The most important single events which occurred during the period of the Hojo regents were the repulse of the two invasions of Mongols sent by the infamous Khabilai Khan, who had become the Emperor of all China in 1263 and immediately set about reducing all neighboring kingdoms to a state of vassalage. When the Japanese rejected his overtures, he invaded, first in 1274 and again seven years later, on both occasions unsuccessfully. The Mongols evidently did not know that August is the month when typhoons may be regularly expected, and extraordinary coincidences saved the Japanese both times, when storms wrecked the Mongol fleets.

The changes effected by Yoritomo and the Hojo regents from 1192 until 1333 were tremendous: among other things a new capital, a new social structure, even new styles in art. In a single century four new Buddhist sects came into existence: Jodo, Shinshu, Nichiren and Zen. The new Bakufu administration had more sympathy with the newer sects, in particular with the first two.

One peculiar development in religious tradition that seems to have become more Japanese than anything else was the Amidism of the Jodo sect. A Mahayana sutra mentions Amida as only one of many Buddhas who obtained enlightenment but refused Buddhahood in order that many others could share his exceptional merit by admitting into Paradise all who called on his name. The cult of Amida began in India, perhaps as early as the first century B.C., where it was introduced from the Iranian districts lying to the north, but it was unknown to the oldest literature of Buddhism written and preserved in the Pali and Sanskrit languages. Early Buddhism expressly repudiated salvation by others. Amida seems to have become one of the Buddha figures of Mahayana Buddhism although he was, so to speak, slipped in much later. His worship was introduced into China as a definite sect by Hui-Yuan (333-418). It was never formally introduced into Japan but became a part of every sect, and the Jodo and Shinshu sects made the most of it. Amida was most closely associated with the Pure Land sect (Jodo) but even more with the True Pure Land (Shinshu). In 1952 Shinshu was twice as popular as Shingon.

Genshin had recommended the endless repetition of the Amida Buddha's name without meditation, but Honen Shonin (1133-1212) was the real founder of the Jodo or Pure Land sect. In 1175 when he was forty-three he declared that the best way to obtain salvation (maybe the only way) was to strive to be reborn to the perfect bliss of the western Paradise. All that was needed to follow Shodo, for the holy path was a simple faith in Amida Buddha and a repetition of the formula, *namu amida butsu,* or "homage to Amida Buddha", a practice called by monks *nembutsu.* If a man repeats this formula at least ten times, Amida will appear to him at the hour of his death and personally conduct him to the Pure Land, which he will own as a Buddha in paradise where he will be certain of obtaining *nirvana*. As for the women in paradise, they will be reborn as men.

The sect was very successful and soon numbered hundreds of followers. Although of a placid disposition Honen had many enemies among the more established sects which made greater demands on their followers, but his sect survived and flourished, and as late as 1932 could boast more than sixteen million members. A dispute broke out among his followers as to whether "one calling" or "many callings" of the formula were necessary, and there are many tales of the devout, including even emperors who repeated the formula millions of times. Honen himself preferred many callings and is said to have repeated the formula 60,000 times a day.

The Japanese dearly love to subdivide sects, and that of the Pure Land was no exception. Honen's disciples alone were responsible for six subsects. The most famous of these, in the end more famous than Jodo, was that of his favorite disciple, Shinran, who in 1224 founded the Jodo Shinshu, the *"True* Pure Land" sect, mentioned above. Shinran, born in Kyoto in 1173 to a court noble who had descended from both the Fujiwara and Minamoto clans, insisted that a single sincere invocation of Amida Buddha was quite sufficient and that all repetitions merely amounted to praise which while devout were not necessary. That was one departure from Honen's Pure Land sect, which insisted on many repetitions; another was that in the Jodo Shinshu the priests could marry, and indeed as Shinrin insisted, *should* marry. He himself married a daughter of the regent Kanezane and had six children.

It is not difficult to see how the principle of obtaining salvation by the simple formula of pronouncing one single utterance of the Amida Buddha's name would appeal to people who had been weighted down with elaborate ritual performances and complicated theological systems. As it is a religion for the ordinary man whose intellect is not strained in the effort, its success is readily understandable. G. B. Sansom states that the Pure Land doctrines were so popular that they passed into the language of everyday speech. Thus *sammai* means whole-hearted effort, and *ojo* rebirth in paradise. Sansom writes that a man run over and killed by a railway train would be said to have experienced *kisha-ojo*, or "train salvation."

The worship of Amida Buddhism is far from the Buddhism of the Buddha. All prophets are betrayed in the end by the beliefs and practices of the religions which bear their names, and Buddhism was no exception. It must be remembered that before Buddhism in Japan was, like all Japanese imports, altered there, it had already been filtered through the Indian and Chinese cultures and also sometimes through the Korean.

It will not do to end the description of this period without a brief word for Nichiren (1222-1282). Born to a poor fisherman's family, with aristocratic forbears, on the eastern sea coast of Japan, he decided, after much study and meditation, that the *Lotus Sutra* upon which the earlier Tendai sect had been based was the only correct version of Buddhism. Accordingly he founded in 1253, the Hokke, or Lotus, sect. Unlike most Buddhist priests who were known for their tolerance, Nichiren was outstanding for his intolerance, attacking his rivals in the most ferocious terms, and of course making many enemies. He was twice saved from execution by miracles, it is said.

If a strong man fails in his endeavors he is said to have been stubborn; if he succeeds he is credited with great strength of character. Nichiren petitioned the emperor to outlaw the other sects, and as a result of his pains was himself banished several times, but he did have followers, and each times the decree of banishment was lifted to allow him to return. He was undoubtedly a disagreeable man, who would brook no difference of opinion and, absolutely sure of his own beliefs, he even condemned Saicho, who had founded the sect he found most congenial, and Honen, the most influential Buddhist of the day.

His was a stubborn, intractable nature, and he probably owed his success to the fact that he had successfully predicted a foreign invasion some years before the Mongols came for the first time (perhaps because he had been advised of it by Chinese priests of his acquaintance). Another, more lasting factor which contributed to his success was that he saw religion in national terms. He thought his version of Buddhism the only true one and believed that it ought to be established as the official religion of Japan; and his ambitions went even further, for he dreamed of a spread of worldwide Buddhism under Japanese leadership. This was a program sympathetic to the leaders of the time.

The Nichiren sect as late as 1931 had upwards of three million followers and may have contributed to that militant nationalism which led the Japanese people into the disaster of the second world war. But as late as 1952, the adherents of Nichiren still had some 1,704,000 members. The head temple of Nichiren is today Kuonji at Minobu, in Yamanashi Prefecture.

The last of the four Buddhist sects which were introduced at this period in Japanese history has been so important that I shall devote the whole of the next chapter to it.

Chapter XXXIV
Zen Buddhism

The most influential of all the Buddhists sects in the history of Japan is Zen, the Japanese name for *Ch'an*, which was the Chinese equivalent of *dhyana*. First imported into China from India by Bodhidharma, the twenty-eighth patriarch in the succession, who arrived at Canton in A.D. 520, Ch'an Buddhism was no doubt heavily influenced by Taoism, of which it may almost be said to be an adaptation were it not for the influence of Buddhism. It is known that Chinese Buddhists at the time studied Taoist texts. As Ch'an Buddhism developed it is possible to see in it the elements of both religions.

The Japanese seem most anxious to show that Zen has no foreign origins or counterparts, and yet how different is Zen from the Chinese Ch'an Buddhist school? Zen made its own way in Japan and had its own masters, but the chief of these as we shall see had studied in China. The fact is that all Japanese religious sects, other than Shinto, had their origins either in Indian religions which had been transformed in China or in native Chinese religions.

By the time of the Sung dynasty in China (960-1279), Ch'an

Buddhism was the only Buddhism that had survived the religious persecutions of 841-846, and consequently had a strong influence on Chinese culture, especially in philosophy and the arts. Another characteristic of the Sung period was a large increase in overseas trade, and this may be the reason for the arrival of Ch'an Buddhism in Japan in the twelfth and thirteenth centuries. There had been several earlier attempts to introduce it into Japan but they did not succeed. The Northern school of Buddhism in China insisted that enlightenment must come slowly, but in contrast Hui-Neng, the sixth patriarch of the Southern school, insisted that it comes suddenly when it comes at all. The difference was a large one, because sudden enlightenment makes institutional religion unnecessary by getting rid of all ritual and indeed of all learning.

The two Zen masters who succeeded in bringing Zen to Japan were Eisai in 1215 and Dogen in 1253. Eisai began his religious life in the monastery on Mount Hiei but made two trips to China to complete his studies and returned to Japan in 1191 as a Zen Master of the Rinzai school. He also introduced tea into Japan and urged that both Zen and tea were good for the Japanese, but met opposition from the established sects in Kyoto and so moved to Kamakura with support from the Hojo regents there. Because Zen was the kind of simple doctrine that the war-lords were looking for, he enjoyed the favor of the military leaders. Later when he returned to Kyoto to preach during his last years he was forced to give the teachings of the other schools a place in his program.

Under his tutelage the Rinzai school of Zen had developed a method of attaining sudden enlightenment by the use of the *koan*, which involved cryptic questions and blows, both intended to shock the student. Koan originally meant in Chinese *Kung-an*, the platform document, but it came to be used in Japan for a puzzling question or deliberately illogical statement put by a Zen master, such as "What is your original face, before you were born?" or a puzzling action, such as Hakuin's holding up one hand and asking, "What is the sound of one hand clapping?" It could also be a slap, a hit with a stick, or a kick.

The disciple, it was supposed, could be brought to the edge of sudden insight by substituting nonsense for sense, thus putting a strain on his mind. Enlightenment is understood as the instantaneous impact of a flash of feeling by means of which reality reveals itself in ordinary experiences. Zen is the art of the ordinary—the basis of its great appeal. By the use of some such technique as the *koan* a subject is shocked into grasping the immediate and total independence of the object, an empathetic feeling of how it is in itself, as a fair sample of how all things are.

In a lighter vein I report that my late Uncle Max was a Zen Buddhist of the Rinzai school (without knowing it, of course). As evidence I offer a sample conversation: "I think the stock of U.S. Steel is going up," he said. Later in the same conversation he suggested that the same stock was going down. When I faced him with the contradiction, he assumed a condescending air, and explained patiently, "That is what I was trying to tell you".

Eisai was easy-going but not so his successor Dogen whose determination and air of independence may have been due to his aristocratic origins; he could look back upon an emperor in his father's line and a Fujiwara prime minister in his mother's. Dogen also trained at first on Mount Hiei but did not find the pure religious spirit that he craved. Shortly before Eisai died, Dogen visited him and then followed his footsteps to China, where he sought the perfect Zen master in vain for years, but just when he was about to give up the search he met Ju-ching, from whom he obtained enlightenment.

Dogen thought that he was returning to the sources of pure Buddhism and that he himself was simply carrying on the Buddhism of the Buddha, and went back again and again to the Hinayana texts. He took issue with the suddenness of enlightenment advocated by Eisai and rejected the use of the *koan* to achieve it because he thought that method was directed too much toward obtaining something and was far too self-assertive.

The method preferred by Dogen was called *zazen*, or "sitting in meditation," without any thought of a particular goal or special problem, a discipline embracing the entire organism, both body and mind, including the moral as well as the intellectual, with no thought of an end apart from the means and looking toward gradual enlightenment.

The Zen enlightenment, called by Japanese scholars *satori*, is the same as *wu* (from the Chinese *wu nien*), the tranquillity to be achieved through the absence of thought, consisting in the serenity of the awareness of nothingness. When the mind has no content, it is believed by Zen Buddhists, it is the pure mind itself that is the subject of contemplation, and a direct experience of the essence of mind occurs. But unlike Eisai's version, which ended with enlightenment, Dogen believed it should issue in a fullness of living through productive labors. In the large monasteries which the success of Zen enabled the monks to build they were expected to arise early and do their share of farm labor as well as to beg food from neighboring houses in the morning.

Zen appeared in full strength for the first time long after the Hojo regency had abandoned formal relations with China, but when the success of the Mongolian conquests threatened Japan, it was necessary to have an intimate knowledge of China, and so Zen monks were chosen as advisers. Later when the third Ashikaga Shogun, Yoshimitsu (1358-1408), engaged in extensive foreign trade with the Ming dynasty, he felt it necessary to build a new Zen monastery, and to make the monks into almost a ministry of foreign affairs.

The influence of Zen soon spread beyond the domain of politics. The result was that it has meant much to every branch of Japanese culture, from the tea ceremony, flower arrangements, incense judging, landscape gardening, painting, the seventeen-syllable poem known as the *haiku*, to say nothing of the art of archery and the military arts. By its simplicity and its humble approach to the most ordinary activities, Zen early on gave new dignity to the most menial of pursuits, and therefore came to be valued highly by the medieval Japanese. Zen is also credited with the style and success of the *No* plays with their rhythmic posturing, and with the tableau of the popular drama of their poor relation, the *kabuki.*

Zen has done well in the arts and stimulated their production considerably. Perhaps the reason is that it must have an external focus; nothing in itself, it has no purely religious content, and must be looked at therefore through other interests. One of the best examples available to western readers is contained in Eugen Herrigel's *Zen in the Art of Archery* in which he shows how the study of archery in the hands of a Zen master can be made to reveal the essential meaning of Zen.

It was Seami (1363-1443) who transformed the No drama from a representational theater to a symbolic one. It was very evident, in his emphasis on the moments of "no-action" which are more stimulating to an audience than the course of the action, which is linked in this way by mindlessness, that he was influenced by Zen.

In archery, as in swordsmanship, and in painting, too, the element of Zen simply means that with practice the interval between effort and execution can be eliminated. The technique, according to Herrigel, consists in a kind of purposeless detachment operating as instinctive evasion. The subject becomes an almost passive agent in whose presence one object has an effect upon another, the bow on the arrow, the sword on the opponent, the brush on the canvas. In such objective efforts as originating works of art, Zen means concentrating on the immediate task as though the object had no other connections; and the artist is obliged in a final struggle to behave as though it had no connections with him either. Zen resembles the *sumiye* method of painting which must be executed in a single action, once and for all, without hesitation and without making any later changes. One Zen master advised a pupil who wanted to paint bamboos, to spend ten years observing bamboos, next to become a bamboo himself, and only then to paint bamboos.

Westerners familiar with philosophy will immediately think that they are looking at an eastern parallel of European idealism, and particularly at an example of Fichte's "ego" or of Husserl's "phenemenology." But this would be to miss the spirit of Zen, which is not a search for the *content* of consciousness but rather for the *discipline* of the conscious state. Looking inward according to Zen is quite different from taking up the viewpoint of German idealism. As Dogen explained, it means to forget yourself, to have the objective world prevail in you, for only when you look straight into yourself can you recognize that the objective world has a reality apart from you. German idealism is passive while Zen has its active side. The activity of German idealism is misleading, for it allows the idealist to suppose that no external changes are needed because the world already conforms to his conception of it, a disastrous point of view and one which results in the most brutal of awakenings. Zen, on the other hand, wishes to influence events without taking part in them, simply through the exercise of deliberate effort in which one external thing is compelled to affect another in the desired ways.

Where did the notion arise that the illogical is more vital than the logical? Given the achievements of applied logic and mathematics in the west, there would seem to be no truth to this claim. Zen was an illogical philosophy which, like that of Nichiren, led the Japanese militarists straight to national ruin in the second world war.

Zen is an idealistic philosophy (in the mental sense of idealism, not in the Platonic sense). Everyone entertains ideals, but the trouble with the absolute idealist is that he mistakes ideals for the external reality. He who believes that things are as he says they are, always suffers for it when he encounters facts to the contrary. This was the fate alike of Hitler's Germany and of Tojo's Japan. The idealist philosophy with all its limitations had deep roots in the irrationalism of Zen.

Two examples, both from the recent Zen master, D.T.Suzuki:

Zen, he declared, is a religion of love and mercy. A Zen swordsman, therefore, could never kill anyone. Only it happens sometimes that a victim presents himself and the sword does the rest. Clearly, from this argument, it would be possible to conclude that there is a point at which rationalization falls over into hypocrisy.

Another example: Suzuki quotes a Zen master to the effect that while logic requires that 'A is A', Zen would say instead that 'A is A' because 'A is not-A'. If we pursue this statement into Zen itself and Zen doctrine, then the denial of the value of Zen is as true as Zen, and so Zen could have no superior claim.

The social acceptance of Zen probably dates from the Ashikaga Shogunate, which ran from the middle of the fourteenth century to the sixteenth. It was a period shaken by widespread feudal wars. The Ashikaga Shoguns were not the rulers that the Hojo regents had been. They were enthusiastic patrons of Zen, though the self-discipline it calls for did not exactly govern their way of life. They lived in extreme luxury and extravagance. But for all others it was a period when Zen was reflected in every department of living. Everyone consulted the masters, not only emperors and statesmen but also literary men, artists, singers, merchants, swordsmen and wrestlers. They came to learn the mystic powers of Zen discipline because it was said to hold the key to the secrets of the universe.

We come to the inevitable question: just what is Zen?

The immediate answer of most practitioners is that Zen cannot be explained. They then proceed to give an explanation which is wholly irrelevant or to undertake an indirect explanation by stating what Zen is not. Suzuki was particularly good at this. It is not nihilistic, not illogical, and at the same time it is nothing in particular and also super-rational, he explained; but his profuse denials and superlatives are in the end not much help. As Sir Charles Eliot said, no one who has adopted Zen knows just what it is and none can tell the others. Unfortunately there is lots of room in it for fraud and fakery, and though it lends itself easily to charlatanism, and separating out the valid elements in it is especially difficult, there is something there. Perhaps the closest any outsider can get to Zen is through the understanding that it manages to combine cruelty with beauty in its effects, as for example in the combination of the swordsmanship displayed in the ceremonial execution of enemy aviators with the elaborate details of flower arrangements. That there is a common strain running through these activities that sets them apart from their opposite numbers in other countries there can be no question; if we can isolate it we shall have penetrated not only to the secret of Zen Buddhism but also to the essence of Japanese civilization.

The idea of enlightenment, called *satori* in Japanese, came from Buddha's original claim of sudden insight into the truth which came to him while he was sitting under the Bo-tree. But he announced quite clearly what that was. The Zen Buddhists have more trouble with it. Whether come at suddenly as Eisai insisted or more slowly as Dogen claimed, it is an insight.

And what is that insight? I should say that it is a counsel of how perfection may be obtained through a degree of concentration which makes it possible to rise above the temporal by arresting time, a kind of instantaneous representation of eternity, like the figures on the Grecian urn in Keats's ode.

Zen is essentially an encounter with nothingness, for that is what a moment by itself always is, and also a reconcilation with nothingness. In this respect it resembles the European philosophy of existentialism as propounded by the Dane, Kierkegaard, though of course there the resemblance ends. There are serious differences, but the basic similarity must be accounted for, and all dogmas eliminated. Zen is essentially a negative method, and can reach nothingness only by dispensing with the last and most recent something.

How much of the pure Buddhism of the Buddha is there left in Zen? Very little, I should say. There may be a remnant of Buddhism in the Zen reverence for existence without preference, expressed mutely by the absence of statement. But the roots of Zen penetrate deeply into later Buddhist thought, probably originating in Mahayanist doctrine, itself far from the Buddha's teaching, as for instance in the doctrine that while action is superior to inaction it must be disinterested action and not directed to any selfish end.

But the shadow of Buddhism lay across most if not all the religious endeavors of the day. That is perhaps why Dogen thought that Zen was a variety of Buddhism. It is on the whole difficult to see the connection, all but impossible to specify the development. Zen is an independent philosophy, owing much to Ch'an Buddhism perhaps, but still a uniquely Japanese religion.

Zen refuses to discriminate between scenario and scripture, and in the end will have nothing to do with either because it seeks to go beyond rational understanding. The description of nothing is not itself nothing, as anyone who has attended a Zen master will testify. Here we are on the dangerous ground involved in the metaphysics of being and non-being, as for instance Plato presented it. The Japanese characteristically will deal with metaphysics, however, only in practice, never as a set of abstractions, and that is perhaps why they always shy away from precise description.

The Japanese Zen masters are always eager to claim that Zen cannot be explained in words. And they would accept rather than reject that statement because they are always willing to embrace contradiction as though it were the very essence of Zen. In their resolute opposition to the use of abstract terms they are close to the position of Henri Bergson, for whom reality was always concrete, but like him they always seem willing and even eager to explain their opposition in the very abstract terms they so much deplore.

Suzuki manages to say a very great deal about what he has claimed cannot be said. But to argue that a doctrine cannot be expressed in words or otherwise reduced to reason does not mean that it is irrational but only that not enough is known to show that in a more inclusive system the inconsistencies would appear as consistent.

In an essay on the historical background of Zen Buddhism Suzuki went so far as to complain about the Buddhism of the Buddha. It was too simple, he said, there was nothing in the doctrines that would lead one to expect the development that later schools made of it. In other words, he considered the Buddhism of the later Buddhists to be a better Buddhism than the Buddhism of the Buddha himself. In particular the Zen masters offer a better Buddhism than Buddha did. Suzuki said that it was the "inner spiritual life of the Buddha himself rather than his exposition of it" that accounted for its success. But, one may ask, how could anyone ever know what that inner spiritual life was except the Buddha himself since his death in 483 B.C.? Suzuki applauded the process of deification which took place during the elaborations of his teachings by the Mahayana, which bore little or no resemblance to the original. The name Buddhism has been retained by Zen; everything else has been altered.

In the end it must be said that for the Zen Buddhist as for most oriental philosophers nothing seems worthy of investigation, because nothing is real, apart from the depths of consciousness and the self-consciousness of the knowing subject. Even a material object can be investigated only in this subjective way, cut loose so to speak from the knower, which still keeps the focus on him and his knowing. It is a way, incidentally, which stands in sharp contrast to the scientific method in the west, which is conducted on the assumption that spirit is a property of matter and that consciousness is always the awareness of something material by something material.

If my reader will take the trouble to look back in this book briefly at the Buddhism of the Buddha on p. 54, at the chief principles of the Tao on p. 146, and finally at Ch'an Buddhism on p. 177, and then read again my explanation of Zen, he will be a party to an approach to reality not native to western civilization but certainly not trivial, and profound in an altogether different way from what the history of western philosophy has accustomed him to. There is a line of development on exhibit here; it is an authentic aspect of reality which we ought not to ignore despite its difficulties and its often crude and distasteful details. Zen Buddhism after all has managed to survive the disastrous military and political defeats suffered by the Japanese nation in the second world war. Of the eleven Buddhists sects in Japan in 1952, with a total of 72,918 temples and 20,466,700 adherents, Zen alone could account for 20,839 temples and 3,361,500 adherents, far more than any of the others except Shin-shu.

Chapter XXXV
Shinto

The Shinto religion was the only native Japanese religion. The practice of Shinto survived through centuries of neglect as Ryobu Shinto when it was almost absorbed into Buddhism. The Shinto priests collaborated in the identification of Buddhist gods with native divinities, thinking, for instance, of Dainichi, the primordial and eternal Buddha, as Amaterasu, the sun goddess. There were throughout Japanese history, in every village and in every scenic spot, Shinto shrines attended by lay priests on festive occasions when they were the center of recreational activities and tournaments.

It is possible that Shinto might not have survived in a climate in which Buddhism was so overwhelmingly successful, had it not been for the compromises that were made by declaring that the Buddhist gods were indestructible while the Shinto gods were their temporary appearances or reincarnations. In this way Shinto fitted into the general picture which remained largely Buddhist. According to Ichijo Kanera (1402-1481) the various Shinto gods were in reality only the one god as seen in his various activities.

The revival of Shinto came as the result of the political revolution which was the response to challenges from western powers. It contained strong Confucian elements but relied heavily upon national character and above all on national history. It was probably Kada Azumamaro (1669-1736), a lay priest at the Inari Shrine in Kyoto, who moved to petition a Tokugawa for the support of a study of Japan's ancient literature which he called "The National Learning", that sparked the revival of what came to be called "Pure Shinto." The pioneer, Motoori Norinaga (1730-1801), revived the study of that ancient document the *Kojiki* and worked for thirty years to establish it as the Bible of the movement. He defended its highly improbable tales on the grounds that the behavior of gods and goddesses lay beyond human understanding. He also went back to the literary classics for which he claimed a high position; not only to the *Tale of Genji* of Lady Murasaki, for which he claimed a closeness to the "sensitivy of things", but also to the *New Collection of Ancient and Modern Poetry* (the Shinkokinshu) made in 1205. He wished the *Tale of Genji* to be the scripture of the National Learning movement.

Despite its difficulties and disorganization, the *Kojiki* was the basis of Motoori's claim of a primitive kind of purity for early Japanese life, which he said represented the best of all humanity from the divine ages. His ideal was the dwelling of the gods from whom the Japanese claimed to have descended. Motoori's work was continued by a disciple who never met him but continued his religious revival, Hirata Atsutane (1776-1843). His vehicle was Shinto, and he wished it to be considered supreme, asserting its supremacy not only over the other two religions but actually over all other forms of knowledge which it was to include. According to Hirata the creator of the universe lived near the Pole Star and directed the other deities who worked for the good of mankind. Japan, he said, lay the nearest to this star and therefore had no need to formulate its morality or codify its laws, for its people always retained the divine purity in their hearts, and quite naturally were inclined to live according to the Way of the Gods. Since the emperors had always been said to have descended from the sun goddess, these ideas were perfectly consistent with the authority of the throne.

Shinto had never entirely disappeared in all the centuries of Japanese history; for a long time it had survived in mountain fastnesses whence priests who had preserved the tradition emerged to affirm their existence only in times of troubles when nothing more organized held sway. When the Tokugawa Shogunate looked as though it would fail Shinto priests began to appear again in public and so constituted a source of religious strength which could always be drawn on.

To look ahead of our story a little, the Meiji Restoration, which lasted from 1868 to 1912, was conducted by a man and his advisers who sought to modernize and liberalize the government. The reorganization of political Japan meant the end of the semi-independent fiefs and provinces and the centralization of authority under the throne and the state. In 1877 the wearing of swords was made illegal and loyalty was henceforth due only to the emperor. The restoration of imperial rule was conducted under favorable auspices, for the choice of emperor fell upon a man who could not have been better suited to the tasks which lay ahead. It was Japan's answer to the demand to "enrich the nation and strengthen its arms."

The Meiji leadership undertook to reconcile two quite different forces; they wanted to try new methods but they also wished to preserve the ancient ideals: on the one side a readiness to change when something suggested in the west offered an improvement, and on the other a tenacious nationalism inherited from Tokugawa times. Toward the latter goal, a reconstituted Shintoism seemed the perfect vehicle, and was accordingly made into a nationalistic cult centered upon the God-Emperor, with the help of Neo-Confucian ethics which was incorporated in the new form of the old faith—a modern chief of state who could claim the authority, so familiar for centuries in China, of the sage-king. The Meiji leadership in this way brought Japan out of its feudal condition and into the modern world, but at the price of an increased militarism which in the second world war was to be its undoing.

The most surprising development was the distinction between state Shinto and sect Shinto. State Shinto as taught in the schools was, they said, "no religion." In the 1930s with the rising military caste more and more in control, state Shinto was thought to be a justification that the generals could use. The book required in all teacher training courses was the *Kokutai no Hongi (Cardinal Principles of the National Entity)* which taught the traditional myths, the legends of the imperial ancestors, the saints of Shinto and the holiness of the national shrines. It recited the history of Japan from the age of the gods, and it included the worship of the emperor. It was supported and regulated by the government. Though it had a high social value and was a comfort to those whose relatives died in battle, it was of no use to a family in which a member had met with, say, an accidental death. It was a national morality, not a private faith. There were over 110,000 state shrines, from the Ise Shrine, the temple of the sun goddess, to the small local shrines; sect Shinto was on a par with Buddhism and Confucianism and was the concern of the Bureau of Religion.

Sect Shinto included those claiming to be "Pure Shinto" because they continued the ancient doctrine in its purest form; the "Mountain Sects," some of which were based on Mount Fuji and also on Mount On-take; the "Purification Sects" which could get rid of sickness and cure moral evil; and the "Faith Healing Sects."

After the American occupation the Shinto religion was disestablished and the Emperor made a broadcast renouncing the divinity which had always been attributed to him. In 1945 because of its militaristic and nationalistic bent, in conformity with the demands of the American occupation, official support for state Shinto was abolished, but its shrines were all supported by their lay followers. As of December 1949, however, there were 87,802 shrines belonging to state Shinto and priests to the number of 14,874. Of sect Shinto at that time there were 160 different varieties.

More recently there has been an effort to reconstitute the importance of Shinto as a deliberate undertaking. Since the defeat of the Japanese in the second world war, as we shall see, Shinto has been a way of seeking a national unity through outward observance without the support of a fundamental belief. In 1973 for example the Grand Shrine of Ise was rededicated; there are now Shinto shrines on the rooftops of department stores, one even on the roof of Tokyo's airport. Shinto penetrates to every corner of Japanese life, but it is a curious religion indeed, and from the point of view of philosophy a most significant one.

Chapter XXXVI
Confucianism

It is time to leave the history of Shinto, which we have followed into modern times, and return to conditions as they were at the outset of the seventeenth century. Medieval Japan, which can be said to have lasted from the twelfth through the sixteenth centuries, was notable chiefly for internal wars. More than sixty feudal houses which struggled with arms for supremacy were reduced in the first half of the sixteenth century to a few powerful families. Finally, three generals divided the country among them; of these one was victorious, so that Japan was suddenly and unexpectedly united. The remnants of feudalism did not vanish overnight, but there were certain clear developments, one of the most important being the supplanting of Buddhism by a new rational version of Confucianism. The teachings of Confucius in the seventeenth century once again dominated Japan.

Broadly speaking, Buddhism was a philosophy for the individual, Confucianism a philosophy for society. The former may be characterized as psychological, the latter ethical. Confucius, like Buddha, had a strong influence on Japanese culture. Confucianism, like Shinto, had its ups and downs. Although Prince Shotoku (573-621) was an ardent Buddhist, it must be remembered that he turned to Confucian models when he introduced his seventeen-article Constitution. The subsequent reform movement which began in 645 was Confucian.

For a long time the work of Confucius was incorporated with that of Buddha and Shinto, and was not particularly powerful in its own right. The leader of the movement to break with the diluted Confucianism of the Japanese past and return to the sources of Confucianism was Ito Jinsai (1627-1705), who followed the example of Confucius in rejecting the offers of administrative posts in order to confine his efforts to teaching. The school which he founded with his son was devoted to the study of the *Analects* and of Mencius. He was in search of universal human values rather than a narrow nationalism. He thought that the universe in all three of its divisions, heaven, earth and mankind, was characterized by the same vital force; it had a dynamic character. The individual could fulfill himself to the utmost and by developing the life force within him achieve his greatest manhood. The virtue of humanity, he held, was love, by which he meant the four virtues: loyalty, good faith, reverence and forgiveness.

But this gentle and individual approach was soon to change. It was during the Tokugawa Shogunate at the beginning of the seventeenth century that a settled social order rather than a settled state of mind became the ideal. No wonder then that officials looked to a Confucian revival for help. The result was that neo-Confucianism joined with Shinto in sparking a vigorous nationalism which rejected Chinese influences and looked only to Japanese models.

The Japanese who have always shied away from metaphysics and indeed from all abstract speculation, were only concerned with that part of the Confucianism system of philosophy which had to do with social matters, in a word, with ethics and history. Moreover, these were not adopted exactly as the Chinese had left them but adapted to Japanese institutions. Accordingly we find a new conception of the role of the samurai and a reinterpretation of Japanese history. As a result of that fact the tradition of the samurai has proved unusually vigorous and enduring, especially in court and military circles, which were always the dominant feature of Japanese society. It may have been given the first turn in this direction by Muso Soseki (1275-1351), the "national master," who served on request as the spiritual mentor of Ashikaga Takauji, the new shogun, who built an impressive monastery for him. But it was continued centuries later as the movement known as *bushido*, "the way of the *samurai* (warrior)." It embraced ideas of the soldier's duty as far back as the days of the Fujiwara domination from the end of the eighth to the middle of the tenth centuries, and it embraced neo-Confucian elements, but the guiding idea was the self-discipline demanded by Zen. *Bushido* was formalized in the seventeenth century by Yamaga Soko (1622-1685), who had special ideas about the devotion to duty of the warrior in peace time, and who wrote a series of works dealing with the warrior's creed (*bukyo*) and the way of the samurai *(shido)*, thus providing a basis for the military traditions which dominated feudal Japan.

The role of the samurai in peace-time according to Yamaga was to embody the Japanese ideal. By living a life of austerity and temperance, by his willingness to die at any time, by discharging his loyal service to his master, by his fidelity to his friends, by considering his own station in life and devoting himself to duty, he fulfilled the lofty mission of the warrior class and set an example for everyone to admire if not to follow. But the samurai was not to be taught merely the arts of war, he was to be familiar with the fine arts and with humanistic studies in the Confucian tradition. Indeed Yamaga held up the teaching of Confucius as the standard to which everyone should refer.

The Confucian who turned the studies of his school away from the individualism of Chu Hsi which Ito Jinsai had promoted to the social emphasis of Hsun Tzu was named Ogyu Sorai (1666-1728). Confucius' ethics was the absolute truth, Ogyu believed, and his support for it was perfectly consistent with the rising awareness of the Japanese that they had a national culture. Ogyu saw Confucius as a man who had devised a practical way to meet social problems, not as one who had imposed an order from outside society. Confucius' approach, which included such immediate affairs as law enforcement and political administration, was what might be expected from one who was internally a sage and externally a king. It is no wonder that he had looked back to the early kings for his model, for that is how he found out what was in conformity with nature.

Accordingly Ogyu gave to the Japanese morality of the seventeenth century an institutional turn. Man's individual nature, inherently evil, can be curbed only by a vigorous appeal to social institutions. His utilitarian thinking featured political administration among social institutions, The eighth Tokugawa Shogun, Yoshimune, was greatly impressed and offered Ogyu a role in government, which his untimely death foreclosed.

Chu Hsi was not without a defender in the later philosophy of Muro Kyuso (1658-1734) who though he had no ideas of his own, saw that the older doctrine could have its Japanese uses. The Tokugawa were very pleased with him for what they rightly considered his support of the government. All individuals, according to his Chinese mentors, owed it their allegiance.

Chapter XXXVII
Empiricism

It would be fair to argue that my account of the religions and philosophies of Japan was over with the description of Shinto and Zen. Shinto was an entirely native product, while Zen, although Indian and Chinese in origin, was changed sufficiently to make it Japanese, but Confucianism was not altered to that extent, and as we are about to see, neither was the scientific empiricism of the west, which in Japan was altered little.

Science, which by now has transformed every large country in the world except India, did not reach Japan like lightning out of a clear sky. It came slowly, and did not replace the Japanese religions when it did come, but merely moved them over to make room for itself. The method of science, called "empiricism," is the search for the laws of nature by means of objective experimental techniques. (In the west empiricism means one thing to the scientists but quite another to the philosophers for whom it took a more subjective turn, referring chiefly to the sense perceptions of the individual.) In Japan empiricism was preceded by a simple respect for reason and fact. Consider for example the work of Seki Kowa (1642-

1708), who already in the seventeenth century independently discovered the integral and differential calculus of Newton and Leibniz (each of whom discovered it independently also). Applied mathematics was certainly stimulated by the need for it in calendar reform, trade and navigation, and schools to promote it were quickly organized.

Another to feel the effects of empiricism was Arai Hakuseki (1657-1725), an adviser to the ruling Tokugawa, who accomplished many practical feats, such as systematizing the basic law of the Shogunate, stabilizing the currency, establishing an accounting and budgetary procedure, and regulating the trade with China to ensure a favorable balance—all that in his six years in office. When the death of his master and the installation of a reactionary ruler ended his power, he retreated to scholarship and wrote in many fields, among them language, archaeology, geography, and history. It is particularly in his remarks about history that Arai's empiricism comes to the fore. He was well aware that the two great chronicles, the *Kojiki* and the *Nihongi*, were not reliable, and contained only accounts of events of a miraculous nature. The true history of Japan, he declared, had never been written; there were no books which gave a critical examination of actual events, and all that existed was only "an account of dreams told in a dream." What he proposed to do, then, was to write a history which would serve as a reliable record—a plan made in his old age, which he never lived to complete. But that he understood the need is very pertinent to our purpose, for he saw it in terms of reason and fact.

The application of the method of historical criticism was applied to religion by Tominaga Nakamoto (1715-1746). In one of his books the *Testament of an Old Man* (Tominaga died when he was thirty-one), he attacked the Buddhist sects and was of course attacked by them. There were at the time thirteen such sects, with a total of sixty-three subsects operating throughout Japan. The many splits, Tominaga said, were caused by followers who invoked the authority of the founder to push beyond the others and so to make names for themselves. This was true but sure to be taken badly, as indeed it was.

Tominaga's empirical criticism of historical religions suggests that of Spinoza, who made the first such criticism in the western tradition. Tominaga pointed out that religions were organized by mortal men, that they were related to the stage of the culture in which the work was done, and that they fell into different classifications according as they were mere assertions, broad generalizations contradictory in nature, reversions to earlier themes, or transformations and modifications. Sounding like a twentieth century agnostic, Tominaga cut through what he regarded as the shortcomings of the traditional religions with a criticism which relied only upon a reasonable examination of the facts. As to Shinto, he said that it was the way in which the medieval Japanese had dressed up ancient traditions in order to construct a national religion to compete successfully with Buddhism and Confucianism. Buddhism was mostly magic, Confucianism mostly rhetoric. Consider the Chinese sage for example. In the tradition he began by being merely an unusually intelligent man, but he was developed into the highest type of humanity and finally credited even with working miracles.

Tominaga's final effort in the religious direction was to try to synthesize the three most powerful religions in Japan: Shinto, Buddhism and Confucianism. He wished in this way to design a kind of ethical culture which had no need of supernatural elements and would serve as what he termed "the religion of true fact."

It was Miura Baien (1723-1789) who took the next step toward confining knowledge to what could be verified. The son of a village physician who carried on his father's profession, he was known far beyond his native village for his scholarship and his championing of the new empiricism (though of course it was not known then by that name). He stated that nature is the only proper object of investigation, and he considered man a part of nature, which is objective, but that man mistakenly thinks of all the things that he studies in terms of himself; he must get rid of this smug sense of his own importance, which can produce only illusions, for reliable knowledge can come, not from the study of books but only from the study of nature, which must be undertaken by means of a series of hypotheses, one after the other being tried until one is found to fit.

The same empirical approach which Miura had used in the study of nature, Kaiho Seiryo (1755-1817) applied to the study of human society. Kaiho spent most of his life traveling and observing, never married, and lived frugally, talking with farmers and shopkeepers, and reaching the conclusion that society rests on the production and exchange of goods. He was a hundred years ahead of Marx and lacked the spectacle of the early factory system from which Marx drew his conclusions. Yet Kaiho thought that everything could be viewed as a commodity: rice fields, the sea, gold; moreover everyone must be productive. Buddhist priests and Confucian scholars constituted a class which could be eliminated, and warriors could be retained so long as they were regarded as human merchandise which had been sold to feudal lords.

It is most interesting that he thought in terms of the rule of law rather than the rule of men, of established laws which the ruler himself would be obliged to obey. About legal codes, he said that there should be a minimum of statutes with a maximum of enforcement.

Chapter XXXVIII
The Nineteenth Century

The eighteenth century had seen the beginnings of reason and fact in the intellectual life of Japan. A sort of native empiricism was discovered and carefully cultivated, though not of course without meeting opposition. The nineteenth century saw the development of this movement in four directions: the rise of an intense nationalism which took form in a search for national identity, the restoration of the monarchy, the introduction of parliamentary democracy, and an eagerness to learn about western culture generally.

The leading advocate of a native Japanese culture was, as we have already noted, Hirata Atsutane (1776-1843). Sato Nobuhiro (1769-1850) another nationalistic figure, wished to see to the economic improvement of Japan in order to save its people from poverty, but he was more concerned to encourage the expansion of her military power to enable her to resist the visiting naval vessels of the western powers. This was in a sense prophetic for, three years after his death, Commodore Perry of the United States Navy arrived at Uraga Bay not far from the Shogun capital and demanded that Japan be opened up to foreign trade. The shogun reluctantly agreed to permit two open ports, an unpopular decision throughout Japan which did much to hasten the fall of the shogunate.

Kido Koin (1833-1877) who did as much as anyone to lead the coalition of forces which overthrew the last Tokugawa shogun, saw that if the new government of the emperor replaced that of the shogun and if he was to rule in fact as well as in name, the old feudal system would have to be abolished.

In 1868 the last of the Tokugawa clan was finally defeated and the young Emperor Meiji was enthroned, thus ending the long history of dual rule. The Meiji Restoration, as it came to be called, was an affair of moderation and a novelty though it came in the name of the old order. With the help of the Neo-Shinto movement, and with the support of an ethics borrowed from Confucianism, nationalism grew quickly into a cult centered upon the God-Emperor which received the enthusiastic support of a willing people. Meiji was promoted as the latest example of the Chinese type of sage-king, destined to bring Japan out of its feudal past and into the modern world. His long reign, which lasted until 1912, was as enlightened and progressive as had been expected and indeed as was required if Japan was to learn about western institutions and adapt them to native needs.

The Charter Oath of 1868 supported the progressive side of the new emperor's reign by calling for deliberative assemblies, while the Constitution of that same year in addition to reaffirming the Charter Oath introduced a separation of executive and legislative powers. It also required public balloting for all officials and for limiting their terms of service to four years. The tax base was to be broadened as well as strengthened, and there was to be a uniformity of laws throughout the land.

One thing that had not changed very much was the popularity of Buddhism. According to the census of 1891 Japan had about 40 million inhabitants, of whom more than 30 million were Buddhists. The Shin-shu sect alone claimed 10 million, with 19,208 temples, 11,958 preachers, 10 chief priests and 3,593 students.

The increasing demands for western trade grew in strength and frequency and finally could not be denied. The Japanese, having looked to Asia for more than twelve hundred years, now in the nineteenth century wheeled about to face Europe and America in what must have been, culturally speaking, too sharp a turn-around. But the mysticism of the east could not compete successfully with the artifacts of the west, and the products of applied science and technology had an appeal which proved too strong to resist. And so Japan succumbed to scientific industrialism, though in her unique way complete with Shinto shrines and Buddhist stupas. But the nation was paralyzed by the suddenness of the 180-degree turn, shocked, so to speak, into cultural silence, so that as a result nothing original has been produced in the islands: no fresh insight, no powerful, innovative philosophy, in a word, no new and important contribution to culture.

Given the possibilities and limitations of a particular environment, there are so many directions a culture could take that one can only say that the way it did develop was remarkable. That the Japanese have been able to adopt the scientific-industrial enterprise, and to live the life of a modern technological culture as eagerly and as completely as they had once embraced Buddhism, proves not only their adaptability but also the fact that all individuals are culturally determined to an extent that we do not ordinarily admit.

Chapter XXXIX
Recent Philosophy

The story of twentieth century Japan is the story of the attempt to adopt western ways, and this applies to everything in the culture from motor cars to baseball. Japan is conforming to the scientific-industrial culture while at the same time trying to retain something of its ancient traditions and folkways. The result is a mixture; the business man who in the daytime wears the same suits as his opposite number in New York or London but who on returning home in the evening resumes Japanese dress. This attempt to manage the best of both worlds runs all through the society.

The fate of philosophy is no different. We have seen that the old religions still flourish mightily, but at the same time in the universities there has been an undertaking to develop native philosophies of the European and American varieties. These have been on the whole rather weak and inadequate. The physical sciences have fared much better.

Japan in the nineteenth century has developed its positivists, its German idealists, its pragmatists, even its Marxists and Wittgensteins. Here unfortunately the ability of the Japanese to successfully adopt western culture reached a dead end; they have failed to produce a powerful philosophy of the western type. The only man to score even a moderate success in the attempt to develop an original philosophy along western lines was Nishida Kitaro (1870-1945), who undertook a combination of eastern and western ideas which on the whole can only be said to be unsuccessful. He began with what he called a "logic of place" which he meant to stand to oriental philosophy as Greek logic stood to western culture. The chief category of the logic of place is "nothingness" or the void. (Suzuki said that the only way to prepare to understand Nishida's thought was to learn Zen Buddhism, but then Suzuki thought that of everything.)

Nishida began with "pure experience" or the direct awareness of things as they are without excluding from the process the contribution of thought itself, a kind of Kantian version of realism, impossible on the face of it. Reality as it turns out is a self-conscious affair, and even from nothing something can be experienced. But all ways of looking at things are partial and only the whole is real (as Hegel had said). Different stages of consciousness are capable of grasping different personifications, for all things are animate in some sense.

Will and knowledge, he claimed, are really not separate; hence knowledge and action are accounted for in a single operation. But will and matter are different because the will is not material but spiritual, it is free because of the myriad of alternatives open to it. As it represents the deepest stratum underyling all of our actions, it is the unifying element in all experience. The debt to James here is an obvious one.

The many other books Nishida wrote after *A Study of Good*, which contains the above theories, are more or less limited to elaborating the themes stated in this first book. His entire output may be characterized as a variety of that psychological philosophy which was elaborated in Europe and America by the philosophers of the time, everyone in fact from

Mill to Bergson and from Kant to James. It is difficult to see just what the oriental contribution to his system of thought is, when even the concept of nothingness can be traced to Kierkegaard.

There is no need to follow further the fortunes of Japanese philosophy. After Nishida and the American occupation the Japanese turned more and more to the west, studying and being influenced in large measure by European and American philosophy with no marked changes such as those that characterized her importation and alteration of Indian and Chinese religions.

Chapter XL
Some General Observations on Japanese Philosophy

We have come to the end of our brief account on Japanese culture. As usual the key to it was contained chiefly in religion and philosophy. We have to ask ourselves, what does Japanese philosophy, looked at from the western perspective, add up to? The first impression is that there is less there than meets the mind, but then it was not designed as an explanation of existence, a demand which western religions, with their theologies, and western philosophies without religions, aim to supply. Both Shinto and Shin-shu, the two largest Buddhist sects and the largest religious bodies in Japan, have one thing in common: they are simple and therefore they make little demands on their adherents. No need to learn a complex theology, no need to engage in elaborate rituals. In both sects conformity is designed to make things easy for the layman.

There can be little doubt that throughout the world of civilized nations science, with its accompaniments of applied science and technology, has destroyed the old organized religions, perhaps by demonstrating that it can do better what the religions claimed to do but could not do at all. Praying for rain is not as effective as seeding clouds with dry ice; invoking

284

the help of the gods in obtaining the fertility of crops and of women does not work as well as scientific agriculture and the new fertility pills. Healing the sick by religious means has been replaced by inoculations to prevent illnesses. The list is endless, and if many people retain their religious affiliations it is too often on other than rational grounds.

What is true of other countries in this regard is no less true of Japan. The Japanese always have been master adopters and adapters. What they achieved in transforming Indian religions and Chinese ethics to their own needs, they have more recently achieved in transforming western science and technology. Thus while family shrines continue to exist, while there may still be in the home a *butsudan*, a simple family-sized "Altar of the Buddhas," and even a kitchen god, a *Koojin-sama*, or a *kamidana*, a "god-shelf" or wooden box containing a paper inscribed with the name of the *kami* of the shrine, the belief in their efficacy is not what it was formerly; many have given up such observances. In the days of the Toyota motor car and the Sony television set, Shinto and Buddhism still exist. But perhaps after all that is no more incongruous than a Roman Catholic or an Orthodox Jew working on the Chevrolet assembly line.

Behind the observances, Shinto and Buddhist, there still stand the shadows of that primitive set of nature beliefs at the head of which is the figure of the Emperor Hirohito, the 124th in line of succession from the sun-goddess Amaterasu-Omikami, (the Great-heaven-Shining-Goddess) still worshipped at the Daijingu Shrines at Uji-Yamada. He is still in the list of gods and heroes representing nature.

The question of just what constitutes Japanese culture becomes more pressing when we remember how much the Japanese have borrowed from other cultures. All cultures borrow, but the extent of the Japanese borrowing renders it unique. What we are faced with, then, are two questions rather than one: first, why the immense borrowing? And second, what do the borrowings have in common and what does that tell us about the culture?

Why the immense borrowing? Remember that a people of Asian stock, probably acting under the pressure of excess population, suddenly found themselves confronted by a primitive native population, the Ainu. The Japanese certainly came from the Asian mainland, and their taking off place was Korea. They had to fight their way onto the islands and after that fought there intermittently until the Ainu were driven north to Hakkido and finally subdued. This left the Japanese little time for cultural pursuits; all their efforts were devoted to survival.

But once the struggle was over and the battles with the Ainu ended, the Japanese found themselves with a country without a culture. They had left the mainland without one; what could be more natural than to send back for it? The Buddhist priests and Confucian scholars, who, we recall, brought more than religious ideas with them, more even than the knowledge of how to found Buddhist monasteries and how to run Confucian societies: they brought the knowledge of a language, the arts and literature, and such technological information as how to build roads, install water systems, plan agricultural cycles and irrigate fields.

The culture of India rested on the twin pillars of Hinduism and Buddhism. The culture of China rested chiefly on Confucianism and Taoism. The Buddhist leader, Kukai, in 791 wrote a book whose title indicated that it was about three religions: Buddhism, Confucianism and Taoism. But there were four, and we must ask ourselves why Hinduism was not included.

There are two possible reasons. The first is that Japan received all its influences from China. Such Indian religions as reached it came through China, and it was Buddhism, not Hinduism, that penetrated from India into China. There simply was no Hinduism in China which could have drifted up through Korea and so over to Japan.

The second reason is that the Japanese were faced with an

immediately practical situation: how to establish a culture in a strange land. No people can survive very long without fundamental beliefs, but in the case of Japan they were both fundamental and immediately applicable. Now Hinduism, with its transcendental and metaphysical concerns, does not quickly respond to such a challenge; it may meet the first requirement perhaps but not the second. The Japanese wanted to know about the nature of things—that in fact is what is meant by fundamental beliefs—but they wanted to know about the nature of things *here and now*. They wanted a religion which was concerned with facts, not with universal truths. Such a universal philosophy as the Nyaya Vaisheshika of the Indians would have had no relevance for the Japanese even if it had reached those islands, but it did not travel even as far as China.

The Japanese religions and philosophies did have such relevance. Shinto was a religion of pantheism, of native gods whose habitat was purely local, gods who could be found in the neighborhood and propitiated immediately. Zen Buddhism, the most notably original adaptation of a Chinese variety of Buddhism, resembled Shinto at least in the respects that it was local and that its effects could be turned to improvement in the treatment of the tasks in hand.

The Japanese religious peculiarity, then, might be described as *the mysticism of the mind confronted by the here and now*.

Here may be the answer to our second question. *The mysticism of the mind confronted by the here and now* was employed as a guide to govern the selection of imports. Thus the Japanese imported what they needed and made of it what they could to meet the problems they had to meet without delay. This may be the key not only to their borrowings but also to the alterations they made in them. The religion of the present, the philosophy of the present, the culture generally of the present: these are the elements which probably account for their readiness to wheel and face in a new direction on what is, for a culture at least, very short notice. It explains why they could so quickly substitute the influences of Europe and the United States for their ancient sources on the Asiatic mainland.

Nations get set on a course for basic reasons, but they tend to continue on that course long after the original reasons are no longer valid. Preoccupation with the present must leave a nation at the mercy of future contingencies. It makes planning impossible.

Expediency can never be raised to the level of national policy over a long period of time. To survive as an independent nation they will have to find their way out of temporizing policy, which can be done only through the discovery of a more extended philosophy.

Empiricism has been the policy of the west and is now in danger of being changed. With the whole world, so to speak, at the crossroads, Japan has an excellent opportunity to re-evaluate its position and to look for a more effective substitute for expediency. Everyone regards the economic transformation of Japan as a latter-day miracle, and so it has been. But now still another miracle is called for, to bring with it a firmer basis of stability.

Some Thoughts in Conclusion

My interest is chiefly in the differences between east and west. The first is the attitude in both camps with respect to the prospects of personal immortality. The Judeo-Christian is afraid the soul is *not* immortal but wants it to be. The Hindu-Buddhist is afraid that the soul *is* immortal and wants it *not* to be. Each advises taking the appropriate steps to reach exactly opposite goals.

Another difference: The oriental wants to lose himself in the universe, to embrace non-being by forgetting what he knows. The westerner on the other hand wants to enlarge himself by increasing what he knows. This vast difference in approach has different consequences.

The aim of the oriental is to follow the avenue of sense experience backward, as it were, to reach the starting-point of consciousness. He wants to be conscious only of consciousness itself because he believes that at its core lies the essence of true being. If he can reach that essence, which he believes never changes, then he can remain eternally at one with it and need never die.

The westerner believes that the greater the number of his encounters with the environment the richer he will be; for every thought, feeling and action which is externally caused will bring him in touch with a wider world, and he thinks he can survive in that world by becoming one with it.

Thus the way of the west is a mirror image of the way of the east; the eastern quest is inward-bound, the western outward-bound. The easterner pursues consciousness for its value without content, the westerner is convinced that its content *is* its value, and knowing that such content comes from the external world, concentrates on examining the world, endeavoring to experience always more of it and even to change it in order to intensify experience. The westerner seeks to control his environment, the easterner to control himself. No doubt the greatest achievements through the millennia have been eastern religions and western science.

Yet there are also broad similarities which cannot be overlooked. We have seen a few of the differences between east and west, but the east is a large area, and the basic similarities between India, China and Japan have often been noted. With a few changes, the writings of the Taoists could have been those of the Buddhists, while the Japanese Zen were frankly influenced by both. How is one to explain the more or less simultaneous appearance of Buddha, Confucius, Zoroaster and Socrates, all in the sixth to fifth centuries B.C.?

We are far from understanding the world movements which sweep over peoples, engulfing them in scores of impossible beliefs and leading them into all sorts of outrageous behavior, from individuals setting themselves on fire in a holy cause to whole societies engaging in wars with those whose beliefs are not the same. The hope is that this book may provide some of the evidence to illuminate the wide-ranging nature of human behavior.

Acknowledgements

My debt to the orientalists of east and west, both scholars and translators, is so great that to name them all would require another book at least as long. The titles listed in the following pages I found particularly helpful, though they were by no means the only ones. I should add that I owe a special thanks to Mr. Ben Raeburn for many helpful suggestions and improvements.

Suggestions for Further Study

India

Hirayanna, M., *Outlines of Indian Philosophy* (London 1932, George Allen and Unwin).

Jennings, J.G., *The Vedantic Buddhism of the Buddha* (London 1948, Oxford University Press).

Muller, F. Max, (trans.), *Upanishads*, 2 vols. (Delhi 1969, Motilal Banarsidass).

———, (trans.), *Vedic Hymns*, 2 vols. (Delhi 1973, Motilal Banarsidass).

Radhakrishnan, S., *Indian Philosophy*, 2 vols. (London 1948, George Allen and Unwin).

——— (ed.), *History of Philosophy Eastern and Western*, 2 vols. (London 1952, George Allen and Unwin).

Rapson, E.J., (ed.), *The Cambridge History of India*, vol. I New York 1922, Macmillan).

Sen, K.M., *Hinduism* (Baltimore 1973, Penguin Books).

Thomas, Edward J., *The History of Buddhist Thought* (London 1933, Kegan Paul, Trench, Trubner and Co.).

Wheeler, Sir Mortimer, *India and Pakistan* (London 1959, Thames and Hudson).

Zaehner, R.C., *Hinduism* (New York 1966, Oxford University Press).

China

Confucius, *The Confucian Analects,* trans. by William Jennings (London 1895, George Routledge and Sons).

———, *Analects of Confucius,* trans. by William E. Soothill (New York 1968, Paragon).

Creel, H. G., *Chinese Thought: From Confucius to Mao Tse-tung* (Chicago 1953, University Press).

Fung Yu-lan, *A History of Chinese Philosophy* (Princeton 1952, University Press). 2 vols.

Gallagher, L. J., (trans.), *China in the Sixteenth Century:* The Journals of Matthew Ricci (New York 1953, Random House).

Galston, Arthur W., with Savage, Jean S., *Daily Life in People's China* (New York 1975, Washington Square Press).

Hughes, E. R. *Chinese Philosophy in Classical Times* (New York 1944, Dutton).

Kai-yu Hsu, *Chou En-lai:* China's Gray Eminence (New York 1969, Doubleday).

Latourette, Kenneth Scott, *The Chinese: Their History and Culture* Two vols. in One (New York 1946, The Macmillan Company).

———, *A History of Modern China* (Baltimore 1954, Penguin Books).

Lin Yutang, *The Wisdom of Laotse* (New York 1948, Modern Library).

Mao Tse-tung, *Quotations from Chairman Mao Tse-tung* (Peking 1972, Foreign Languages Press).

Needham, Joseph, *Science and Civilization in China* (Cambridge 1936, University Press), especially vol. H.

———, *The Grand Titration* (London 1969, Allen and Unwin).

Schram, Stuart, *Mao Tse-tung* (Baltimore 1972, Penguin).

Schwartz, Benjamin I., *Chinése Communism and the Rise of Mao* (New York 1967, Harper and Row).

Spence, Jonathan D., *Emperor of China: Self-portrait of K'ang-hsi* (New York 1974, Knopf).

Stein, Sir Aurel, *On Ancient Central-Asian Tracks* (New York 1964, Pantheon Books).

Swearer, Howard R., "Higher Education in Contemporary China" *The Key Reporter*, Phi Beta Kappa, 40, 2-4 (1974-75).

Wing-tsit Chan, (trans.), *The Platform Scripture* (New York 1963, St. John's University Press).

———, *A Source Book in Chinese Philosophy* (Princeton 1973, University Press).

Japan

Barnett, A.D., *Communist China:* The Early Years 1949-55 (New York 1964, Praeger).

Chang, G.C.C., *The Practice of Zen* (New York 1970, Harper and Row).

Duncan, R., (ed.), *Selected Writings of Mahatma Gandhi* (London 1951 Faber and Faber).

Eliot, Sir Charles, *Japanese Buddhism* (London 1935, Routledge and Kegan Paul).

Gandhi's Autobiography (Washington, D.C. 1948, Public Affairs Press).

Piovesana, G.K., *Contemporary Japanese Philosophical Thought* (New York 1969, St. John's University Press).

Sansom, G.B., *Japan:* A Short Cultural History (New York 1962, Appleton-Century-Crofts).

Suzuki, D.T., *An Introduction to Zen Buddhism* (New York 1964, Grove Press).

Tsunoda, R., de Bary, Wm. T., and Keene, D., *Sources of Japanese Tradition*, 2 vols. (New York 1964, Columbia University Press).

INDEX